Paul and Elaine Lewis

Peoples of the Golden Triangle

Tribal village in the morning mist

Paul and Elaine Lewis

Peoples of the Golden Triangle

Six Tribes in Thailand

Thames and Hudson

Above the stifling heat of the valley

First published in Great Britain in 1984 by
Thames and Hudson Ltd, London

First published in hardcover in the United States of America in
1984 by Thames and Hudson Inc., 500 Fifth Avenue, New York,
New York 10110

First paperback edition 1998

Copyright © 1984 Paul and Elaine Lewis and the photographers

British Library Cataloguing-in-Publication Data
A catalogue record for this book is available from the British
Library

ISBN 0-500-97472-1

Library of Congress Catalog Card Number 84-50047

Printed in Thailand

Contents

Source of 'black gold' in the Golden Triangle

Preface

Tribes

The Thai Government recognizes six groups of 'hilltribes' (*chao khao*, literally 'mountain people') in Thailand: Karen, Hmong, Mien, Lahu, Akha, and Lisu. These are the groups we describe, although since many tribal people no longer live in the mountains we use the term 'tribe' rather than 'hilltribe'.

Each of these six tribes has its own language, dress, religion, and historical background. Within some tribes, such as the Lahu, there are sub-tribes with divergent dialects, different forms of dress, and varied religious patterns. Even so, the members of each tribe have an ethno-consciousness which leads them to recognize one another as belonging to the same ethnic group.

There are some who object to the use of the term 'tribe' for these people, as they are not located in a single area and have no tribal organization. However, terms that have been used as substitutes are not satisfactory. For instance, if 'minority' or 'ethnic group' were used, that would include such groups as Chinese, Indians, Malaysians, and Laotians. 'Highlanders' or 'People of the Hills' would include Thai and Chinese hill-dwellers. When the term 'tribe' is used in the sense described above, there is little chance of misunderstanding.

Descriptions

We use three methods to portray these tribal groups: field photographs from tribal villages in Thailand; studio photographs of the Mayer-Lipton Hilltribe Collection; and a written description of the people and their culture based on our own observations, consultation with specialists on each tribal group, and anthropological studies. The bibliography lists the main sources consulted.

Although a single chapter on each tribe cannot give a complete picture of these rich cultures, we hope that enough of the characteristics and traditions have been captured to present them to the reader as the fascinating people they are.

Tribal terms

In describing each group, we include the use of certain terms from their languages in cases where we can find no English equivalent. The tribal word is given with an approximate translation in quote marks, e. g. *dzoe ma* ('village priest'). This indicates that much is lost in the translation, so the reader must depend on the description to get the precise meaning.

When a term in a tribal language translates at almost full value into English, such as blacksmith (*ba ji*), quotes are not used.

The Tai

We use 'Tai' as a generic term for those who speak a Tai (or Daic) language, including Shan, Lao, Zhuang and all dialects of Thai. The term 'Thai' refers to the citizens and country of Thailand.

Change

Among these six tribes a great deal of change is taking place. The extent of change differs from group to group and even from household to household. Not all of this can be reflected in this book, especially when the full implications of that change are not possible to comprehend. We describe the major cultural patterns common to the tribal groups between 1948 and 1983. When we say 'the Lisu do this', or, 'the Mien pattern is that', we are simply stating the traditional pattern for the majority of that group – as we see it.

Thanks

We are most grateful to those who have aided in producing this book:

For the patient help of many tribal friends who have helped us in so many ways;

For the field photographs: John Hobday, Michael Freeman, Jacques Lemoine, Paul Lewis, Hansjörg Mayer, Heini Schneebeli, Friedhelm Scholz, Ali Sumlut, and those who have helped: Frank, Sascha Holzer, Beate Kaupp, Thanongsak Laohavisudhi, Li Pi, Tee, Christa Weber;

For reading and commenting on the entire book: Ted and Adele Anderson, Lucien and Jane Hanks, Mimi Lipton, Hansjörg Mayer, Graham Nicol, Ruth Podgwaite, Theodore Stern;

For reading and commenting on specific chapters: Brad and Jean Abernethy, Ann Burgess, Barbara Good, Sakda Hasuwan, Ed Hudspith, Otome Hutheesing, Nina Kammerer, Judith Knauf, Gary Lee, Jacques Lemoine, Rupert Nelson, Herbert Purnell, Friedhelm Scholz, Nicholas Tapp, Andy Thomson, Anthony Walker;

Heini Schneebeli for the studio photographs of the Mayer-Lipton Hilltribe Collection, made possible by Mimi Lipton and Hansjörg Mayer, and for the aid in making the collection: Elaine Lewis, Thai Tribal Crafts, and Gertrude Heim, Barbara and Julian Harding, Ann and Martin Timmer, Julia Brunskill, Jean Sidwell, Ali Sumlut and Midaw Dzoe Baw, Marisa Suanduenchai, Anong Katika, Satawak Sathit Phiansiri, Nandhana Borissoothi, Ampai Maneesinn, Wichai Pichitkanjanakul, Duangjitt-Thaveesri, Santana, Cherie Aung Khin, Chaiwut Tulayadhan, Anongnart Ulapathorn, Navarat Smitasin, Pusit Eakapong Paisal, Lee Shin Song.

'Peoples of the Golden Triangle' has become a reality because of the vision, the encouragement and the constant support of our dear friends Hansjörg and Mimi, to whom we are deeply indebted.

Paul and Elaine Lewis
Chiang Rai, Thailand
January 1984

8

Main immigration routes of Karen, Hmong, Mien,
Lahu, Akha and Lisu into Thailand

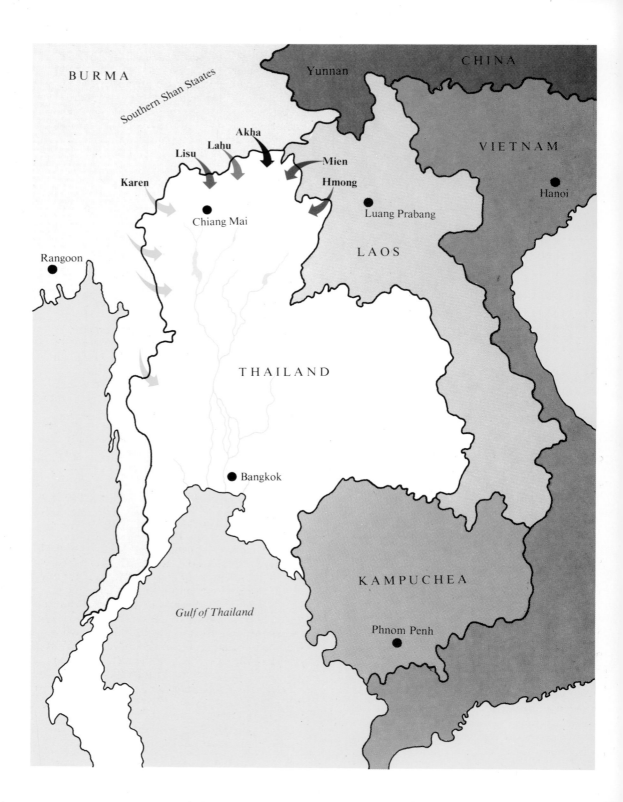

For map of 'Distribution of Major Tribal Village
Settlements' see page 294/295.

Chapter 1

Peoples of the Golden Triangle

Northern Thailand, with its forested hills and fertile valleys, rugged limestone formations and verdant waterways, is the home of some of the most fascinating people to be found anywhere in the world. The lowland areas have for some eight centuries been claimed by the Lanna or Yuan people, generally called the Northern Thai. The mountain slopes are occupied by a variety of tribal people who have converged on this area from the north, northeast, west and northwest, and now eke out a precarious livelihood there. These tribal people are: KAREN (Kariang, Yang), HMONG (Meo), MIEN (Yao), LAHU (Mussur), AKHA (Kaw), and LISU (Lisaw).

These people who now occupy the Golden Triangle area have come from southwest and south-central China, and except for the Karen, large numbers of each group still live there. All but the Karen retain in their culture many residual elements of their historical contacts with the Chinese.

The Lahu, Akha, and Lisu have common linguistic roots in the Yi (Lolo) sub-division of the Tibeto-Burman family of languages. The Lahu and Akha migrated in stages from Yunnan, China, into eastern Burma and northern Laos. From about the beginning of the twentieth century they started to migrate slowly into northern Thailand from Burma – a process that continues to this day. Only a few Lahu and practically no Akha have entered Thailand from Laos. The Lisu migrated from the headwaters of the Salween River in China into northern Burma, and then into Thailand through Kengtung State, Burma. Only minor segments of these three tribes live in Thailand. Much larger populations of each group still live in China and Burma.

The Hmong (Meo) and Mien (Yao), who speak languages of the Miao-Yao sub-division of the Sino-Tibetan family of languages, migrated from south-central China into Laos, and from there across the Mekong River into Thailand. Until the Communist take-over of Laos in 1975, the mountains of northern Laos were dominated by these two tribal groups, the Hmong outnumbering the Mien. Because many of the men fought on the side of the anti-Communist forces they had to flee into Thailand with their families, where they were given temporary asylum in refugee camps along the eastern border. A consequence of that tragic war was possibly the most abnormal migration of tribal people so far known; for many thousand Hmong and Mien, and a small number of Lahu, have been resettled in the United States and other Western countries.

Where the Karen came from remains shrouded in mystery. They probably originated in southwest China or southeast Tibet, but apparently none of them live there today. The vast majority of Karen are domiciled in Burma, totalling some four million. They are by far the most populous tribal group in Thailand. Little or no evidence of association with the Chinese remains in their culture, while their centuries of contacts with the Burmese, Mon, Tai, as well as with the British, have left their mark. The Karen remain profoundly different from any other lowland or highland group today.

These tribal groups still remain concentrated for the most part in the border areas where they first entered the country (see page 8). With the passage of time, however, further internal migration has taken place, so that today it is impossible to divide the region into neat, well-defined districts, and label them as Karen, Hmong, Mien, Lahu, Akha, or Lisu areas. There is a tendency for those who have lived in the country the longest, like the Karen, to be more concentrated and to live at lower elevations, while those who have come more recently, for instance the Hmong, are more scattered and live at higher elevations. Other factors influence the ecological adaptation of the tribal groups, such as their history of making slash-and-burn (swidden) fields, and the need to find areas which provide wild plants for use in religious ceremonies and in medicine. Many tribal people simply like to be high enough to be above the stifling heat of the valleys.

There are areas where two, three, or even more of these six tribal groups occupy the same mountain or district, albeit remaining for the most part quite separate in their own villages. In Mae Suay District south of Chiang Rai town, for example, one can find two kinds of Lahu, plus Akha, Lisu, and Karen villages on the same mountain. Along the banks of the Mae Kok River can be found villages of three Lahu sub-tribes, as well as Karen, Lisu, and Mien. Even as far south as Kamphaeng Phet in central Thailand there are significant numbers of Mien, Lisu, Hmong, Karen, and Lahu living in an area which as recently as the early 1970s had only a few Karen and Hmong villages.

Population

Although it is impossible to know the exact number of tribal people currently living in Thailand, our own studies and other available data indicate the total population of the six tribes to be approximately 416,000 in mid-1983.

Ethnic group	Number of villages	Total population	Average people/house
KAREN	2,160	246,000	5.2
HMONG	246	58,000	8.0
LAHU	318	40,000	5.8
MIEN	140	30,000	7.3
AKHA	155	24,000	6.4
LISU	109	18,000	6.8
TOTALS	3,128	416,000	5.8

Through natural increase (births over deaths) and immigration, the tribal segment in Thailand increased from approximately 100,000 in 1948 to 416,000 by 1983, an increase of over 4% per year, more than quadrupling in 35 years. During the same period the national population went from 15 to 50 million. Although the tribal segment constitutes less than 1% of the total population, this dramatic increase is now placing pressure upon the available land and natural resources. As tribal people are forced to farm more and more marginal land and to shorten drastically the fallow periods essential for the recovery of their slash-and-burn mountain fields, their food supply is not sufficient. Conflicts within and between villages have become more serious as competition for land is stepped up. At the same time Thai lowlanders, also facing a significant land shortage, tend to push their way into the hills, causing increasingly serious tensions between themselves and the tribal people.

Basic Themes

These six ethnic groups have experienced basically the same natural environment, yet there are striking differences in the way they have responded to it. Despite the fact that they share many common features (they are all minorities, all farmers, all live in villages), they have developed cultures unlike one another, and have become distinct ethnic groups.

Through the centuries each group has woven its own tapestry of cultural patterns. For example, each tribe observes the New Year as a very special time of celebration. It is a time for the wearing of new clothes, feasting with one's family, and visiting friends and relatives. The mythology and ritual which accompany the celebrations, however, differ markedly from group to group, because each culture has developed its own basic theme, colouring its outlook and response to a given situation. The themes are reflected in their language, dress, crafts, and other areas of their lives, and in the final analysis make them the unique, well-defined groups we see today.

Just as an intricately woven tapestry has a theme repeated throughout its design, so we can attempt to characterize each tribe by finding a dominant cultural theme distinguishing it from other tribes.

1 **KAREN** A desire for HARMONY is a basic theme in the Sgaw and Pwo Karen cultures. The excellent fallow system they have developed in their agriculture shows their desire for harmony with their environment. The annual celebrations in which they feast the guardian spirits of the village show their desire for harmony with these unseen powers. They attempt to maintain harmony in relationships within the village by submission to the acknowledged leaders, and harmony with their neighbours by avoiding conflict whenever possible.

2 **HMONG** A desire for INDEPENDENCE dominates the lives of the Hmong. They seek economic independence through their industriousness, and liberty to follow their own life style by means of armed force when threatened. In Thailand this desire for independence has led a few Hmong to join Communist factions promising them freedom, while in Laos the Hmong were bitter anti-Communist fighters seeing in Communism a distinct threat to their independence. Most of the Hmong living in Thailand in the early 1980s, however, have found that real economic, social and religious freedom is only to be found within a stable political environment.

3 **MIEN** A desire for PROPRIETY is a driving theme in the Mien culture. They are a dignified people, who prize decorum highly. Whether the endeavour they are engaged in concerns human needs or the realm of unseen forces (including spirits and ancestors) the Mien seek perfection in their orderliness. They desire to avoid open conflict at all costs: for instance if two parties in a village have a disagreement they will discuss it with studied politeness, seeking to resolve the problem before it blocks their joint pursuit of merit and status.

4 **LAHU** A desire for BLESSING is a dominant theme throughout Lahu culture. In their many rites and ceremonies the Lahu pray for such blessings as: health, wealth, freedom from worry, many children and many animals, a stable village, and fruitful return for their labours. Their society is so structured as to maximize the receipt of blessing in their personal and family lives, and even the life of the village. The Lahu call themselves 'children of blessing', since they perform 'customs of blessing'. This desire has led some of them to follow messianic movements in China, Burma, and Thailand, whereas others turned to Christianity.

5 **AKHA** A desire for CONTINUITY is a dominant theme among the Akha, and for them continuity resides primarily in relationship with their ancestors. For this reason they learn the names of their male ancestors in chronological order back to 'the beginning of human beings'. They see themselves as a link in the great continuum of Akha history; everything they do must fit into that chain. The Akha depend on their ancestors for life, food, health, and security. One day they will take their place among the ancestors, and their descendents will then look to them for sustenance and protection.

6 **LISU** A desire for PRIMACY is predominant in Lisu culture. Every Lisu feels that his or her own family, clan, or village is pre-eminent, and will argue vehemently with anyone who presumes to dispute it. A village will claim its young people to be the best in the singing contest, its women the most skillful in needlework, and its families the most adept in growing opium. Competition between individuals is equally intense, and legal disputes are common. A Lisu man involved in a court case will muster all his fellow clansmen, his children's in-laws, and anyone he believes to be indebted to him to fight his case. This spirit of competition is to be seen even in their dress. Through the years women's dress has grown increasingly more elaborate, and their jewellery more ornate.

Clothing

Just the mention of the names Karen, Hmong, Mien, Lahu, Akha, or Lisu will conjure up mental images of the distinctive dress of each group. Their clothing did not at some point in time suddenly appear as we know it today, but evolved generation by generation to become what we now see. There is room within the limits of basic style for each individual to express his or her own personality and preferences, and it is here that innovation occurs.

In each tribe (with the exception of Karen) the young people of marriageable age wear the most elaborate clothing. Teen-age girls devote much time to weaving, sewing, and doing fancywork in order to produce the prettiest costume in the village. Mothers take special care in making clothing for their bachelor sons in hopes they will be attractive to the girls. At the New Year festival the finest clothing is brought out, for it is believed that wearing old clothes on New Year's Day will bring poverty throughout that year. Young married people pay considerable attention to dress, but as they grow older lose interest in decorative clothing. Older people wear clothing with less ornamentation, leaving it to the young to set fashion trends.

Without attempting to trace the historical development of the clothing of these tribes, we portray the style of clothing worn by the group with as little reference to Western influence as possible. However, it should be stated that with the increased accessibility of formerly remote mountain areas, the ubiquitous T-shirt and jeans have become an undeniable reality. No doubt in the future more and more of the tribal people will adopt Thai or Western styles of dress.

New techniques of producing clothing are being adopted, although still retaining tribal distinctiveness. Sewing machines have become standard equipment in the earthen-floored homes of many of the Hmong and Lisu, and it is virtually impossible today to find a hand-sewn set of clothing among them. Furthermore, Hmong women have found that cloth sold in the market with printed batik and embroidery designs imitating their patterns is a great boon in terms of time saved. Lahu Nyi women prefer making their skirts of bright flowered velvet, instead of following the laborious stitching of traditional styles. In some cases, bright red or pink acrylic yarn tassels are replacing the traditional dyed feather tassels on Akha women's headdresses, and strands of cheap plastic beads are used instead of the red seeds which require both time and patience to puncture.

We describe the dress and artifacts of these tribal people as they are (or were, as the case may be) before the onset of such modernization. This is not to be seen as an attempt to deny the realities of the modern world, or even to suggest that it is unfortunate that such changes are taking place. It is rather our purpose to present as nearly as possible those elements of their material and spiritual culture that have made them distinctively Karen, – Hmong, – Mien, – Lahu, – Akha, – or Lisu.

Loimi-Akha woman spinning cotton

Pwo Karen woman weaving skirt

Mien woman embroidering

Tribal Villages

Tribal villages are usually populated by members of only one tribe or sub-tribe. A village with a mixed population would likely be in a state of frequent conflict due to differences in social and religious practices. Generally when an individual or family of one tribe lives in a village of another tribe, they either accept the culture and religion of the majority or remain completely aloof from such practices.

The ideal conditions for a village site are: a gentle mountain slope with a good jungle covering; an adequate water source; and sufficient land for cultivation. The jungle area is important as a source of firewood, building materials, game, wild plants, and marketable products. It also serves as a place of refuge in times of danger.

The design of the houses, which are built of jungle materials, differs from tribe to tribe. As one approaches a village it is often possible to say which tribal group lives there by simple observation of the design of the houses and layout of the village.

The ceremonial head of the village, with the elders, decides the exact area where a village is to be located. Each tribe has its own method of ascertaining whether the spiritual forces – the owner/guardians of the land – agree to a village being located in a given area. The most common practice is to make a small depression in the ground at the desired site and place three or four grains of uncooked rice in it, radiating out from a common centre. The grains of rice are then covered by an inverted bowl and left for a certain length of time. If the rice remains undisturbed it is assumed that the site meets with the approval of the spirits.

The gathering and preparation of the wood, bamboo, thatch and other materials for individual houses is the responsibility of each household. The actual building is normally done communally on a day auspicious for the family whose house is to be built, with representatives of each household in the village working together. The household head kills a pig and provides a feast for all who help. He, in turn, will assist his fellow villagers when they build their houses.

All village members are expected to share certain communal responsibilities. Paths must be maintained leading to the fields, the water source, other villages, and perhaps to the nearest road. Certain services must be rendered to such village leaders as the political headman, the ceremonial head, and the village blacksmith. From time to time local Government officials, Border Patrol Police, or army officers also require certain services. At such times each household is expected to provide one or more persons to share in the labour. When a village function is held each household makes a contribution in money or kind. A tribal village is ideally a very close-knit community in which each member is dependent on the others for the safety and well-being of all.

Lahu thatching roof

Political Patterns

Within the wider ethnic context, each tribal village tends to be autonomous. There are no pan-village or pan-tribal organizations. The village itself is often not a stable unit, because tribal families tend not to show strong loyalty to it. If they decide that by joining kinsmen elsewhere they can improve their economic status they will move, even at the cost of breaking off relationships with the old village. This might mean crossing the border (often ill-defined) into another country.

Each village has territory it claims as its domain, and it functions so as to keep the peace within that territory, and between that territory and the Thai Government. The tribal groups have no written laws, but by means of codes of conduct handed down from generation to generation certain socially binding patterns function as 'law'. Anyone who breaks these codes may be fined, or in the case of serious misdemeanors, banned from the village. At the same time, any household which does not like the way the village is administered can move to another village.

The Karen, Akha, and Lisu have a leader in each village who functions as the ceremonial headman, or 'village priest'. The elders choose for this office the man they consider to have the most knowledge of the mythology and rituals of the tribe and who is conversant with their codes of conduct. He must be a person who can be depended on to carry out their decisions.

Each village must have a political headman who serves as its representative in governmental matters. He is usually called *kae ban* (from Northern Thai), or *phu yai ban* (from Central Thai). This office is an overlay of the Thai system. One man may combine the positions of ceremonial headman and political leader, or a different man may be chosen for each position. Thai officials prefer a headman who can speak Thai, and in some instances they make the choice themselves. As he is often chosen more for his knowledge of the Thai language than for his qualities of leadership, young men who do not have the confidence of the villagers are often selected. Much misunderstanding arises from this fact, creating tension in tribal-governmental relations.

Relationship with Government and Others

Although northern Thailand has been under Thai control since 1874, it was not until after World War II that the Thai Government began to develop active programmes for the tribal people. The Government now recognizes that the tribes are of importance politically due to their vulnerability to Communist and other ideological influences; strategically because they live within long mountainous border areas difficult to defend; and economically because of the impact of slash-and-burn cultivation on the forests and watershed areas.

However, the major problems in border areas are not due to the tribal presence there. For years these areas have been plagued by the activities of smugglers, KMT irregulars (former Nationalist Chinese soldiers), opium warlords, and bands of insurgents. Unsettled political conditions in neighbouring countries also exacerbate these problems for both the Government and the tribal people living in the Golden Triangle.

In 1953 the Thai Government began to develop programmes both to guard their borders and to ameliorate the problems of the tribal populations. Some of the resulting programmes have not been as successful as had been hoped – such as the Hill Tribes Development and Welfare Centres (called *Nikhom* in Thai). On the other hand the Tribal Research Centre at Chiang Mai University has carried out research and suggested constructive programmes to meet the needs of tribal people.

The Thai King and Queen, as well as the Princess Mother, have personally interested themselves in helping the tribes. The tribal people consequently feel they have friends in Their Majesties and Her Royal Highness, and hold them in much affection.

Most of the contacts tribal people have with the Administration are through the local district (*amphur*) offices. The District Officer (*Nai Amphur*) himself may often be sympathetic to their problems and needs, but the tribal people seldom have direct access to him. They usually have to deal with clerks who are so preoccupied with lowland concerns that they find it difficult even to consider tribal problems.

An area of severe tension between uplanders and the Government is that of reforestation. The Government is rightly concerned about the watershed areas and the propagation of the forests in the north. Tribal people, not understanding the long-range ecological factors at work, view this as simply robbing them of their fields, thus threatening their very existence. Many of them are moving from area to area trying to find places they can farm, but with little success.

Of deepest concern to most of the tribal people is the fact that they are not sure where they stand in relation to the Government. As of the early 1980s probably not more than 30% of them had citizenship papers. At the same time, the Government has problems knowing how to deal with these minority groups with whom it is difficult to communicate, and who have little understanding of the nation and its laws. Consequently most tribal people are keenly aware of their peripheral position within the State, and do not feel they really 'belong'.

Better understanding should develop as more young tribal people are educated. It is to be hoped that as they mature and attain places of leadership among their people, the *Khon Thai phu khao* ('Thai people of the mountains'), as the King prefers to call them, will become fully accepted as citizens.

No tribal group exists in isolation. The amount of contact they have with others depends on their geographical location, as well as the degree to which they must depend on neighbouring groups for the necessities of life. The tribal population of Thailand cannot be fully understood apart from a consideration of their relationship with their neighbours.

Members of the same tribal group tend to be loyal to one another, especially when facing what they often consider a hostile world. Since they speak the same language and have similar cultural features, it is normally much easier to relate to fellow tribal members than 'outsiders'. At the same time, serious altercations occasionally break out within a single tribal group. This may be sparked off by disputes over payment of bride price, land rights, theft, or some other alleged infringement of rights. Usually the headman can arbitrate the dispute, but sometimes the case may be taken to the local Thai officials for settlement. This may lead to village splits and long-standing feuds.

Although there are certain differences between the tribal groups and Thai lowlanders, there are also similarities. Almost all are farmers, for example. Moreover, although the lowlanders are mostly Buddhists, a belief in spirits is fundamental to their religion, just as it is to tribal religions. In fact, some of the tribal beliefs and practices in regard to spirits have been learned fromThai lowlanders.

In the day-to-day relationship between tribal people and the lowland Thai, the various ethnic groups react in different ways. For example, the Mien tend to have a good relationship with the Thai, whereas the Akha sometimes find relations strained. Take one case in Chiang Rai Province, where a young Akha man was murdered by a local Thai. Although it was well known who the murderer was, he was never brought to justice, which infuriated the Akha. Some of them wanted to kill the murderer in revenge, but certain Mien leaders in the area dissuaded them saying, 'That would only cause much needless bloodshed of innocent people. Drop it!' In this case the Akha heeded the practical advice given by the Mien.

There are times when tribal people work cooperatively with lowland Thai in projects such as the digging of irrigation ditches to be shared by both, the repairing of roads between villages, and providing help in times of extreme need.

On the other hand, around their fireplaces in the evening one can frequently hear stories revealing the bitterness the tribal people feel at what they consider to be unpunished murder, theft, land-stealing and the like.

Karen farmers around the fireplace in the evening

Large trees are sacrificed in the making of swiddens (Akha)

The Economy

Rice Fields

Swiddens are burned in April

Slash-and-burn (swidden) cultivation is probably the oldest agricultural method in the world. It is so called because it involves cutting down all the trees and underbrush on a wooded hillside, and then when it is thoroughly dried burning it off in preparation for planting. The burning destroys insect pests and disease, and the layer of ash remaining serves as fertilizer for the crop. This type of shifting cultivation is the main agricultural method used by tribal people in Thailand.

There are many Thai who also use swiddening, at least for some of their fields. Many who formerly farmed only irrigated rice paddies are now practicing swiddening because of land pressure in some valley areas. On the other hand, tribal people are turning to lowland irrigated rice farming wherever they are able. McKinnon (1977:1) states that there are approximately four million people in Thailand who depend upon some form of shifting, or swidden, cultivation. If this is true, it means that the tribal population represents only about 10% of the slash-and-burn cultivators in the country.

As rice is the main food for all tribal people, the finding of suitable areas in which to plant it is a vital consideration. They would naturally prefer hillsides clothed with virgin forests, but these have long since disappeared. Therefore they look for a secondary or tertiary forest which has enjoyed at least a ten-year fallow period. However, due to the pressure of population on the land, they are often forced to shorten this to four, three, or even two years. The shorter the fallow period the greater the need for intensive cultivation and weeding. The resulting fields, irrespective of how much labour is expended, will inevitably show decreasing yields.

The traditional method of preparing mountain fields is for the men to go out in January or early February and cut down the trees and undergrowth. The fields are then left for about three months to dry out. As it is necessary for all those villagers with contiguous fields to burn them at the same time, they have to agree on a day for burning. This will be at the height of dry season so as to achieve an even burn. Sometimes lowlanders or other tribal groups set fire to the swiddens before they are thoroughly dry. This leads to serious problems and involves much extra work. In some cases such fields have to be abandoned and areas planted which have recently been left fallow.

Rice is planted after the monsoon rains break in May. The farmer walks laterally across the field punching holes in the soil with a dibble stick (a long bamboo pole with a metal point), while his wife or daughter follows behind dropping six to ten seeds into each hole. Most of the seeds will be covered by the planters walking to and fro over these holes.

Two or three times during the growing season another period of intensive labour is required to weed the field, the work being done primarily by women and children. Swiddens are harvested at the end of the rainy season, usually in October. The stalks are cut with small hand sickles or reaping knives, then laid on top of the stubble in such a way that the heads do not touch the soil. This allows for circulation of air, and prevents the rice from sprouting in case it should rain before it is gathered for threshing. A threshing floor is levelled in the field, a mat laid down, and the grain is threshed according to the custom of each tribal group. After beating the rice to remove the grain from the stalks it is fanned or winnowed to remove the chaff.

Transporting the grain to the village on their backs is heavy work, as the field may be a two- or three-hour walk away. For those with ponies to carry the rice the task is obviously easier. It is necessary to bring the rice to the village as soon as possible so as to prevent it from being stolen.

Each family has its own granary near the house, built off the ground to minimize loss due to domesticated animals and rodents. Often the posts have bands of slippery material, such as a strip of tin or perhaps the sheath from the base of a bamboo stalk, to prevent rodents from climbing up.

Tribal people also plant maize (corn) for both human and animal consumption, and a variety of vegetables: melons, squash, cucumbers, tomatoes, onions, beans, greens, and cabbage. These are often planted among the rice, maize, and poppy plants. It is generally agreed that vegetables planted among the poppies are the most delicious.

Although rice is the main crop for most tribal people, they also plant cash crops in order to be able to purchase needed commodities. Some also have to buy a part or all of their rice. In many villages more than half of the households always have to buy some of their rice, and in bad years the majority may have to purchase most of it. Some who raise opium poppies intensively make no effort to be self-sufficient in rice.

Lahu using rented buffalo to plough irrigated rice field

A dibble stick is used when planting hillside field (Akha)

Field hut provides shelter during periods of intense cultivation

Tender rice shoots respond to early monsoon rains

Threshing paddy in the field (Karen)

Preparing to carry paddy home (Akha)

Winnowing rice after pounding (Lisu)

Fanning the paddy to remove the chaff (Karen)

Mien rice drying rack

Opium

The favourite cash crop of some Hmong, Mien, Lahu and Lisu is opium whereas relatively few Karen and Akha grow it. It fulfills many of the requirements for the ideal cash crop: it has high value for small volume; it can be grown only at a high elevation (there is thus no competition with lowlanders); it will not spoil; and the dealers usually come to the growers to make their purchases. The opium growers feel that these advantages outweigh the risks involved in growing a crop which has been illegal since 1959.

Poppy cultivation is exhausting work. Standard practice is to plant maize and poppies successively in the same fields each year. The maize keeps down excessive weeds and provides feed for the animals. It is grown from about April to August, then with the stalks still standing in the fields, the ground is weeded and pulverized. Just before the end of the rainy season, in successive sowings throughout September and October, the poppy seed is broadcast among the maize stalks, which offer protection to the young plants. The poppies must be weeded and thinned several times during the growing season.

Weeding opium field (Akha)

Scoring poppy pods (Lisu)

Raw opium oozes out of scored pod

Opium is harvested over an eight- to ten-week period, beginning about the middle of December. A few days after the petals have dropped, the harvesters, primarily women and children, go through the fields scoring the green pods with small, curved tools made of two or three very sharp blades bound tightly together. The incising of the pod must be done with care and with a steady hand, preferably in bright sunlight. If the incisions are too deep, most of the white, sticky sap may drip to the ground, and if they are too shallow, the sap will harden in the pod.

The poppies are left overnight, then the raw opium, which will have oxidized and become a yellowish-brown gummy substance, is scraped from the pods with wide-bladed knives. The gum is formed into balls and wrapped in banana leaves or mulberry-bark paper. As the plants in a single field are not all ready for harvest at the same time, and the same pod may be tapped several times, the harvesters work over the same field again and again, always moving backwards so as not to brush against the oozing sap. After the harvest the best seed is kept for the next season.

An addict smokes opium three or four times a day (Hmong)

Oxidized sap clings to pod

Raw opium is scraped from pod

Other crops

Chilli pepper and sesame are both major cash crops. The Lahu are especially adept at growing chilli peppers, which is a risky crop, for if there is disease in the soil (such as wilt), most of the crop will be lost.

Many are now turning to the cultivation of coffee and tea, while others are growing varieties of fruit trees which do well at high elevations: lichee, mango, longan, peach, and citrus trees. However, only those who live near roads leading to major markets can profitably grow them. Other cash crops grown are peanuts, castor beans, soy beans, and tobacco.

Drying tea on open porch (Akha)

Shredding tobacco leaves (Karen)

Coffee and other crops must be sun-dried (Lahu)

Domestic Animals

Pigs and chickens are kept by all the tribes. In addition to being important sources of protein, they are used extensively as sacrifices in rituals related to marriage, death, and New Year, as well as in healing ceremonies.

Customarily chickens and pigs are fed in the mornings and evenings, but through the day are allowed to wander through the village and surrounding area. Chickens are fed paddy (unhusked rice) and sometimes maize. Pig food consists mainly of rice bran, wild banana stalks, jungle greens, and left-over food all cooked together in a large wok on a special fireplace. Those who grow maize add it to the mash. If there is a surplus of pigs they are sold in nearby villages and towns.

Cattle are highly prized, but not for milk, and only occasionally is the meat eaten. They often serve the function of a bank, in that when cash is needed their owner will sell one or more of them. As small boys can herd them to graze in the jungle area around the village they are an investment which will increase with little effort or expenditure. They are given salt water from time to time in order to ensure their return to their owner.

Some tribal people look after cattle and water buffalo for lowlanders, and receive an agreed number of calves for their services. A few who live close to the border with Burma buy cattle there at a low price, then drive them into Thailand to sell at a higher price. This is speculative at best, as they might be robbed in the unpatrolled border areas, or opium traffickers might demand a tax from them. There is risk involved in any type of cattle raising, since cattle are quite often stolen or poisoned by lowlanders; the ensuing enmity will cause the tribal people more often than not to move away.

Water buffalo are highly valued, and are a status symbol. Tribal farmers with irrigated rice fields need buffalo for ploughing and harrowing. All too often buffalo, like cattle, are stolen; consequently many farmers rent a buffalo for the short ploughing season. Buffalo have for some tribes an important ceremonial use. For example, the Akha sacrifice at least one buffalo during the funeral rites of important elders.

Feeding pigs is women's work (Hmong)

Buffalo tied up for sacrifice (Akha)

Ponies and oxen are used as pack animals to transport produce to the village, and for inter-village trading. Ponies, especially prized by groups with strong Chinese ties, are very useful for difficult mountain trails. Chinese-style bells and harnesses are used and the ponies respond to Chinese commands. Buffalo and oxen on the other hand respond to Thai commands, while pigs, chickens and dogs are called in the language of the owner, revealing which domesticated animals are traditional to them, and which have been adopted from other cultures.

Some Karen, particularly those in villages along the western border, keep elephants which they capture in the jungle and train. They use them both for their own work and to hire out in the timber industry.

All tribal people in Thailand keep dogs. Besides being of value as pets, they guard the household, aid in hunting, and together with pigs are useful village scavengers. As there are few latrines, this is an essential service for the health of the village.

Cats are also of value to tribal people because they keep down the rodent population. The Lahu, who often refer to the cat as the 'queen of the household', believe that a stolen cat is the best ratter.

Ponies respond to Chinese commands

Karen are the only tribal people who use elephants

Hunting, Fishing, and Gathering

Tribal people exploit in a variety of ways the plant and animal life in the forests and streams surrounding their villages. Hunting and fishing provide much of the protein in their diet, while jungle trees and plants add food and raw materials for their own use, or for sale.

Tribal men are good hunters. The Lahu are considered to be the most skilled of all, and are called Mussur by the Thai from a Burmese word meaning 'hunter'. In many areas game has become scarce, as there is little understanding of the importance of protecting animals for future generations. Wild pigs and bears are still fairly common, but leopards, tigers, wild elephants, and gaur are now rare. Deer (both sambur and barking), monkeys, gibbons, squirrels, jungle fowl, game birds, snakes, and lizards are all commonly hunted with guns and crossbows or are trapped.

Edible items gathered to supplement tribal diets include mushrooms, bamboo shoots, greens, tubers and roots, fruits and nuts, honey, wasp larvae, and other edible insects.

Taking aim (Lisu)

Ready for the hunt (Lahu)

Dividing the catch (Akha)

Setting a net trap (Lisu)

Bartering and Trading

Although all tribal groups are now within a 'cash economy', bartering still takes place between households within the village. One household may provide labour in a neighbour's field in return for pork; a blacksmith may be paid for making farming implements with a basket or two of rice; or one household might exchange maize for meat. Where opium is grown, it is frequently used as money. Trading between people of different ethnic groups is usually on a cash basis, and at a higher price.

Tribal men living far away from a market town generally make at least one trip a year to stock up on supplies they do not produce, and which are not available from neighbours. This includes salt, iron, kerosene, household utensils, blankets, cloth, medicines, flashlights, batteries, needles, thread, and various ornamental items.

More frequent visits to market towns are made from tribal villages nearby. Villagers do not go empty-handed to market, but take handicrafts, garden produce, charcoal, thatch shingles, broom grass, bamboo shoots, and other forest products to sell.

Many tribal men use the slack agricultural months for trading. Some purchase pigs or other livestock in one village and sell them at profit in other villages. Others purchase livestock and drive them to the market to sell, then use the money to buy a variety of commodities to resell in the villages.

Yunnanese (called *Haw* by the Thai) are inveterate traders, and have provided a model for the more Sinicized groups (all but the Karen). They, as well as Thai traders, travel regularly to tribal villages with articles they know are popular. Prices are high due to the risks, like being robbed on the trail, paying off policemen, or paying protection money to local bandits.

These traders, some of whom speak one or more tribal languages, help to shape the outlook of tribal people concerning the world outside. Villagers realize they are constantly exploited by them and have an instinctive distrust of them. Nevertheless, they look forward to their visits because they can purchase needed items and have contact with the world outside.

Opium-growing tribal groups are more dependent on outside traders than others. They are reluctant to take their crop to market for fear of being arrested. Instead they rely on traders who come to the villages with large mule caravans at opium harvest time. These heavily-armed traders maintain a monopoly of the traffic between villages and markets. They set the price for the opium, which the growers, although often dissatisfied, are forced to accept simply from fear. Occasionally a grower will attempt to market his own opium. If this becomes known to the traders, they might have him ambushed and robbed, or inform the local police, who will arrest him. In such a manner are the opium growers kept at the mercy of the traffickers. As the whole business is illegal, tribal people have no recourse, for they are unable to appeal to the police for protection.

Yunnanese traders have shops in certain opium-growing villages where they sell commodities in return for an appropriate weight of opium. If a villager wishes to pay cash, the shopkeeper calculates how much that given quantity of opium would sell for that day, and charges accordingly.

Villagers often pile up large debts with these shopkeepers, especially households which run out of rice and have to buy it from the shop on credit. If the debt gets too large they may be forced to sell their unharvested rice or opium crop in the fields for a very low price to the trader. This is called 'selling it green'. Obviously many families become heavily dependent upon these shopkeepers as they sink deeper into hopeless debt. In some cases such an unfortunate family will give a child to the trader to help pay off the debt; the child will in turn perhaps be sold to others. If it is a girl, she may be sold to a brothel in central or southern Thailand.

Traditionally tribal people have been independent, living by means of subsistence agriculture. However, nowadays wage-work has become an increasingly important source of income for many of them. They prefer to work for fellow villagers, but a more permanent form of employment is found with those engaged in intensive opium production. Many Karen work for Hmong and Lisu, while poor Lahu and Akha often work in the opium fields of Mien, Lisu, and Yunnanese. This work is usually paid for in opium as many such workers are opium addicts, and those not at first addicted soon become so.

The rice fields of lowlanders provide another important opportunity for wage-labour. Because the planting and harvesting of highland and lowland rice fields do not coincide, tribal people can hire themselves out to the Thai when their

Selling produce at a roadside market (Lahu)

own fields do not require attention. Payment for their labour is often made in rice – a welcome addition to their food supply.

Crafts

Each tribal group has its own distinctive crafts, most obviously observed in their clothing (see chapters 3–8), and jewellery (see chapter 2). Their fine skills can also be seen in their musical instruments, basketry, tools, utensils, weapons, and traps (see chapter 9).

Many articles of everyday use are produced by individual households while others are made by specialists. Clothing is produced by women, while men make tools and utensils. Men and women often share in making baskets and mats. Some articles, such as crossbows, animal traps, and musical instruments, are produced by artisans who specialize in making those products. Tribal groups accord considerable status to their blacksmiths, on whom they depend for the production and repair of their tools and weapons. Most tribes have an annual ceremony in which each village pays special tribute to its blacksmith. The Yi (Lolo) groups (Lahu, Akha, and Lisu) believe that a village cannot exist without a blacksmith, and each village has at least one. Silversmiths are also men of considerable status. A highly-renowned silversmith attracts customers from considerable distances.

Tribal people have not traditionally considered their crafts as marketable. A few products, however, which are made well by people of one tribe, are purchased by others lacking the necessary skill. People from many tribes purchase the sturdy and attractive shoulder bags and baskets produced by the Lahu. Karen betel boxes are much sought after by the Lisu, while Lahu and Akha frequently have Lisu silversmiths make their jewellery.

In recent years 'tribal handicrafts' have taken on a new significance in the economy due to a growing world market. Three organizations specifically geared to the improvement of the economic situation of tribal people by furthering such trade are: the Thai Hill-Crafts Foundation, under the patronage of HRH the Princess Mother; Bordercrafts, sponsored by the Border Patrol Police; and Thai Tribal Crafts, owned and managed by Karen and Lahu church organizations. Many tribal people have developed into skilled entrepreneurs, purchasing craft products from villagers and selling them in the colourful 'Night Bazaar' in Chiang Mai, or to shops in Chiang Mai, Chiang Rai, and Bangkok.

Lahu blacksmith forging machete

Hmong silversmith making ornament

Karen craftsman weaving basket

Family and Clan

Among all tribal people the family is the most important social unit. It may be made up of three or more generations (an extended family), or of just two (a nuclear family). In the case of the patrilocal Hmong, Mien, Akha, and Lisu, the normal household consists of a man and his wife, their unmarried children, and their married sons with their wives and children. Karen and Lahu households, however, being matrilocal, generally include the families of married daughters rather than married sons.

Normally tribal people marry within their own ethnic group. The majority of tribal families are monogamous, but polygyny* is acceptable in all the tribes except the Karen.

Each tribal group uses specialized kinship terms. When speaking to or about a relative they do not use the person's name, but only the correct kinship term. These terms reflect relative age, the sex of the speaker, the sex of the person addressed or referred to, generational differences, and whether the relationship is through the father's or mother's lineage.

The clan is the next unit of importance to the Hmong, Mien, Akha, and Lisu for it provides a secure base for contact with the outside world. The Karen and Lahu do not have clans, but their lineage ties, both maternal and paternal, are of great importance to them. Kinsmen and clansmen are called upon for help in times of economic need and in other crisis situations.

Religions

As the languages and dress of these six tribes are different from one another, so are their religions. To lump them together under the convenient term 'animism' is to over-simplify.

It is not clear how these religions have evolved, but among the factors that have influenced their development are: their ecological setting; the need for people to explain sickness and tragedy; and contacts made with neighbouring groups. When tribal people are unable to find obvious explanations for illness and other phenomena, they are inclined to attribute them to the activity of spirits. Although unseen, these spirits are as real to them as is the visible world. Despite their great diversity all tribal religions display a profound belief in this unseen spirit world.

The influence of outside groups on tribal religions is seen in its most extreme form in the Taoism which the Mien took over from the Chinese. Lisu and Akha display characteristics of Chinese religions, and much Tai religious practice is found among the Karen and Lahu.

Outside influences continue to affect tribal religion. For instance, those who have recently moved down into the valleys to try irrigated rice production have taken over both the Tai systems of irrigation ditches, and the Tai rituals which ensure successful harvests. Karen, Akha, and Lisu borrowed a ceremony from the Tai which honours the 'Lord of Land and Water'.

Most groups possess two types of religious specialists: a 'village priest' or religious head who presides over the ritual life of the village, and a shaman with special power to communicate with the spirit world. We describe each religious system in greater detail in the chapters on the tribes.

* Polygyny. Marriage of one man to two or more women.

Mien priest burns paper money in Taoist ceremony

Lisu father and son make sacrifice to ensure a good opium crop

Akha spirit priest repeating spirit incantations at funeral

Altar in a White Hmong home

Missionary Activity

Buddhist missionaries have been active among the tribal people in Thailand since the end of World War II. Monks travel to many villages both to teach their doctrines, and to provide medical services; in some instances Buddhist temples have been built in tribal villages. Buddhist monks in Central Thailand have developed programmes to detoxify tribal opium addicts. The temple of Wat Srisoda, at the base of Doi Suthep mountain to the west of Chiang Mai town, is now used for the education of young tribal men. As many as 400 from all six tribal groups have been in residence there at the same time.

In 1882 Karen Christians from Burma began missionary work among the Karen in Thailand. Several missions from the West have been active among the tribal groups since the end of World War II. As Kunstadter writes (1967: 22), Western missionaries often help to 'widen the horizons' of people in remote areas, especially as they combine educational, medical, and agricultural programmes with religious instruction. Some tribal Christians organize their churches into associations and conferences, providing contact with others in their tribe. These are virtually the only tribal pan-village organizations in Thailand.

The Christian churches among tribal people are generally under the leadership of pastors from their own tribe. The pastor, often the best educated man in the village, usually has had some theological education. Many are partially supported by their local church, but also work as farmers. These men, who are respected as religious practitioners by the villagers, often have considerable influence in the affairs of the village.

Lahu Christian church

Communications

The tribal groups do not have an indigenous form of writing. The Mien have used for many centuries a modified form of Chinese script to record their complicated ceremonies. Only Mien males, and not all of them, learn this script. It has not been widely used other than in their ritual.

For each language a script has been developed by missionaries. Apart from Karen, which is written in Burmese characters, all used at first the Roman alphabet, but most are now changing to Thai characters. A growing number of tribal people are becoming literate in Thai because of the introduction of schools in many tribal villages.

The customs and rituals of the people, except in the case of the Mien, have been handed down by oral tradition. Cassette recorders, popular among tribal people, now make it possible for these traditions to be recorded; songs and legends are sent to the tribal radio stations in Chiang Mai and Mae Chan to be broadcast on each tribe's daily programmes.

These radio stations are proving to be an important link between tribal villages and the world outside, as radios have now found their way into virtually every village. The broadcasts include newscasts by announcers from each tribe which acquaint the people, even in the most remote areas, with news from within Thailand, as well as major international events. Health, agricultural, and village development programmes are making some impact. The radio ranks, together with roads, as a major break-through in communications for tribal people.

Travel by paths to the fields, between villages, and from villages to towns is very important for communication and commerce. Narrow foot paths, as well as wider trails for ponies, mules, and oxen must be maintained by the villages they serve.

Roads are being constructed through the tribal areas at a rapid rate. Though primarily intended for logging, forestry, mining, and strategic purposes, the tribal people living in their vicinity clearly benefit from them. Roads, however, are a mixed blessing. Sometimes tensions develop when the road builders pay little heed to the local culture and so cause offense to the tribal people. As a result of these roads lowlanders, tourists, and curiosity-hunters can explore (and often exploit) the hill areas, breaking into the cherished privacy of the tribal people. Alien factors that tend to erode their culture are sometimes introduced by these visitors. Finally, valley-dwelling Thai are tempted by roads to move into the hills and lay claim to territory considered by the tribes to be their domain.

Tribal people living along rivers like the Salween and Mae Kok use 'long-tailed' outboard motor boats to transport themselves and their produce to market, and carry supplies back to the villages. Some of them have become owners of boats or pick-up trucks, and operate transport businesses.

Health

Tribal people have a shorter life-expectancy than their lowland neighbours. The main reasons are remoteness from medical facilities for most of them, and a lack of public health services, such as inoculations for their children. Other factors include poor sanitation; inadequate or contaminated water supplies; lack of knowledge about the human body and its care; occupational hazards; opium addiction; and poor nutrition.

Specific ways of curing illness have been developed by the tribal people:

1. *Ritual curing.* Each group has rituals to discover the cause and effect the cure for both physical and psychological illness. Shamans or other specialists usually perform such rituals.

2. *Traditional medicine.* People in each group have learned from medical practitioners of their own tribe and from other ethnic groups (such as the Yunnanese, Tai, and Burmese), how to use medicines obtained from herbs and animals in the treatment of a variety of diseases. The most commonly used herbal drug is opium. The majority of opium addicts first used it as medicine when ill, and ultimately became addicted. They have learned that opium can control diarrhea, coughs, and pain, so the temptation to use it is considerable when other treatment is not at hand. Opium addiction has become a major health and social problem among some tribal people.

3. *'Injection doctors'.* There are many 'injection doctors', mostly Thai and Yunnanese, who roam the hills with their syringes and bags of drugs. Although sometimes their services are beneficial, most have a limited understanding of Western medicines and at times misuse powerful drugs or use unsterile equipment, with the inevitable serious consequences.

4. *Western medicine.* Tribal people have a growing confidence in Western medicine. They take patients to clinics and hospitals with increasing frequency. All too often, however, they try other methods first, and resort to taking the patients to the hospital when it is too late for them to be saved. There is a growing tendency now for many tribal people to perform curing rituals simply to avoid offending the spirits, but actually to rely on Western medicine.

It is not at all uncommon for the tribal people to use a combination of methods, in the hope that at least one will be effective.

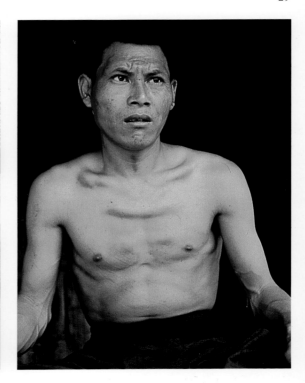

Top left:
The soul of a sick Mien woman is called to return over a ceremonial bridge

Middle:
Paraphernalia used by a Hmong shaman, with sacrificial pig's head

Right:
Causing raw welts to rise on the body is believed to bring healing to the affected parts

Bottom left:
A string is tied around a Lisu women's neck following a soul-calling ceremony

Daily Life

Reality today

The picture of peaceful tribal people living in the pristine beauty of cool, quiet hills – away from urban congestion and pollution – is misleading at best. From January to April the hills of the Golden Triangle are enveloped by smoke from burning fields, and roads are deep in dust. While the monsoon rains clear the air, they also turn the earth into sticky mud. Women and children must trudge increasingly greater distances to find enough firewood for every-day use. Land, once plentiful, is now scarce and unproductive. A woman with an opium-addicted husband must not only provide food and clothing for her family, but opium for her husband as well. There is no glamour in staving off hunger, caring for sick children, being victimized because of one's illiteracy, being denied citizenship, or being gawked at by tourists and laughed at by townspeople.

Yet there are compensations. To watch the charred hillsides take on new life as the rains coax tender green rice shoots out of the soil; to look up at the bright stars on crisp evenings; to be part of a large household and feel the warmth and support of grandparents, parents, siblings and children; to sit by the evening fires and listen to old men tell the legends and lore of your people and boast of tribal heroes – all this makes it possible to bear the burdens and to hope for better days ahead.

Daily Routine

A day starts early in a typical tribal village. Roosters announce the coming of a new day well before sunrise. The women and girls are first to rise and roll up their sleeping mats. Their initial task is to pound the paddy (unhusked rice) to be eaten by the family. The rhythmical thud of the rice pounder is soon joined by the sounds of squealing pigs, barking dogs, mooing cows, whinnying ponies, and clucking chickens as they make known that they are awake and ready to be fed.

Children carry water from a spring or stream, or perhaps from a bamboo aqueduct which brings water right into the village. Then the women cook the morning meal, which consists of rice with vegetables from the garden, or roots and herbs from the jungle, all eaten with salt and chilli peppers. On their luckier days there is also a meat dish, often prepared by the men.

The morning meal is usually eaten sometime between seven and nine o'clock, but at times of peak activity in the fields – such as harvest time – the family will have had their morning rice and be on their way to the fields by five A. M.

During busy times in the fields cooked rice wrapped in banana leaves is often taken in their shoulder bags and eaten in their field hut or under a shady tree when the family takes its noonday break. Then work is resumed, often continuing until almost sunset. On the way home they collect firewood and pig food, as every trip must be fully utilised to provide the essentials of every-day living.

Families living long distances from their fields may spend several days at a time working by day and camping in their field huts at night, rather than walking back and forth every day.

The evening meal may be eaten at any time between six and nine o'clock, followed by a time for visiting and relaxation. The women congregate in groups around smoky kerosene lamps or pitchpine torches where they can find enough light for sewing and fancywork. The men gather in one another's houses to discuss the happenings of the day or share news gleaned from traders, as they smoke their tobacco pipes and drink tea. Small children play around their fathers until they become drowsy, then crawl onto their laps and drift off to sleep.

The village sounds gradually diminish, until by ten or eleven o'clock everyone is asleep. The silence of the night may occasionally be broken by the stirring of livestock, the barking of dogs at real or imagined foes, or the cry of a baby, who will be comforted by its mother's breast.

Another day has ended. The weariness is slept away until, all too soon, a rooster crows, the livestock begins to stir, and another day starts its rhythmical cycle.

Silver items: Chain elements, balls, spindle, clasp, opium boxes, 'flower' coins (a form of ancient Thai coinage) used by Karen as pendants, Indian silver rupees and Chinese coin

Chapter 2

Jewellery and Ornaments

What would tribal women be without their jewellery? They are resplendent in their full regalia of silver chains, beads, buckles, earrings, and finger rings. The ornamentation jingles and sways, dangles and glistens. They feel happy and secure when they are loaded down with silver, beads, and other valuables. This represents the wealth of the family; adds to their status; and attracts suitors to the young women. Such a display shows that a man provides for his family. Excitement and colour are added to an otherwise hum-drum life.

For many the value of almost everything is measured in terms of silver. They do not trust ordinary money. In former days the paper money held by them became valueless overnight. Silver, however, whether in the shape of coins, jewellery, silver pipes, tobacco boxes, or silver ingots, always retains its value. Therefore, the price of a field or a pig, a pony or opium crop, is generally quoted in terms of silver coins or ingots. Bride price is also negotiated in terms of silver. Any spare funds are often converted into silver, which in effect becomes a family's bank account.

Silver jewellery takes many different forms according to the ethnic group. The Hmong and Mien favour massive pieces of jewellery; the Lisu add tier after tier until they are covered with silver; while the Lahu and Akha prefer to attach it to their clothing.

Brass and copper are also used for jewellery, and more recently aluminium has gained favour as a substitute for silver. Beads are used by all the tribes. Some use them only as decorative additions to tassels, while others wind them around the neck in massive amounts. Seeds, shells and other natural products are also used for ornamentation.

Collection of neck rings, bracelets, anklets and button for small children

Glass beads are worn in great profusion by Akha and Karen women. The large beads are of Chinese origin and date back from one to several centuries. Some of the smaller beads are of European origin and were used as barter by early traders from Europe. Lahu Nyi and Lahu Shi women wear red and white bead necklaces, while

Lahu Sheh Leh wear many strands of white beads wrapped around their necks. Lisu use beads on women's turbans and to make a net of beads to ornament the young man's 'courting bag'

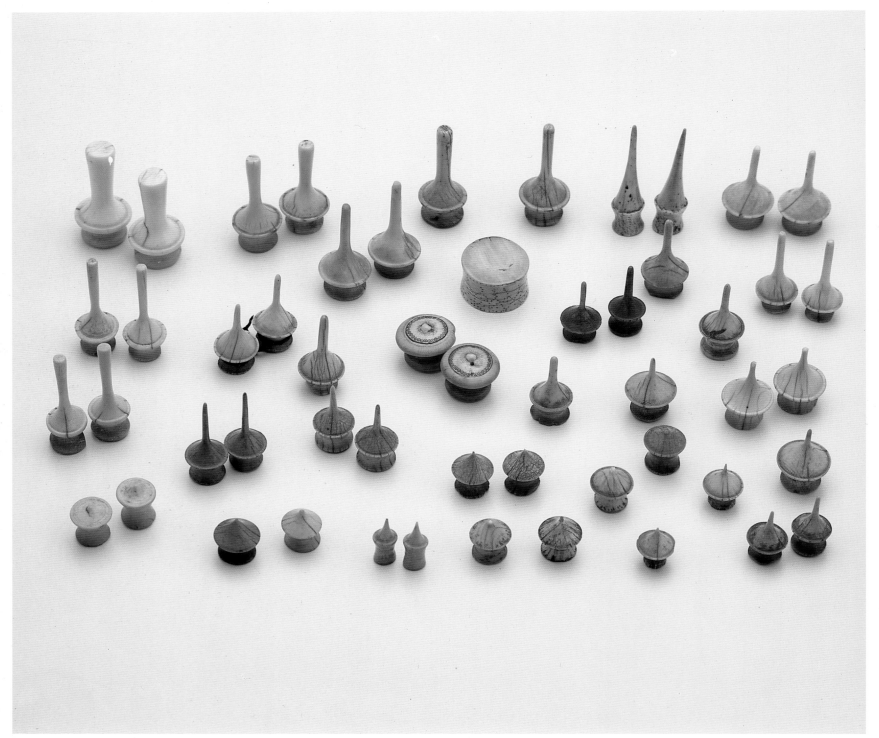

Ivory ear ornaments consisting of plugs to be inserted
into the ear lobes with projections of varying lengths
were formerly worn by Karen men and women

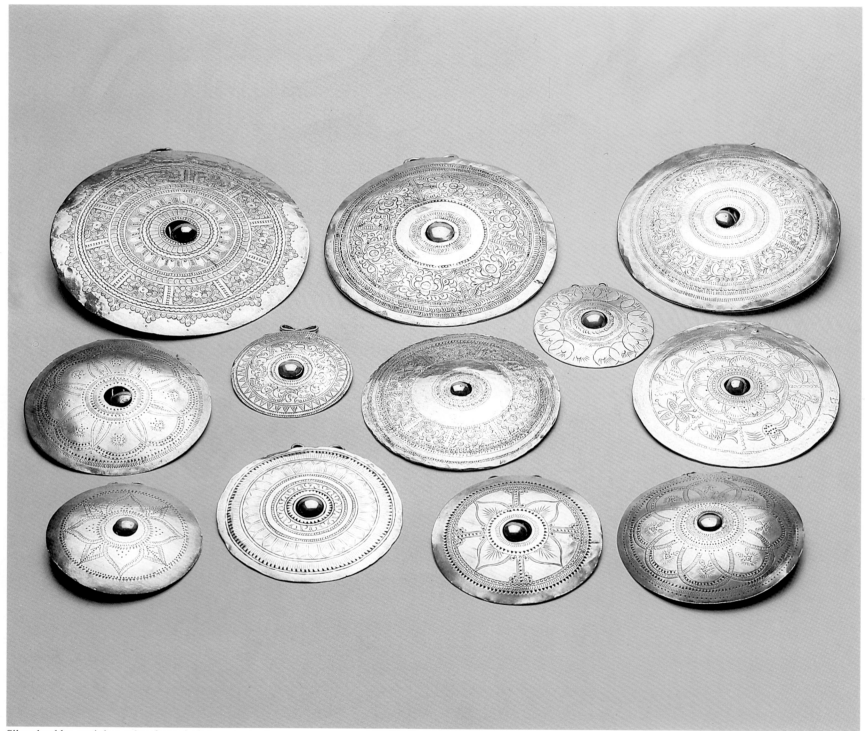

Silver buckles, mainly used to fasten jackets or tunics by
Lahu and Akha, and sometimes by Lisu

Flat silver bracelets, mostly with engraved designs,
mainly worn by Lahu, Akha and Lisu women

Top row: Silver Shan or Wa/Lawa bracelets with wire embellishment. All others have a variety of engraved designs imitating the wire embellishment and are mainly worn by Lahu, Akha and Lisu women

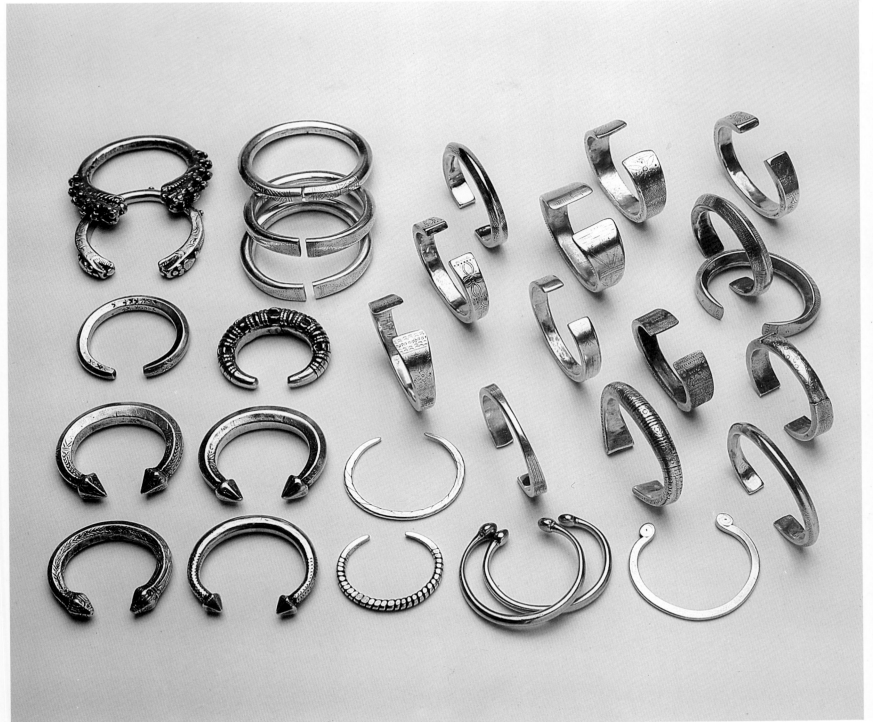

Solid open bracelets – usually silver, but can be of copper or brass. Those in the upper left section are worn by Lahu, Akha and Lisu men. The ones with pointed ends are worn mainly by the Wa/Lawa groups, and those on the right with flattened ends by Hmong and Mien

Solid silver bracelets and anklets (some expandable)
mainly worn by Wa/Lawa people

Silver spiral bracelets are mainly worn by Wa/Lawa people. Twisted wire bracelets are mostly of Chinese origin and are worn by several tribal groups (in Thailand mainly by Phami-Akha women)

Hollow silver bracelets, plain or with engraved designs,
were mostly made by Shan or Chinese silversmiths, and
in Thailand are worn primarily by Lahu and Akha men

Hollow silver bracelets were made in a great variety of
designs mostly by Shan or Chinese silversmiths, and in
Thailand are primarily worn by Lahu and Akha men

Hollow dragon-bracelets are treasured particularly by
old Akha men. A grain of silver, called the 'heart',
rattles inside the bracelet and has religious significance

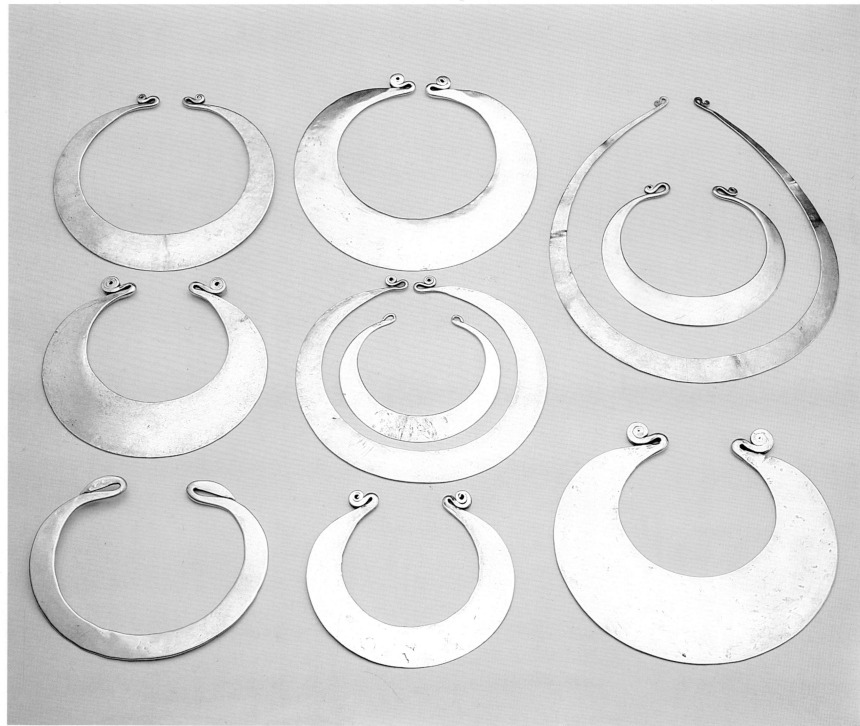

Flat plain silver neck rings are mainly worn by Akha women

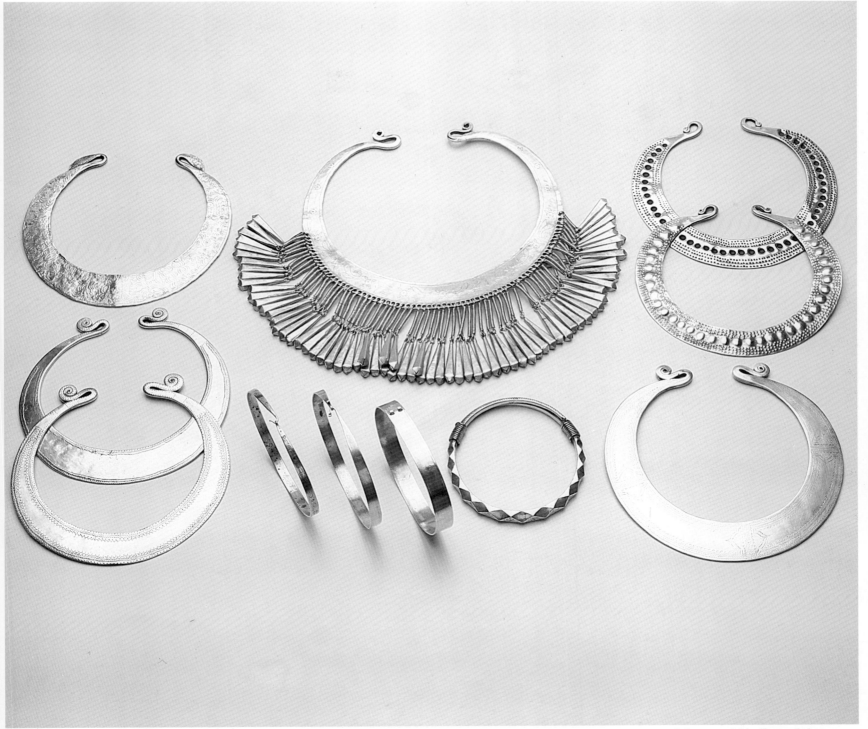

The engraved silver neck ring with club-shaped dangles is worn by Lisu women, the flat engraved ones by Akha women and the repousséd ones mainly by Akha and Lahu children. Closed flat silver neck rings are worn by Karen women, and the expandable diamond-shape patterned one by the Wa/Lawa people

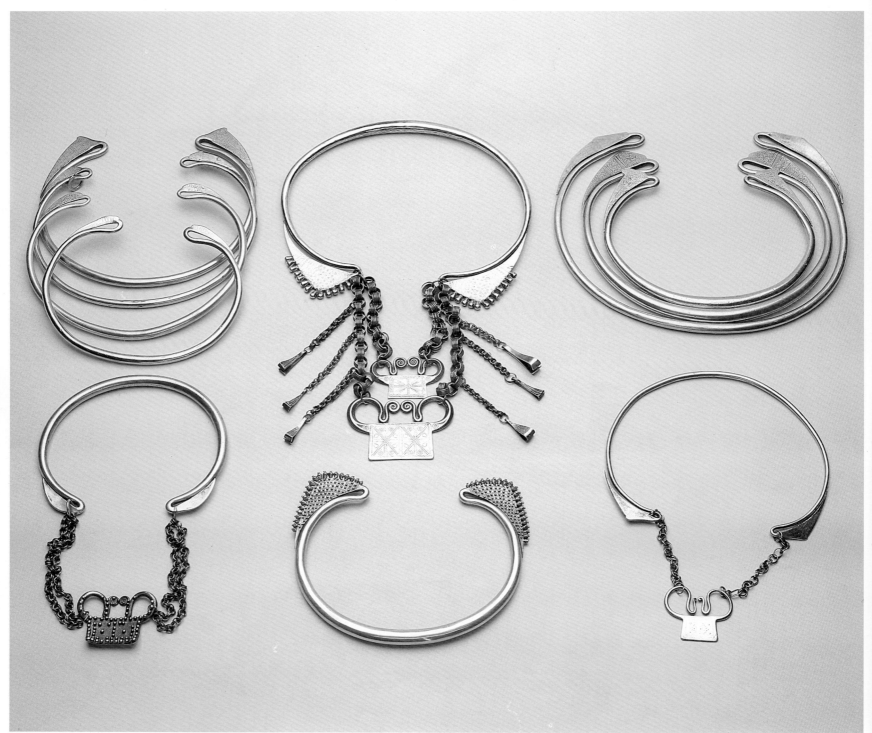

Single silver neck rings, solid or hollow, are worn by
Hmong, Mien, Lahu and Akha. Hmong neck rings often
have chains and pendants attached

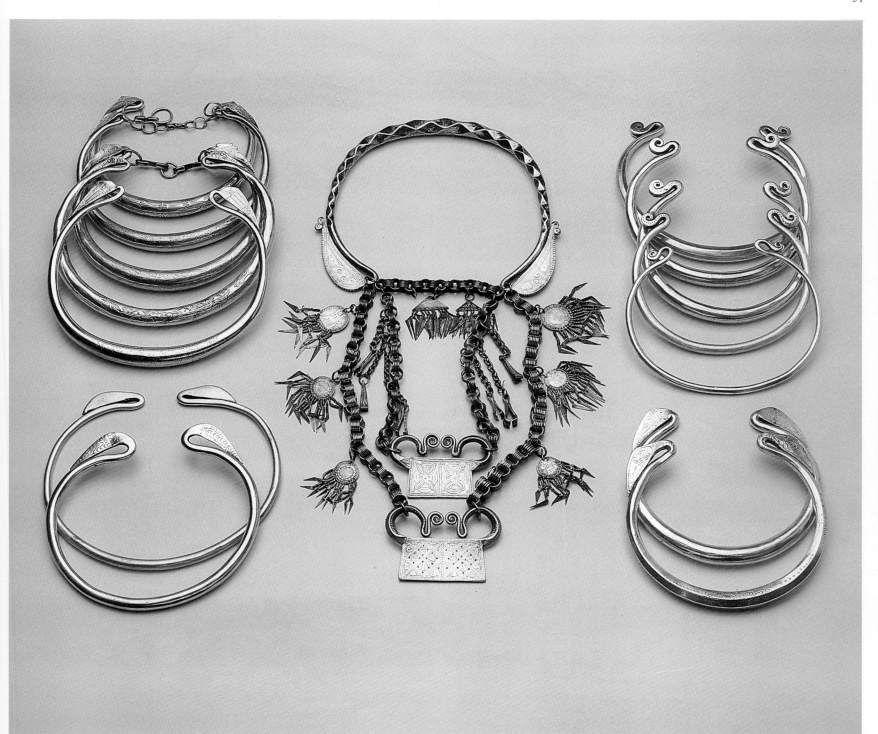

Torques (twisted neck rings), (*upper left and centre*), are worn by Hmong. Those on the *right* are worn mainly by Lahu.

'Three-metal' torques (*lower left*) are used by Hmong in healing ceremonies

Multi-tiered neck rings are worn by Hmong and Mien.

They may be either solid or hollow, plain or with engraved designs

Lock-shaped pendants, suspended by heavy chains from neck rings, are used by Hmong in soul-calling ceremonies to 'lock' the soul of the patient into his or her body

Hollow, single silver neck rings are mainly worn by
Hmong and Mien, and sometimes by Akha

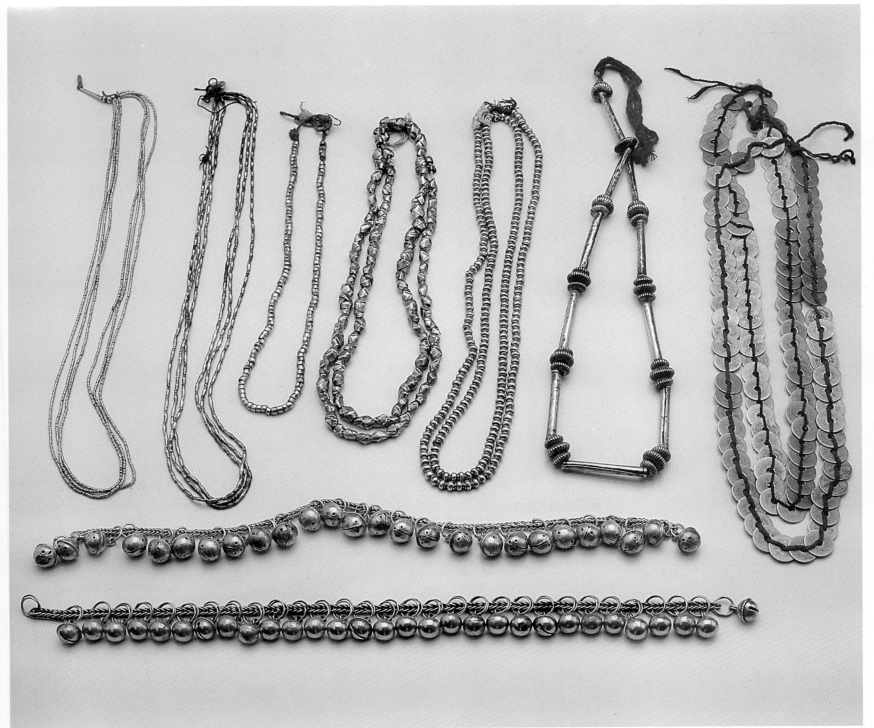

The top row consists of Karen necklaces of various designs. The two on the far right are bronze coins tied together by red and blue string. All others are of various types of silver beads. The third from the left is made of old silver 'bullet' coins which were used in Thailand for several centuries

The two silver bell necklaces at the bottom are worn either by Akha women on their headdresses or sewn to the front opening of an Akha man's jacket

Mien chains

The large piece is suspended from a woman's neck ring
and covers her back to the waist

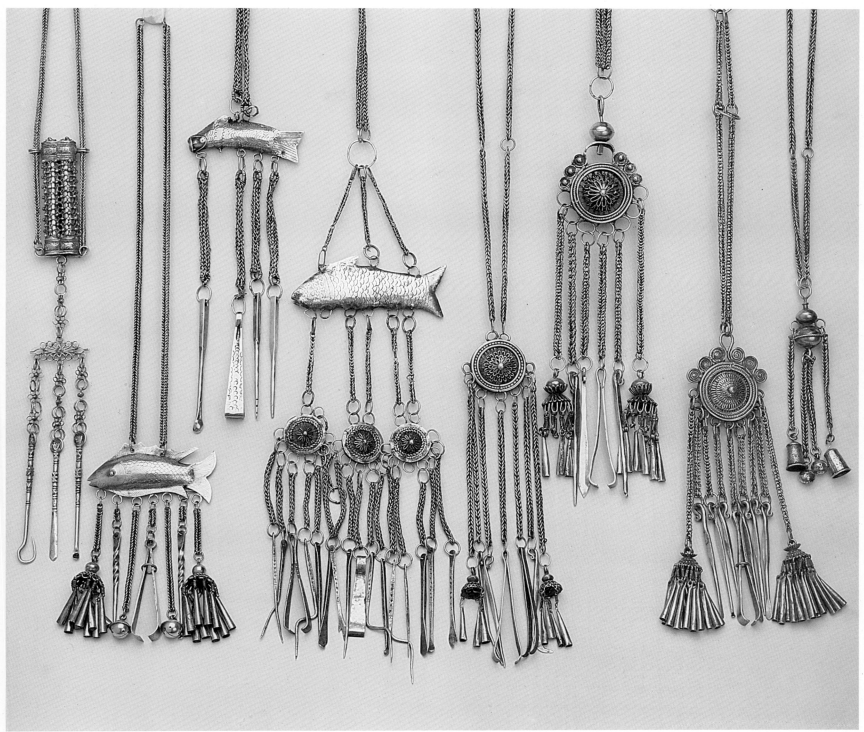

These silver chains with pendants are worn primarily by Lahu, Akha, and Lisu. They may be worn around the neck, but are more often suspended from a loop on the shoulder or from the back of a neck ring

Long hook-shaped Hmong silver earrings

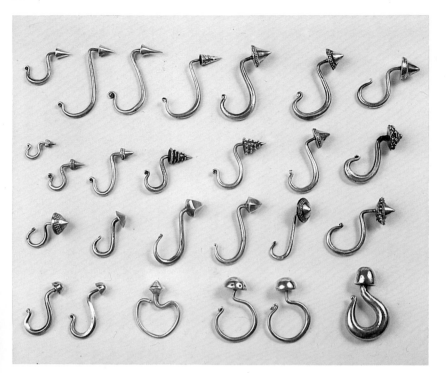

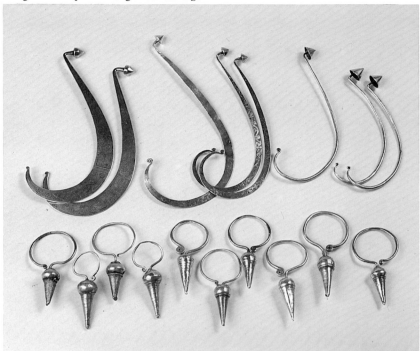

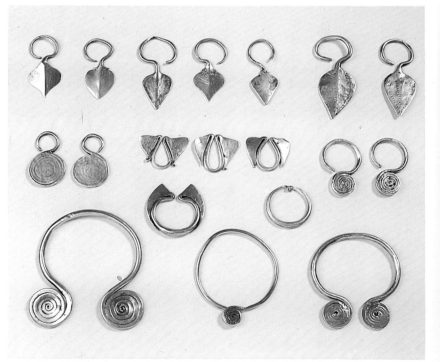

A variety of Hmong earrings. Mien and some Lahu also wear the bent-arrow type, and some Lahu may wear the round ones with dangles

The leaf and scroll-shaped earrings are mainly worn by Lahu Nyi women. The oval-shaped rings with wide flanges are probably of Hmong origin. Horseshoe-shaped ornaments as shown at the bottom are suspended from Akha headdresses

The dangle earrings with hooks are worn by Lahu and Lisu women. Akha women wear the larger types on their headdresses.

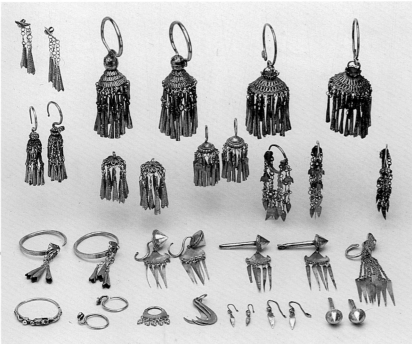

Bottom row, second left is a pair of Lisu women's earrings. Others unknown origin

Hair ornaments. Those with repousséd crowns are of Shan or Wa/Lawa origin

The cylindrical-shaped ear ornaments are Lahu Shi, the cup-shaped ones Karen, and the capped plugs are Shan. The whorled ear ornaments are probably Karen

The crown-shaped rings are worn by Lahu, Akha, and Lisu as well as Wa/Lawa people as finger rings and as ornaments on turbans and belts. The double-pointed rings are worn by Hmong and Mien. The bottom row of rings are Mien

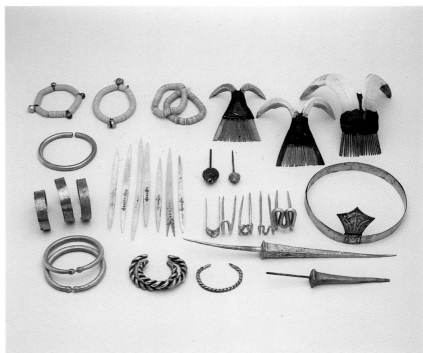

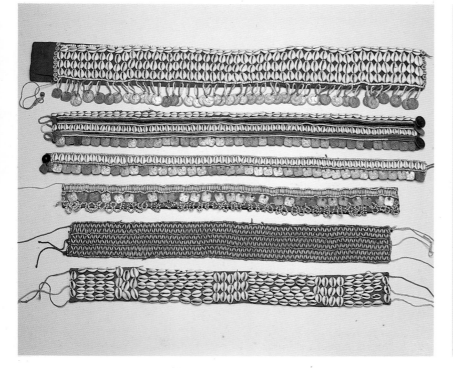

Page 62, top left: Karen make these necklaces out of coconut shell. The bracelets are lacquered string or rattan

Right: These Karen ornaments include bracelets made of white buttons; boar's tusk combs; brass and aluminium bracelets; aluminium hairpins; a silver tiara; a silver hairpin; a brass hairpin; and bone and aluminium hair spikes

Page 62, bottom left: Akha shell, seed and coin belts. The wide belts are worn by young unmarried women, while young matrons wear the narrower belts. A belt encrusted only with Job's-tear seeds (second from bottom) would be worn by a poor young woman who cannot afford to buy cowrie shells

Right: Many kinds of silver belts and chains are worn by tribal people

Knives and swords ornamented with silver and/or ivory are important status symbols for tribal men. They are made by Chinese, Shan, or tribal craftsmen

Silver knives with ivory, horn, bone, animal tooth and wood handles

Examples of carved ivory handles

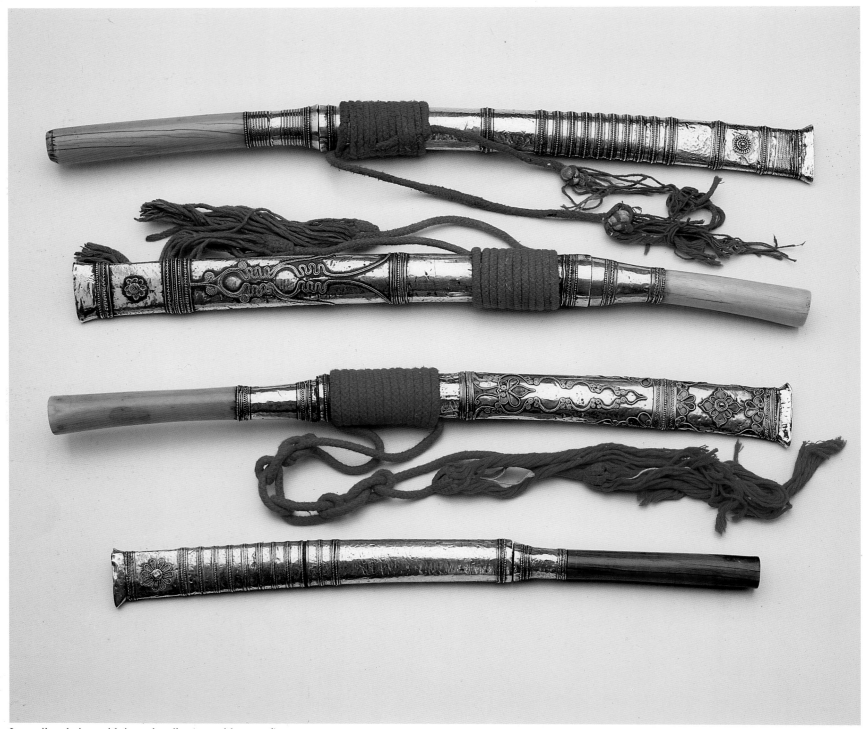

Long silver knives with ivory handles (one with enamel)

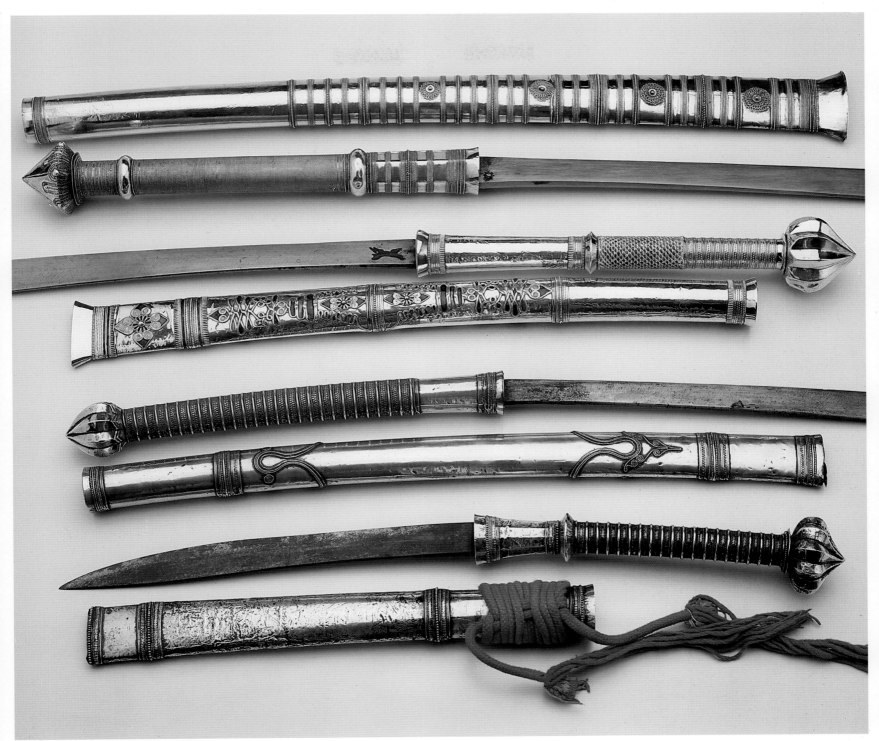

Silver swords, Shan style (one with enamel)

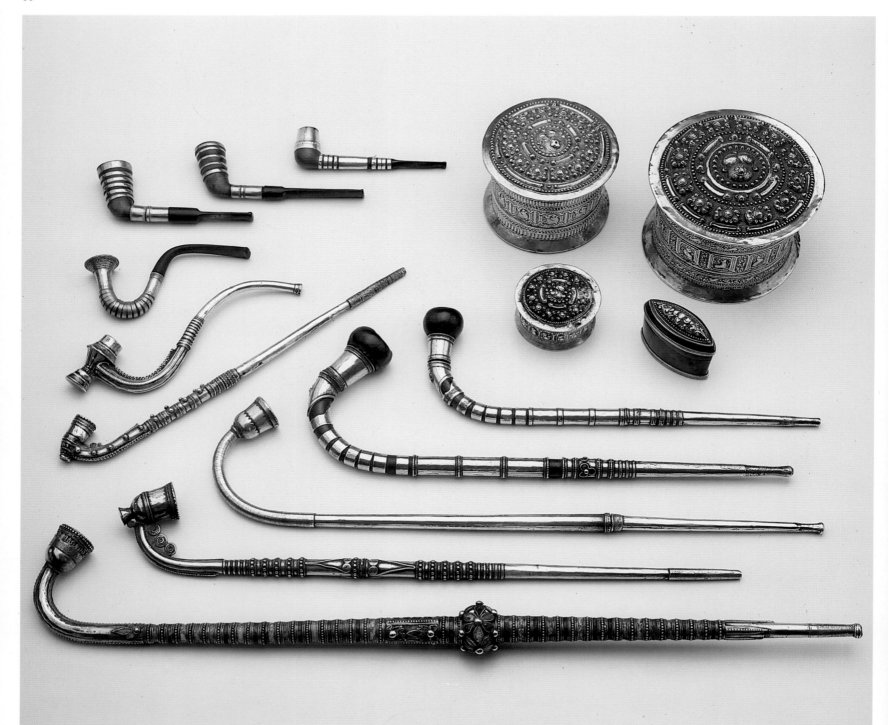

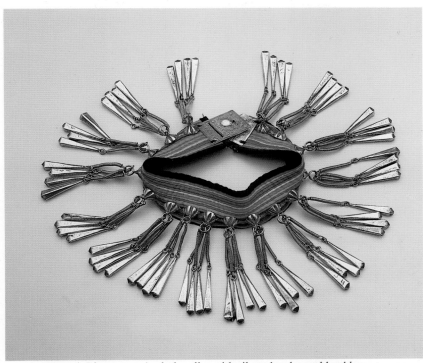

A Lisu woman's cloth collar with silver dangles and buckle

The wood/horn and silver pipes in the upper left are
used by Karen men and women, and the curved one
with silver wire by the Lawa people. Akha elders like to
use silver pipes, and might use any of the others
pictured. The three solid silver pipes at the bottom
could be the proud possession of almost any of the
Chinese-oriented groups. Shan-made silver boxes are
used for tobacco and betel-nut paraphernalia

Pwo Karen children

Chapter 3

KAREN (Kariang, Yang)

Pwo Karen girl

Desire for Harmony

A blackened teakettle bubbles lazily over the glowing coals on the fireplace in the middle of the room. Red-shirted Karen men sit cross-legged around the fire for the second night in a row, discussing where to move their village. Smoke curls up from the tobacco pipes of some, while others chew their quids of betel-nut, leaning over from time to time to spit streams of blood-red saliva through the slatted bamboo floor.

The elders are meeting in the home of their new village priest, the brother of the priest who died a month ago. He agreed only last night to take his brother's place. Now they must decide on a new village site, for the new priest might not be able to maintain harmonious relations with the 'Lord of Land and Water' of the present location.

'I think we should move closer to the new road', says one of the younger men. Silence. The host busies himself stuffing tea leaves into the kettle of hot water. He does not want to move close to the road. The harmony of the village would be threatened. All kinds of people might come in and out. Those foreign tourists might find the young Karen women too attractive.

The father of the first speaker clears his throat, 'Hmong have already moved near the road. Let's not get too close to their territory'. Relieved, the priest pours scalding tea into cups and passes them to the oldest members of the group.

Another long pause with smoking, chewing, and tea-drinking. The blacksmith puts down his teacup, shifts his position, and voices his thoughts. 'Let's just move to the other side of Rocky Ridge. That way we can keep our gardens and continue to work our fields'.

Silence again. More puffing, chewing, sipping. At last the young man defers to his elders. 'Maybe it wouldn't be too good to live close to the road', he says. It is late, but no one makes a move to leave. One elder after another begins to support the 'other side of Rocky Ridge' proposal. Other heads nod in agreement. A murmur of satisfaction moves across the room.

The embers of the fire are growing dim. 'Does anyone else wish to speak?' asks the priest. Silence again. It is imperative that they all agree to the move. Any who cannot go along must find another village. The host ejects a quid of betel-nut from his mouth, clears his throat loudly: 'Then we'll move to the other side of Rocky Ridge. Everyone start getting ready tomorrow'.

Name

The largest tribal group in Thailand is called 'Karen' in English (emphasis on the second syllable). They are called 'Kariang' by the Central Thai, while the Northern Thai refer to them as 'Yang'.

There are two major divisions of Karen in Thailand: Sgaw and Pwo. Two other Karenic groups found in very small numbers in Mae Hong Son Province are the Pa O (Taungthu, or Tongsu), and the Kayah (Karenni, or Bwe). This book does not deal with these two groups, as they represent less than 1% of the total Karen population in Thailand.

The Sgaw (sometimes written S'kaw) Karen refer to themselves as 'Pg'a Kanyaw Sg'aw', which means 'the Sgaw people'. (Note: The g' indicates a fricative g.) They call the Pwo 'Pg'a Kanyaw Pg'o'. The Pwo, however, refer to themselves as 'Phlong', or 'Phlong Shu'.

The Karen are the only group for which we are not using the name they call themselves, since they have no generic term to cover all the sub-groups of their tribe.

Population

Karen live in both Burma and Thailand. There are no recent census figures, but we estimate that there are about four million members of the Karenic group in Burma, the majority being Sgaw and Pwo.

There were approximately 246,000 Sgaw and Pwo in Thailand in mid-1983, about 20% being Pwo. Karen villages are found from the northern provinces of Chiang Rai, Chiang Mai and Mae Hong Son all the way down the western border of Thailand to the Isthmus of Kra – scattered throughout 15 provinces.

If a line were drawn from Mae Sariang through Hod (Chiang Mai Province) and on into Lamphun Province, most of the Pwo Karen in Thailand would be south of the line, including pockets of Pwo in Tak and Kanchanaburi provinces. Throughout the rest of the Karen areas the Sgaw are predominant.

Language

The Karen languages are difficult to categorize as to linguistic family. They differ from other Tibeto-Burman languages in certain aspects, and yet they do not seem to fit other classifications. Many linguists now refer to them as the Karenic group of the Tibeto-Burman family.

There are many Karen languages and dialects, especially in Burma. The two main languages spoken in Thailand, Sgaw and Pwo, are not considered to be mutally intelligible.

Karen borrow words widely from Burmese, Mon, Shan, and Tai, depending on where they live. Unlike other tribal people, they have the reputation of not learning other languages readily. When Karen are hired to work in Hmong poppy fields, it is the Hmong who learn Karen rather than the other way around. Many Karen can speak a limited amount of Northern Thai, but usually with a heavy accent.

History

The Karen reckon 1983 to be their year 2722. This means that they look to BC 739 as the year of their founding. Unfortunately they cannot remember where it was. In their legends Karen speak of coming from the land of 'Thibi Kawbi', which some have thought may indicate Tibet and the Gobi desert. According to some the Karen probably originated farther to the west than the other five tribes.

No doubt there have been Karen living in Burma for many centuries. It was in the 18th century that the Karen began to make their way across the Salween River from Burma into Thailand. This is verified by some Karen still living in Mae Hong Son Province who can calculate the time of the first wave of Karen settlers into the area. During the last half of the 18th century and the early years of the 19th, Karen communities along the eastern border of Burma were undoubtedly caught up in the turmoil of events when Burmese and Thai armies pursued each other through their territory. They would have suffered the oppression such people endure even today when caught between hostile forces – having to feed the marauding troops and serve them as porters and guides. When accompanying these armies they would have discovered vast areas of virgin forest on the Thai side where they could perhaps live in peace. There is evidence that the Karen of that period established a symbiotic relationship with the Yuan (Northern Thai), and may have moved across the river with some of them.

It was the Yuan who were at that time ruling the areas along the eastern bank of the Salween River. The Lawa (Lua') were then moving out of certain areas in the Yuan principality (especially in the Lannathai areas of Mae Sariang and Chiang Mai), and it seems quite likely that the Yuan rulers welcomed the peace-loving Karen into the resulting vacuum.

The Lawa had not moved out of some areas, so the Karen asked for permission to live near them, or in some cases even in their villages. The Lawa, who seemed at the time in no danger of being outnumbered by these relatively small groups of immigrants, graciously gave permission – only to find that in time the Karen had taken over the area and crowded them out. To this day, however, some Karen and Lawa live along side each other in Mae Hong Son Province. There is much evidence of Lawa influence in the dress, ornamentation, and implements of the Karen there.

There have been successive waves of Karen immigrants moving into Thailand since then. There is no significant immigration taking place within this generation, although there are even now groups of Karen from Burma taking temporary refuge on the Thai side of the border due to unrest in their own country.

Mythology

Karen mythology has many themes typical of minority people who have felt the pressure of having little, if any, political identity and power. Attitudes of resentment and distrust are prevalent in their folklore. This can be seen most clearly in the many Karen stories with the 'orphan' theme. Although the orphan is poor and trodden upon by the rich and mighty, he finally triumphs through his cleverness.

One Karen myth states that when the different tribal groups were created they were all brothers. The Karen was the 'oldest brother', and therefore deserving of respect from all the younger siblings, reflecting another theme in their culture. The 'White foreigner' is considered to be a younger brother. When God (or Buddha, depending on who is relating the myth) handed out writing to the brothers, the Karen lost his, thus explaining their relative poverty today. However, the myth also expresses the hope that the younger 'White brother' will come from across the sea and bring the writing to the Karen. When missionaries first came to Burma with the Bible, some Karen interpreted this as a fulfillment of the myth.

Karen are excellent story tellers, and love to sit around the fire in the evenings regaling their children with stories and myths. Many such tales revolve around how some gracious deity wished to give the Karen special gifts of wealth and wisdom, but the Karen were often sitting in the shade or were about their own business, thus they failed to receive the bounty intended for them.

Drawing on the testimony of their own folk tales, Pwo regard themselves as the guardians of the entire Karen culture. They consider the Sgaw to be of the male lineage, whereas the Pwo are of the female lineage of the tribe. This gives them the responsibility of holding the culture together. The Sgaw dispute this, pointing out that when the Pwo court, recite poety, and eulogize the dead, they use the Sgaw language, proving that the Sgaw are the 'senior' of the two groups!

Sgaw Karen woman

Clothing

The name 'Karen' has become almost synonymous with 'Weaver', so outstanding are the products of Karen looms. Their unusual embroidery and seed work make for widely varied types of clothing worn by those groups coming under the general heading of 'Karen'.

The upper garments worn by men, women and children are made in the same basic way, differing only in length, colour, and embellishment. They are made of two strips of hand-woven cloth, the width depending on the size of the wearer. These strips are folded in half, the fold forming the shoulders of the garment. They are then stitched together, leaving openings for the head and arms which are bound with braid of a contrasting colour. Karen make the most of their stitching. It is seldom hidden, but rather becomes a part of the decoration.

Originally all clothing was made of homespun cotton cloth. Even now many mountain-dwelling Karen still spin thread from their own cotton. Weaving is done on simple back-strap looms using a single-warp technique.

Pwo woman weaving skirt with intricate pattern

Sgaw woman embroidering with seeds

Sgaw woman weaving blouse

Pwo woman spinning cotton

Pwo girls weaving their wedding garments

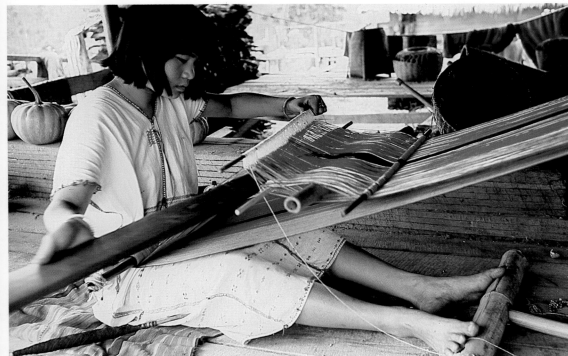

Pwo girl weaving tie-dyed skirt

Sgaw woman sewing

Single girls' dress

From the time they are tiny tots until they marry, Karen girls wear long white cotton shifts. Girls as young as ten years of age learn to make their own dresses, consequently they are of simple design. As the girls grow older and become more skilled, they often weave more ornate designs into their dresses.

Sgaw girls weave a band of red or pink just above the waist. That same colour is used in all the stitching. (All shades of pink are considered variations of red.)

Pwo girls embellish their dresses more elaborately. One style is similar to the Sgaw dress, but has scattered red diamond-shaped patterns woven into the lower portion of the skirt, with other colours used for accent. Another style has an all-over diamond-shaped pattern in red covering the lower portion of the dress. Traditionally the design extended from the knees to the hemline, but some girls are today weaving the pattern from the waist down, perhaps indulging in a little game of 'one-up-manship'.

Another style of the Pwo girl's shift has a wide red yoke, a strip of colour down the shoulders, and a wide border from the knees down. All of these designs are basically red. The yoke is woven in the usual manner, but designs on the shoulder and border are chenille. This is done by inserting thick tufts of thread while weaving, and later cutting them off short to give a fuzzy effect. For ceremonial occasions (primarily funerals) the girls insert long strands of red thread all around the dress at the yoke, making a fringe that hangs to below the knees. (See illustration right.)

Head coverings

Traditionally Karen girls have worn their hair long and tied in a knot on top of the head, although many girls today wear their hair short. Women wear their long hair in a bun at the nape of their necks. Both young women and adults use two styles of head coverings. One is a hand-woven red or white turban with a long fringe. The other is rather like a veil. It is a rectangle of white or pink cloth almost one metre wide, tied around the head and left to hang loose over the shoulders in back. Often a young woman ties a beaded headband with bright-coloured pompons around the crown of her head to hold the veil in place.

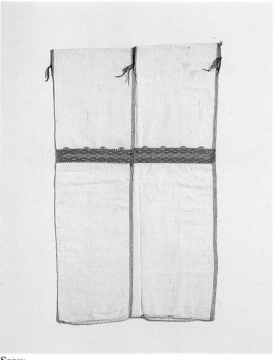

Sgaw

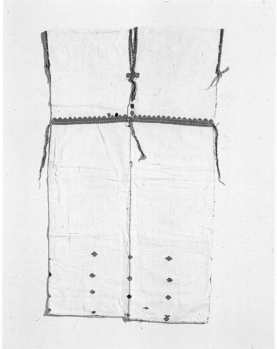

Sgaw

Woman's turban

Pwo

Pwo

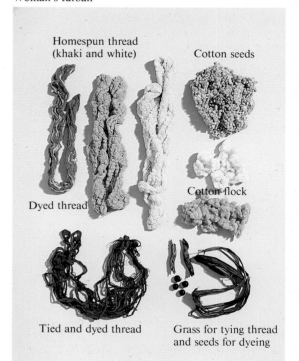

Homespun thread
(khaki and white)

Cotton seeds

Dyed thread

Cotton flock

Tied and dyed thread

Grass for tying thread
and seeds for dyeing

Tie-dye (Ikat) technique

Married women's dress

All married women wear sarongs and over-blouses. A young woman contemplating marriage makes her own wedding clothes, as well as a shirt for her prospective husband. The woman's outfit is made in a wide variety of designs, depending whether Sgaw or Pwo, mountain-dwellers or valley-dwellers, living in the north or south, and how recently they have arrived from Burma. It is therefore difficult to classify Karen women's clothing.

Sgaw women living in the mountains wear blouses woven of indigo-dyed homespun cotton. They embroider the lower portion of the blouse with bright red thread, and embellish it with white Job's-tear seeds.* The borders may vary from rather simply embroidered patterns over the lower third of the blouse to very elaborate solid embroidery covering two-thirds of the garment. On some of the blouses the seeds are used sparingly, and simply accent the design of the embroidery, while on others they form a major element in the pattern. Often a strip of red cloth three or four fingers wide is appliquéd near the bottom edge.

Other Sgaw women wear blouses with a woven pattern. The top part of the blouse is plain black or indigo, and the design forms a lower border. It can be a rather narrow border or extend two-thirds of the way up. Again it is predominantly red, with other colours used for accent. The lower section has large all-over diamond-shaped patterns and above that is a section blocked out into vertical rectangles. Most of the patterns within the rectangles are variations of diamonds, zigzags, vertical lines, and dots.

Pwo women generally wear blouses with bold patterns. A style worn by Pwo living in the Hod Valley uses black thread for the basic cloth, but it is totally overlaid with a pattern of alternating red and gold-coloured stripes and squares, often accented with Job's-tear seeds. Another style of Pwo Karen blouse has an all-over design in the upper part of the blouse – across the shoulders and down about half way, just the opposite of the Sgaw style. Blouses are sleeveless but the cloth falls over the shoulders with a cap-sleeve effect. While working, women often wear long detached sleeves of dark blue or black cloth to protect their arms.

Married women wear sarongs made of two strips of material sewn together horizontally, then stitched together to form a tubular skirt. Being narrow, the sarongs do not have enough overlap to be folded and tucked in like Thai-style sarongs, therefore they are either bunched around the waist or wrapped with a pleat in front, and held up with a cord or metal belt. Sarongs are worn anywhere from knee- to ankle-length, being hitched up shorter when doing certain types of work, and worn longer for more formal occasions.

Homespun skirts using ikat (tie-dye) patterns are worn by mountain-dwelling Sgaw and Pwo women. Each woman has her own way of tying the thread to produce her special pattern, and she carefully guards her secret. It is said that the tie-dye process is associated with spirit worship, and each woman does hers in the forest, away from curious eyes. (See Campbell 1978: 133 for a description of the process.) The brick-red dye is made from the *kho* plant. After the threads are tied and dyed, the warp is set up using strips of ikat alternating with bands of kho-dyed thread, accented with strips of indigo thread.

Plains-dwelling Karen generally weave their skirts of market thread, with narrower strips of tie-dyed pattern and wider strips of solid colours in order to save time and work.

Some of the plains-dwelling Pwo women wear very bright-coloured skirts. The basic colour is usually red. They commonly have narrow strips of tie-dyed design of the rust or brick-red colour, separated with strips of an intricately woven pattern, alternating stripes of gold, green, and black or blue.

Sgaw women in the Mae Sariang plains weave skirts of still a different type. The borders are red, while the central panel is of an intricate all-over pattern of various colours.

---

* The white, pearly seeds of a hardy, annual tropical grass.

Sgaw woman's blouse with embroidery and seed-work

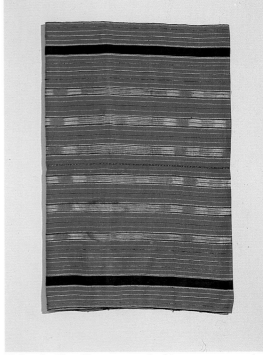

Plains-dwelling Karen woman's skirt

Sgaw blouse with seed-work

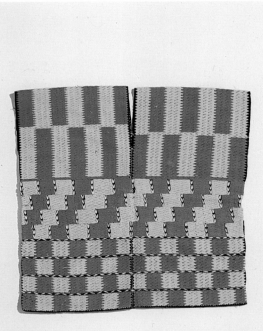

Pwo woman's blouse

Pwo woman's blouse

Tie-dyed market thread sarong

Plains-dwelling Pwo sarong

Plains-dwelling Pwo Sarong

Sgaw blouse with embroidery and seed-work

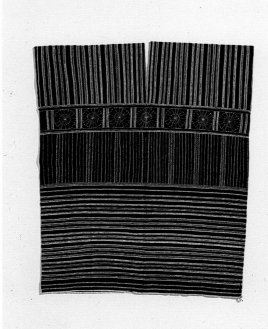

Pwo embroidered blouse from Rachburi Province

Old-style blouse with seed-work (Sgaw from Burma)

Sgaw blouse with woven design

Old style Pwo blouse with embroidery and seed-work

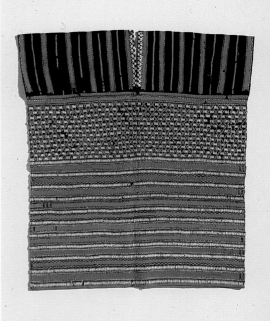

Old-style blouse with seed-work (Sgaw from Burma)

Men's clothing

Karen men's shirts generally hang to the hips, although some Pwo Karen wear shirts that reach almost to the knees. They are either of unbleached homespun cotton with red or blue stripes, or red with white stripes accented with yellow and green. A decorative cording effect is made in the lower portion of the shirts by inserting many strands of red thread at regular intervals while weaving. For ceremonial occasions, the cording threads are left several centimetres longer than the width of the cloth to form a fringe when the garment is stitched together. In such a case, instead of hemming the shirt, the warp threads are left as a fringe around the bottom. The braiding around the neck and arm holes is often of green, yellow, and white thread. Shirts worn by young bachelors at funerals often have a long fringe hanging down to the knees.

Some Pwo men wear jackets of unbleached homespun cotton which open at the front. The neck is shaped and bound and is edged with braiding. Elbow-length sleeves are set in.

Both Pwo and Sgaw men wear either sarongs or Thai peasant-style pants. The knee-length sarongs are made of two panels, and are either white or red with one wide blue stripe in each panel. Pants are black and reach to mid-calf.

Men often wear turbans consisting of turkish towels or phakamas (the cloth Thai men wrap around their waists). Young Pwo bachelors wear their hair long and often pull it sleekly across the head to tie in a knot over one ear. They anchor the knot with a huge hairpin, and sometimes an ivory comb. For special occasions they neatly wrap a band of red silk cloth around their heads.

Older men usually wear their hair in a crew cut. On special occasions they may wear pink silk turbans – Shan style.

Older boys wear the same style of clothing as men, while most small boys wear over-sized shirts and no other garment.

Sgaw shirt

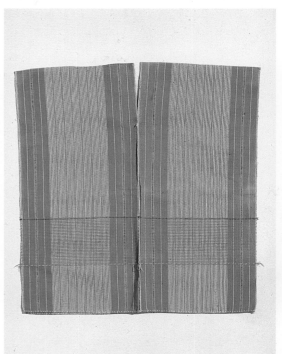
Pwo shirt

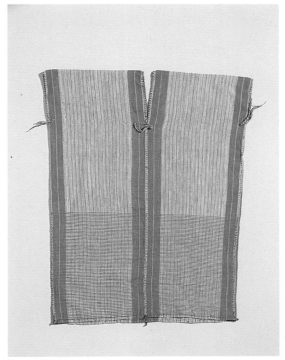
Pwo shirt

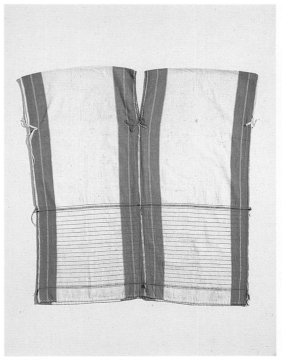
Man's homespun work shirt

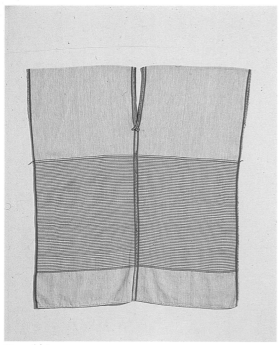

Pwo shirt

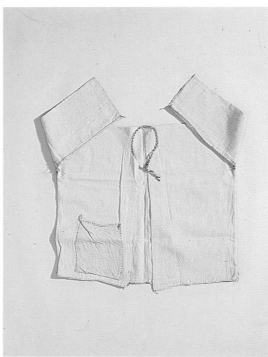

Pwo homespun jacket

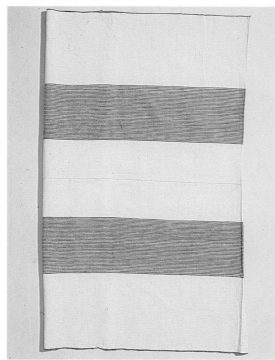

Man's sarong

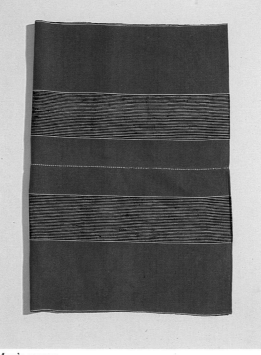

Man's sarong

Shoulder bags

Plain canvas-like bags made of unbleached homespun with only narrow stripes of red, indigo, or black down the sides are used for every-day work bags. Finely woven ones, usually of market thread, are more decorative.

Pwo bags are woven with a top border of designs similar to those used in the women's blouses. Sgaw bags have designs which are either geometric or stylized animals or flowers. These bags were traditionally red or white. Now, however, they are often black, and when made for sale may be any colour.

Blankets

Hand-woven blankets are of red and white stripes. Now sometimes they are other colours, such as the ones which are woven of natural homespun white thread and natural khaki cotton thread in alternating stripes.

The panels of the blankets are about 40 cm wide and are woven in four-metre lengths. These are then cut in half, and panels are sewn together to make the desired width. One end of the blanket has a twisted fringe, and the other end is hemmed. The fringe end must always be used at the foot, because when a corpse is covered with a blanket the fringe is placed at the head. This is one way of letting the deceased know he is dead!

Pwo women weave small red blankets with white pinstripes. About half of the blanket has horizontal stripes of yellow and green, and there is a trim of these two colours plus pink. The yellow and green threads are allowed to hang from the panels and edges of the blanket in a fringe when sewn together.

Pwo blankets can be made into 'singing shawls', used at funerals. Half the shawl is covered with white buttons arranged in groups of three or five. An elaborate singing shawl has strings of the bright iridescent wings of green beetles attached, with tiny bells at the ends.

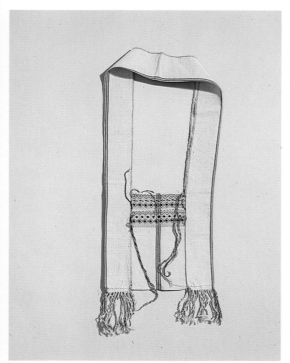

Pwo bag

Pwo blankets

Pwo blanket and bag used at funerals

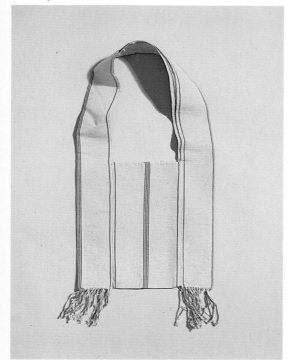

Sgaw work bag

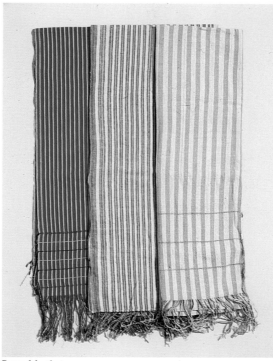

Sgaw blankets

Pwo singing shawl

Ornaments

Beads

Sgaw women and girls wear multiple strands of small beads which hang anywhere from mid-chest to waist length, favouring red, white, and yellow. Pwo women, on the other hand, wind extremely long strings of beads around the throat and down to mid-chest. These are mostly black. Young Pwo bachelors wear bead chokers, and on special occasions multiple strands of longer beads as well.

The Karen use an astonishing variety of beads. Many wear small glass seed-beads used as barter by European traders centuries ago. Others are Chinese glass beads, and no doubt some are from India and other Asian and European countries.

Tiny pierced beads are made from coconut shells cut out with metal tools by a technique known by the Karen for hundreds of years. These feather-light beads become very dark and shiny with use.

Silver jewellery

Karen do not wear the heavy types of silver jewellery used by some other tribal groups. The most common type of silver necklace is made of the old 'bullet coins' which were used by the Thai for hundreds of years. These come in several sizes, the one-baht size being the most numerous. The five-baht size is sometimes used as a pendant in the centre of a string of one-baht coins. Bullet coins are usually strung on braided red thread.

Another style is the 'rice grain' necklace. Delicately-made hollow, elongated silver beads alternated with tiny spherical ones are worn in multi-strands.

Karen neck rings are small in comparison with those of other tribes. Some are thin bands of silver which hook around the neck. Others are flat, round or twisted. Many are etched with plant, animal, or geometric designs.

Bracelets

Pwo women like to cover their arms with a variety of bracelets. Some are flat and narrow, while others are round and smooth, twisted or coiled. They may be made of silver, copper, brass, or aluminium. Several kinds are often worn together.

In some areas it has become popular among the Pwo to wear bracelets made by stringing ordinary white shirt buttons back to back, with tiny brass bells attached. Others wear bracelets made of plaited rattan or lacquered thread. Sgaw women are much more moderate in their use of jewellery. A few men, both Sgaw and Pwo, wear simple bracelets of silver, brass, or aluminium – one on each wrist.

Earrings

Both Sgaw and Pwo women wear silver earrings having a cylindrical part which is thrust through the holes in the ear lobes (bevelled so they will stay in the ear) with a cup-shaped outer part. These vary in size. Often brightly coloured tufts of wool and other decorative objects are attached.

Some Pwo men wear rhinestone earrings with wool tassels. In some areas Pwo men and women used to wear ivory ear plugs with a stick-like portion extending to as much as ten cm. These are now rarely seen.

Karen girls like to wear lots of beads and bracelets

Some wear head bands, and tufts of wool yarn in their earrings

Pwo women

Villages

The majority of Karen in Thailand, both Sgaw and Pwo, live in mountain villages, although at a lower elevation than other groups. They have become renowned for their sound methods of swidden agriculture. Ideally they have followed this method:

1. A field is used for only one year, then left fallow for six to twelve years.
2. Elaborate steps are taken to contain fire so that fallow areas are not destroyed.
3. A belt of forest growth is left intact on the slope above the cleared fields, and saplings are allowed to stand.
4. Weeds are scraped off and the soil is not turned when preparing for planting.

As a result of these measures, Karen fields have not eroded significantly and there has been a minimum of cogan (thatch) grass in their fields while lying fallow. However, population pressure is forcing Karen farmers to violate their own rules, with consequent loss of soil fertility.

Lowland, or valley-dwelling Karen, usually live in villages of their own, but there are also Karen settlements in towns like Sankhlaburi, Mae Sariang, Hod, Chiang Mai and Nam Lat.

There are considerable differences between mountain villages, plains villages, and settlements in towns. Karen living in the hills prefer an isolated area where they can live in peace. They look for a site sheltered from the weather and near a good water supply. They prefer an elevation of between six hundred and one thousand metres.

Karen living in the valleys tend to imitate the Thai farmers' agricultural methods, house design, and for the men, clothing. Most women, however, continue to wear their own distinctive dress. Karen is still the language spoken, and their own ceremonies are regularly observed. The lowland Karen have developed a somewhat different dialect from their brothers and sisters in the mountains, and borrow vocabulary freely from the Thai.

The few Karen living in towns significantly influence the values and outlook of the Karen as a whole, for they include the best educated and most affluent of their tribe.

Karen villages in the hills develop in clusters. Each cluster begins with a single village, the population of which doubles about every 24 years.

As a village becomes larger, some of the people have to walk ever-increasing distances to make their swidden fields. Eventually this becomes a burden, and those who have fields in a given area far away will start their own satellite village, although they usually continue to relate to the leadership of the 'mother village'. Those, however, who start making irrigated rice fields often choose their own leadership, and do not maintain as close a tie to the mother village as would otherwise be the case.

There may be as many as seven or eight satellites clustered around the mother village, some comprising no more than two or three households, while others may grow to a size of thirty or more houses – occasionally even exceeding the size of the mother village.

A satellite must receive its village spirit from the parent village, and if the satellite is large enough to warrant a priest, it will probably secure a son or younger brother of the village priest from the mother village. A close relationship is usually maintained. This cohesion can be seen most clearly at the time of a funeral, when boys and girls of marriageable age from the entire cluster gather together to sing and enjoy each other's company.

Anthropologists are concerned that due to population pressure there are no longer sites into which satellite villages can move. Swidden areas have virtually been exhausted, especially in the Mae Hong Son and Chiang Mai provinces. It is now recognized that the system of satellite villages breaking away from the mother village has not only been of value in providing for the agricultural needs of the people, but has also served as a means of restoring harmony to a village torn by disputes.

On the whole, Karen villages are more stable than those of other tribes. Hinton (1973:245) found that 92% of the Hmong, 77% of the Lahu, 75% of the Lisu and 74% of the Mien villages studied had moved at least once over a ten-year period. During that same time only 24% of the Karen villages had moved, partly due to the fact that Karen have been domiciled in Thailand over a longer period, and have their territory well staked out.

There are times when a Karen village must move, such as when the village priest dies, but it seldom moves very far. Sometimes only a token move of a few metres is made. Since the village does not move far, they do not have to abandon everything they have developed. For this reason Karen can grow such permanent crops as jackfruit, mango, and citrus fruits. Some also develop extensive garden areas and tobacco fields. This is in sharp contrast to most other tribal groups.

Anyone who wishes to move into a Karen village first requests permission from the village priest and elders. If accepted, he must make the appropriate sacrifice at the village shrine. Until twenty years ago most villages welcomed the opportunity to enlarge their community, because it gave them added security and a broader social network. By the 1970s, however, the jungle belt surrounding many of the Karen villages was shrinking as more land – some of which was quite marginal – was being brought under cultivation. As a result, nowadays the village priest and elders are not always eager to accept new people into their village.

Sgaw women threshing paddy

Sgaw house

Feeding piglets (Sgaw)

Street in a Sgaw village

Drying rice (Pwo)

Carrying water in bamboo section (Sgaw)

Cleaning rice (Pwo)

Village Leaders

Village priest

The most important person in a Karen village is the village priest, called *sapwa hi akhu* by the Sgaw, and *shasha g'ae akhu* by the Pwo. His is a herditary position, and according to Karen tradition succession can only take place when he dies. The office is passed on to the oldest willing male resident of the village who is related to the deceased priest on his father's side. This would include his younger brothers, his sons, and sons of his father's brothers.

The priest is the ritual leader of the village. He sets the dates for and officiates at the annual village ceremonies, the most important of which is to the 'Lord of Land and Water'. This ceremony periodically confirms the village as a social and religious unit, and involves all the villagers.

As spiritual leader of the village, the priest watches over the moral conduct of its members. The Karen are particularly concerned about sexual mores, and believe that a breach of their moral code will result in repercussions from the offended spirits, such as disease, crop failure, or the loss of livestock to predatory animals. It is the task of the village priest to restore harmony in such situations by requiring a sacrifice (usually of a large pig or buffalo), and by imposing other sanctions on the offending party.

Just as it is the responsibility of the village priest to admit people into the village, it is also he who requires a person to leave who has broken taboos or in other ways jeopardized the harmony of the community.

The priest, in consultation with the elders, allocates fields to the households. Before a villager can sell his fields he must have the permission of the priest. In certain areas where the Hmong have moved in and are pressing the Karen to sell land to them, some, particularly opium addicts, are selling at a very low price without first obtaining the permission of the priest. This alarms the custodians of Karen tradition.

When there is a village dispute the priest arbitrates, for he holds in his hands the harmony and well-being of the village. The quality of life depends in large part on his skill in fulfilling his priestly functions. Some prove to be negligent and incompetent. As there is no provision in Karen tradition to remove him from office, the only alternatives are to start a new village with a male relative of his as priest, or to move out of his village into one which has a good priest. In some cases an entire village has moved away from its priest. This is tragic for him, because as the 'senior' priest he could not move with the village and be under one who would be his 'junior'.

Village headman

From the Karen point of view the village headman has little power or authority. His duty is to determine the village consensus and then to follow it carefully. This can put him in a difficult position, as he needs to remain a 'good Karen', while at the same time carrying out whatever duties the Thai authorities require. Most Karen do not aspire to this position because of potential conflicts that might arise.

Karen house plan

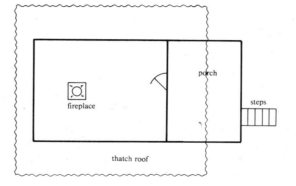

fireplace

porch

steps

thatch roof

House and Household

Karen in mountain villages build simple houses on stilts, usually using split bamboo for walls and floor, and thatch or large leaves for the roof. Chickens, pigs, and cattle are kept under the house at night. In some villages wide-seated swings are suspended under the house for the enjoyment of family and friends.

Every house has a spacious covered veranda which is used for preparing food, for weaving and doing other work, and as a place to chat with friends and accommodate overnight guests. There is often an uncovered section which extends from the porch, especially among the Pwo.

The traditional Karen house has only one room, although there may be a screened-off area in one corner to provide privacy for an adolescent daughter. The family sits and sleeps on mats laid on the floor. In the centre of the room is the fireplace, where the fire is often kept going day and night. A mat is suspended above the fireplace for drying and storage.

The granary is built separately from the house, but from the same materials. It must not be in front of or behind the house, but must be placed diagonally to it. If the house is on a slope, the floor has to be lower than that of the house, otherwise it is believed illness would result.

Not every house has a rice pounder, for one pounder is used by several households. Consequently it is a focal point for social gatherings.

There are certain rules about where houses are built. First of all, they are grouped according to matrilineages, with a great deal of care being given to assure that no household spirits are offended by people of another matriline building between two houses of the same matrilineage. No three houses should ever be constructed so they form an equi-distant triangular pattern. Failure to observe these rules would be *'chai'*, a situation where something horrible happens due to someone breaking Karen taboos.

There is no altar in a Karen house, nor are there any centres of worship in a traditional Karen village. The only sacred areas are the burial ground and the special shrine to the 'Lord of Land and Water' outside the village.

The household is an independent economic unit which holds rights over the land it is tilling and over its own wealth, whether cash, goods, or livestock. Each values its autonomy and tries to be totally self-sufficient.

Most households are made up of a husband and wife and their unmarried children – a nuclear family, unlike other tribal groups which usually have three generational households. This difference can partially be explained by the fact that women who are not related to the wife and mother of the household must not live there, as this would lead to 'conflict of the spirits'. There is a case where a widowed woman came to live with her son, and because of their fear of *chai* he built a small hut near the house for her to sleep in, but she took her meals with the family. Later when the son's wife died in childbirth the villagers felt it was because his mother had been taking her meals with them, causing conflict between their spirits.

This fear of *chai* also explains why Karen men do not take second wives, and widowers do not remarry, at least until their children are grown-up and are living on their own. This places a severe burden on men who lose their wives and are left with small children, as the father must take care of them and also work in the fields.

There are strict rules as to who is allowed to sleep in a Karen house. Unmarried sons past the age of puberty should not sleep in the same house with their sisters of marriageable age. They spend the nights on the verandas of friends who have no mature sisters. Guests are usually expected to sleep on the veranda.

Threshing basket on porch of Pwo house

Pwo mother and children at mealtime

Sgaw women pounding paddy

Sgaw woman preparing meal

Courtship and Marriage

Karen like to extend their social network through marriage. While marriages of related people are not totally banned, they desire to keep down the number of unions between couples related on the female side. They believe that if successive unions take place between two matrilineages, those parties to the earlier marriages who are still alive would suffer soul loss, and thus become sick and die.

Marital regulation of both Sgaw and Pwo follow this pattern:

- first cousins should not marry (although Pwo sometimes marry parallel paternal cousins);
- a man must not marry someone he classifies as 'older cousin';
- marriage between aunt and nephew or uncle and niece is prohibited.

The intricate details of these regulations are discussed exhaustively when a couple is contemplating marriage.

Courtship

There are many opportunities for young people to become acquainted with one another, although elders frown on young unmarried couples meeting privately on any occasion. Young men and women sometimes hold thatch-making parties on moonlit nights, which afford opportunities for chatting and teasing. They also work together during times of communal planting, weeding, and harvesting, and enjoy meeting around rice pounders and on verandas in the evenings. During the agricultural lull of December and January young men visit other Karen villages. These are times of informal contacts, and serious courting does not usually take place.

Courting is mainly done at funerals, when all work stops in the village of the deceased, and everyone gathers for the rites. Many come from neighbouring villages as well. The young people, dressed in their finest clothing, gather around the bier and sing, making the most of the many hours of contact. When there are long periods between funerals, youth are sometimes heard to wish out loud that someone would die!

A girl is taught to be shy. She is not supposed to show any outward sign of interest in a boy. When a young man, for instance, offers food or drink during a work break at harvest time, she probably will not even speak to or look at him. This does not indicate a lack of interest, but simply that she is a proper Karen young woman.

When a boy wishes to call his girl friend to come out of the house, he may sing a song like this:

Oh Miss Flower, Miss Budding Flower,
Miss Yellow Budding Flower.
Your dress is embroidered with diamond designs,
Lovely tassels hang from it.
See the seven-star constellation setting,
Untie your loom and come down to the boys.
Cut down leaves by the village well.
Cut down bamboo by the well of the village.
Cut down wood to whittle a harp.
Cut bamboo from which a harp can be whittled.
Strum it in the house, it is heard in the open;
Strum it in the open, it is heard in the house.

After such a period of informal courtship, a young man may propose to the young woman of his choice. It is not unheard of, however, for her to propose marriage. Being a society which stresses matrilineage and practices matrilocal residence, this is permissible. In either case the proposal may be made directly or through an intermediary. If it is accepted, the couple may exchange tobacco pipes to symbolize their commitment, and an announcement is made to the village.

If some believe that a union of this couple might result in soul loss for some or all of the villagers, they voice their objections to the parents of either the boy or the girl. Such objections, raising fears in the couple themselves lest their union might lead to sickness or even death for them or others, often block the marriage.

Despite Karen prohibition against pre-marital sex, and even against the couple being alone together before marriage, some 15–20% of the bridegrooms pay a fine at the time of marriage for having broken this rule.

Wedding

The wedding ceremony includes festivities lasting for two or three days, the bride's community hosting the groom's. On the wedding day the groom goes with friends in a procession to the bride's house, singing and dancing to the accompaniment of horns, drums and gongs. On their arrival the bride's mother ceremonially sprinkles water on the feet of the groom, thus cleansing him from the spirits of his natal home, and ensuring future harmony in the new home. The bride brings a bowl of water and washes the groom's hands as a further blessing upon their union.

A special dish will have been prepared by cooking a hen and rooster together, adding little spice, thus symbolizing the desire for a union free from hot tempers. The bride takes some of the chicken, mixes it with rice, and spoons it into the groom's mouth, after which he feeds her in the same way. Those present cheer, and everyone begins to eat. Sometime during the feast water is poured over the groom, who wears old clothes for this occasion – then his bride presents him with the new shirt she has woven.

Later the groom pours a glass of liquor for his bride. After she has taken a sip, all those present drink. The bride, if she has not done so earlier, changes from her long white dress to her two-piece ensemble. This change of dress style at marriage is unique to the Karen.

Following the wedding the couple performs a three-day 'thanksgiving ceremony', first for the bride's parents, and then for the parents of the groom. The first evening they feast on a rooster and hen, the second on a small pig, and the third evening on fish. The parents eat first, followed by the newly weds, and finally by their younger siblings, who represent their future children. Thus a three-generational relationship is established: the newly married couple, their parents, and the children yet to be born.

Ideally the couple lives for at least two years in the bride's village, either with her parents or in a home of their own. This practice used to operate with few serious difficulties, but because of the population explosion the land factor now influences the choice of place of residence. The couple tends to live in whichever of the two villages has more available arable land.

Divorce

To the Karen marriage is for life, therefore, divorce is strongly disapproved of. Among the hill-dwelling Karen of the north it has been found that the divorce rate is only 5 to 6%. In 75% of these cases an opium addicted husband had deserted his wife so he could become a wage labourer in the lowlands. In valleys and towns the rate of divorce is about double, but still much lower than among the other tribal groups and the Thai.

When divorce occurs the absconding party is supposed to pay token compensation to the other. The house stays with the wife, who also keeps the children. Other property is equally divided.

Adultery is strongly condemned and occurs more rarely among the Karen than other groups. They believe that if adultery is committed, the spirit of the 'Lord of Land and Water' will punish the entire community, causing crop failure, disease, pestilence, or even death from marauding tigers. When adultery occurs, the offending parties must sacrifice a large animal, and salt must be ritually distributed to each household in the village. The guilty pair or party must then be driven from the village.

Birth

Pregnancy

When a Karen woman becomes pregnant, she must observe certain restrictions which it is believed will prevent complications endangering both her life and that of the baby. Diet is of primary concern. The expectant mother must avoid food to which she is unaccustomed, or has been bought from others. To drink liquor might cause a miscarriage; to eat jackfruit could cause the baby to be born with a skin disease.

There are other taboos not related to diet. The pregnant woman must not go to a funeral, lest the baby's soul go to the afterworld with the soul of the deceased. If she even looks upon a corpse, a soul-calling ceremony must be held for the unborn baby.

Others in the community need to be careful that nothing is done to cause problems for the pregnant woman. For instance, if she comes upon a tree felled across her path, it is believed she will have an obstruction during birth; consequently whoever felled the tree must give her a chicken.

Birth

Ideally a woman should give birth in her own home. At a normal delivery, her husband, mother, or some other relative assists. During delivery she squats, clinging for support to a rope suspended from a roof beam. Those assisting gently massage her abdomen to help ease the baby downward.

After the baby has been born, the umbilical cord is severed with a freshly cut sliver of bamboo. The placenta is wrapped in cloth and put in a bamboo tube. The father hangs this in a tree just outside the village, or buries it at the foot of the steps leading up to the veranda, depending on the area in which they live.

Karen women greatly fear complications at the time of birth, knowing this is one of the most common causes of death. In a difficult delivery a midwife (either woman or man) is called to press and massage the baby into the correct position. Magical spells might be used, such as spewing 'lustral water' over the body of the woman in labour, and giving her the remainder to drink. If this does not help, the midwife divines to discover if some animal is causing the difficulty. If so, it will be killed. If it is a spirit causing the problem a ceremony is held to placate that spirit.

Some midwives are held in such high regard that they may be called to other villages to assist in deliveries. They maintain contact with many families and villages and are an important inter-village communications link.

Post-natal

After the birth of the child, the mother sits by the fire for three days before leaving the house. She is afraid to lie down for fear her blood will run directly to her head and cause her death. She often holds a hot stone wrapped in cloth to her abdomen. During this post-natal period she generally eats only rice and chicken.

To protect the mother and child from evil spirits, a bamboo basket is often overturned and placed near the door with a large knife on top of it.

The day after the birth a ritual specialist is called in to chant spells and spew lustral water over the mother. Following this her husband or father ties a white cotton cord around her neck to avert sickness and worry. Two or three days later the new mother presents to the midwife a chicken, a bottle of liquor, a strand of beads, and some acacia seeds. The midwife puts the acacia seeds in water and uses the solution to wash her (or his) hair, thus becoming purified from any contamination due to the birth.

The day after giving birth the mother chews up a mixture of rice, salt, and water and offers it to the child as a ritual feeding. When the navel has healed, the child's wrists are bound with cotton strings and small stones are hung around its neck to foster healthy growth. At the naming ceremony, which is usually held a month after birth, the parents tie cotton strings on the baby's wrist, and pierce its ears to show it is human and not a monkey, and say, 'Now you have become a Pg'a Kanyaw (human being)'.

If within a few days of birth the infant falls ill, the parents may go to the site where the placenta was placed and invite the child's soul to return to the body. If the child is more than two weeks old, however, they may need to buy back the soul from the spirits, which involves trading a chicken for the soul of the child. When they return home after sacrificing the chicken they knock on the steps leading up to the house before entering. Then they hurry inside, believing the soul has been restored to the baby's body.

Various amulets are tied around the necks of infants to protect them from illness. These may be of Karen origin or purchased from the Thai. In areas where Karen are followers of the 'White Monk' (see *Religious Movements*) it may be an amulet containing his picture.

Karen children

Karen mothers and children

Pwo

Pwo

Pwo

Pwo

Sgaw

Pwo

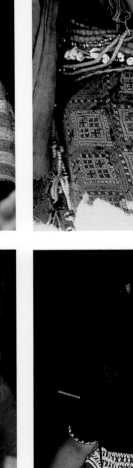

Pwo women

Young Pwo bachelor with traditional hairstyle

Sgaw headman winding silk turban

Making bamboo ties

Karen elders

The tattoo needle provides the main adornment for Karen men

Death

At death a person enters the place of the dead, ruled over by the 'Lord of the Dead' (Khu See-du). The after-life is a mirror of life on earth, and those who have gone there make fields, care for livestock, and participate in other activities similar to what is done in life. When the sun sets for the living, it rises for those who are in the place of death. Khu See-du, they say, grants permission to those who have lived worthily to enter the higher realms, but condemns to the lowest hell those who have offended Karen custom.

If an unmarried Karen girl dies she is buried in a married woman's outfit, because if an evil spirit knew she were single it would prevent her from walking to the higher realms of the dead. Wearing the clothes of a married woman she can simply say, 'My husband is coming just behind', and the spirit will not detain her. If an unmarried girl dies away from home her parents go and dress the body in the appropriate attire.

The family of a deceased person first washes the body, then dresses it in the best clothing the person owned. Other clothing, together with personal items, are hung from bamboo branches prior to the burial or cremation.

The deceased is eulogized by young men and women who sing songs to aid in the journey to the land of the dead.

Just as the bamboo clump is affected when one stock dies,
A whole community is affected when one person dies.
I said, 'If you were yourself as usual. . .',
But you are in the resting place all yellow.
I said, 'If you were in the house. . .',
But you are all yellow lying in the resting place.
I dreamed of a walking banyan tree with shade-giving branches,
All draped with skirts and blouses.
I dreamed of a walking banyan tree with buds,
All draped with bracelets and beads for the trip.
Before, you went up and down your steps,
Now you are dead and the steps are empty.
I dreamed the moon rose up-side-down,
Because you my brother/sister have died.
If you return you won't have to make fields.

Khu See-du will do it. Eat his labours.
If you return you won't have to work.
Khu See-du will do it. And you'll have more than enough.

Young Pwo women wear 'singing shawls' while walking arm-and-arm around the bier. When the body is carried out for cremation or burial, the young women wear spike-like hairpins of ivory, bone or metal, and cover their heads and faces with a silk veil.

Karen funeral rites are mainly to ensure that the soul (kala) of the deceased will not return to the place of the living. On their return from the burial or cremation ground the villagers erect obstacles to prevent the soul of the dead from following.

Religion

Through their religion the Karen seek solutions to the problem of survival. In it we see their constant striving for harmony between themselves and the spirit realm – 'Lord of Land and Water', household spirits, jungle spirits, or any other forces.

There are certain marked differences between the Sgaw and Pwo, and also between those living in the hills and those in the valleys in the manner in which they observe religious customs. Marlowe (in Keyes 1979:190) quotes one Karen as saying, 'Each river valley does things in the way that the grandparents who settled it said things should be done. . . one cannot generalize from settlement to settlement. For us, no two villages have the same customs'.

Beliefs and rituals

The 'Lord of Land and Water', who owns all the land, water, rocks, trees, paddies and swiddens in a given area, is the most important spiritual force Karen deal with as a village. Once a year the priest leads the men out to the Lord's shrine to perform a ritual ensuring an abundant rice crop and a healthy, harmonious village. After the shrine is repaired offerings are made on behalf of all inhabitants. A prayer, led by the priest, invokes the blessing of the 'Lord of Land and Water' on the whole village for the coming year. The names of any absent members are mentioned to make sure they also receive the longed-for blessings. Ceremonies for this spirit are also held in the swiddens to help the rice grow and to call back the soul of the rice at harvest time.

The ancestral, or matrilineal 'guardian spirit' (bga), provides protection and comes to the aid of all members of the lineage. The oldest woman in the lineage officiates at an annual rite to 'propitiate the ancestral spirit' (awxe awbga), during which all members should be present. If some cannot come, meat from the sacrifice is sent to them, and they eat the meat and take a day off from work. There are other times when a special 'feeding of the ancestral spirit' may take place, as when sickness or some other calamity has befallen a member of the lineage. When lineage members gather to 'feed the bga', they must all arrive the night before, and spend at least three nights in the house. Before the feast, all take a bath and put on new Karen clothing. On the morning of the ritual they assemble in the living area at which time only Karen may be spoken.

The lineage head offers a pair of chickens to the 'Lord Bga', asking that the lineage be free from illness and safe from evil. After the chickens are cooked, she eats a symbolic morsel. The other relatives then begin to eat in order of seniority, having first confessed any act of immorality.

In the case of the Sgaw, a pig is caught after dark, tied up and carried into the house. It is laid on banana leaves by the mat on which the lineage leader sleeps. She places her hands on the pig and says something like this, 'O great family spirit, we are offering you the flesh of swine. Do not harm us. Bless each and every one of us and be with us in the year to come'.

Each member of the lineage then touches the pig and banana leaves. The pig is beaten over the head and body, while care is taken not to shed blood, and then drowned by pouring water into its nostrils. The abdomen is cut open and the gall bladder examined. If full and round, they can use this pig for the sacrifice, and if not, they must select another one.

After the ceremony is completed, meat is divided among them to take home. Before leaving each person takes some dirt and sprinkles it over one of his or her ears to be camouflaged from the spirits.

Today Karen find this ceremony difficult to observe, as members of the lineage are spread out over great distances. Some are therefore turning to a tattooing ceremony (chekosi) in order to rid themselves of their obligations to the bga. This involves roasting seeds of cultivated plants and saying to the bga, 'We will make sacrifices to you again when these seeds bear fruit'. Tattoo marks are made on their bodies to show that they have undergone this rite. Many mountain-dwelling, but few valley-dwelling Karen have accepted this 'medicine tattooing sect'.

Besides the ancestral spirits, the Karen are also deeply aware of the nature spirits inhabiting dominant features surrounding their village. If placated with offerings at proper intervals, they will usually be harmless, but they are known to behave capriciously.

The concept of a 'soul' (kala) is important to Karen. There are many souls which dwell in each human being. The six most important ones are located in the eyes, ears, nose, tongue, mind, and body. These 'Life forces' keep a person alive and well. Should they leave there will be sickness – perhaps even death. The souls of a child are especially susceptible to being enticed away by the souls of the dead. For this reason parents will not allow their children even to look at a corpse being carried out of the village.

Religion and agriculture

Each phase of the agricultural cycle is accompanied by sacrifices to the spirits, made by the 'ritual owner' of the field, who is not always the legal owner. The one chosen each year to preside over the rituals is often a younger member of the family, either male or female. It is felt that younger people are more favoured by the spirits, since they have had fewer years in which to offend them.

> A typical prayer at the time of rice planting is: *'Water Lord, Country Lord, Hill Lord, Mountain Lord, come down! Lord of Laykawkey village, Lord of Laykawkey stream, send us good rice, send us sparse weeds. . .'.*

Karen are careful not to offend the 'Crop Grandmother' (*Phi Bi Yaw*), who sits on the half-burned tree stumps in the field watching while rice is growing. It is therefore taboo to hack or otherwise disturb the stumps until the harvest is over. Offerings are made to her in the field while the crop is growing, and on top of the paddy in the granary after harvest – the latter providing food for her journey back to her heavenly home.

Rice liquor is used for most Karen ceremonies. Marlowe (nd:18) records an incident he witnessed in Baw Keo when an 'official' Thai whiskey distiller came through the district telling the Karen they must not brew their own liquor any more, but buy it from him. They responded with numbed acquiescence, because tradition dictates that each household must brew liquor from its own rice for ceremonial use. The Karen's awe of authority, and their desire for harmony was so compelling that they did not even hold their post-harvest festival that year.

Religious movements

In the 1970s a religious cult developed among the Karen which revolved around a 'White Monk' (*Khruba Khao* in Thai), who proclaimed himself the Buddhist priest of the Karen and Lawa. This man, now dead, had left the regular Buddhist priesthood and put on white robes. His followers were mostly Karen from a large area of north-western Thailand, but included many Thai as well. Although he was mainly a religious leader he also helped to provide schools and was active in other development projects in the north. Karen went in busloads to see him in order to make merit.

He urged no radical political action, but was quoted by many Karen as saying that he would lead them back into Burma where they would have ample land to farm, and would ensure their prosperity by controlling the spirit forces. The objects he blessed are highly valued to this day.

The Karen of both Burma and Thailand have experienced several 'millennial' movements promising a future of peace, prosperity, and happiness. These have emerged as a result of the frustrations created by poverty and lack of political identity, and represent an attempt to arouse a spirit of unity among the Karen. These movements promise that the day of the 'Karen king' will come and they will all live in a magnificent palace in a great city (Stern 1968: 304). One of these millennial sects, the Telekhon, has been active for many years among a small number of Karen in the border area of the southwest section of Tak Province. The deaths of their prophets in recent years has caused this movement to decline in influence.

Large numbers of lowland Karen in both Thailand and Burma practice Buddhism. They have not broken away from all Karen practices, but tend to be eclectic in what they choose of both religions. Kunstadter (in Keyes 1977:134) quotes an old Karen woman as saying, 'I stick to *awxe* (feeding the ancestors) for my own health, but I make merit (with the Buddhist priests) so I will prosper'.

Christianity was first introduced to Karen in Thailand by Karen preachers from Burma over a century ago. The number of Christian converts has grown steadily since. Missionary organizations from the West have worked among them since the end of World War II. In addition to church development these missions emphasize medical, educational, and agricultural programmes.

Sickness and Curing

Cause

When sickness strikes, Karen immediately look for the cause. It is taken for granted that whatever the symptoms, there is some kind of spiritual force causing the illness. Possibly the person inadvertently wronged a nature spirit in the forest, so the angry spirit has snatched away his soul (or souls) and made the person ill. Or a person has been startled by a wild animal or a clap of thunder, causing his soul to flee in terror. Again, it may be that an ancestral spirit is angry and is 'eating the soul'. When a two-month-old baby fell out of a hammock into a fire, the grandfather believed that the accident was caused by the spirit of his dead wife.

In order to discover the spiritual origin of a disease Karen often employ divination by using chicken bones, feathers, eggs, or by counting grains of rice. Even if an injury has obviously been caused by a falling tree, the spiritual cause must be found and rectified before there can be healing. In certain cases it may be divined that the 'Lord of Land and Water' is punishing them for sexual immorality in the village.

Tying strings on a sick man's wrist after soul-calling ceremony

Curing

Once the cause is known a cure can be effected. If the case is relatively simple, members of the household may be competent to perform both the divination and the cure. A shaman is called in for a more difficult case. He is a man who has a close relationship with the local spiritual force, and when possessed by that force communicates the cause and prescribes the cure to the family.

In the case of soul loss a soul-calling ceremony is performed by the shaman. If, on the other hand, the shaman finds a malevolent presence in the patient's body, he offers pork or chicken to the offending spirit, and lures it into a basket which he then abandons in the jungle.

In the case of the two-month-old child who was burned, the grandfather made a special offering of pork, placing some of it on the baby's head, and some in a banana leaf which was left in a corner of the house for the spirit of the grandmother.

When offering it he said, 'Your grandson is very ill. Please leave his soul alone and help him recover. Do not disregard us . . .'.

Social Relationships

Karen are hospitable people. In some instances this may be dictated by caution, for if a family does not offer hospitality it is feared that the visitor, angered by rejection, might curse them or entice away the soul of a member of the family. Yet, in some instances a Karen housewife does not offer hospitality to a visitor, particularly if she might fear that his spirits would conflict with the spirits of her household.

In all social interaction the 'senior-junior' relationship is of vital importance. The young are always expected to defer to their elders, whether in the family, the village, or inter-village relationships. Certain traditions emphasize this relationship, such as when a lineage which has become very large is divided and a new leader is chosen for the branch of the group that breaks away. The woman chosen to be leader of the new lineage must wash the hair of the leader of the original group as an acknowledgment of her own junior status.

Wealth is another factor in the determination of status, but Karen do not count wealth in terms of silver, as in some other tribal groups, but of livestock and rice supplies. The elephant owner enjoys the highest status of all.

Over centuries of contact, many Karen have developed close symbiotic relationships with their Thai neighbours. Marlowe found (Keyes 1979:185) that over 50% of the Sgaw families he surveyed in the Chiang Mai area in 1967 claimed to have a *si-so* relation (called *sahai* in Thai) with non-Karen lowlanders. This is a situation where two families, one Karen and the other Thai, provide assistance to each other and share in social functions. When visiting each other's villages, they stay in the home of the family with which they have the *si-so* relationship, and they invite each other to attend special rituals and festivals.

Conclusion

The Karen in Thailand are faced with overpopulation, depleted soil, limited land, the crumbling of traditional values, and increasing poverty. This is nothing new, for they feel it is their lot in life to suffer and to be oppressed. They also feel, however, that 'their day will come' (a part of the millenarian legacy). The 'orphan' of their myths will one day, through his cleverness and honesty, be victorious. And they will all live – perhaps not quite happily – but at least harmoniously ever after.

Women return from fields

Blue Hmong village scene

Chapter 4

HMONG (MEO)

Blue Hmong man performs acrobatic solo dance while playing mouth organ

Desire for Independence

Yaitong got off the bus and started the thirty-minute climb to his Hmong village. As headman he had been attending the monthly meeting at the District Office. It was hot in the valley, and he had not slept well. What an effort it had been to speak Thai all the time. He could speak Yunnanese without much difficulty, but Thai was another matter as he had never been to school. Then there was the trip back to the village. The first bus he took broke down just outside of town, so he had to walk back and catch another one. Now he was dusty, hungry, and exhausted – but also excited.

That evening one person after another came to chat with Yaitong. 'What did you learn about getting a school?' was the first question each asked as they entered his spacious house. Yaitong told them that in five days the Educational Officer would come to their village to finalize plans. 'Then it looks like we'll really have a school', the younger men said excitedly. They had long hoped that their children could learn Thai. Two or three of the older men complained of possible loss of freedom if a Government school were located in their village. Yaitong retorted, 'But look at the freedom we are denied now because we don't know how to speak and read Thai!'

A cousin of Yaitong, visiting the village to purchase handicrafts, spoke up, 'When I sell these crafts in the Night Bazaar in Chiang Mai I have problems, because I cannot speak Thai properly. Sales are good, and I have almost paid for my truck. But how much easier it would be if I could have had an education!'

Chetso remained silent throughout the discussion. He was of another clan and had been critical from the beginning of the headman's zeal in trying to get a school. He saw the step towards having a Thai teacher living in the village as wrong. The teacher would most likely woo the children away from the great Hmong traditions. Inevitably more Thai and other 'outsiders' would be drawn into the orbit of their village and fields, tightening a noose around them. Chetso wanted no part of it. Tomorrow he would visit his uncle in Mae Hong Son Province. Perhaps he could find land there to farm.

Name and language

The tribe called 'Meo' (Miao, Meau) by the Thai and some other groups consists of two major branches in Thailand: the 'Hmong Deaw' (White Hmong) and the 'Mong Njua' (literally Green Mong, but commonly called Blue Hmong). They are two sub-groups of the Miao people, the majority of whom continue to live in China. The name 'Hmong' (spoken with a slight aspiration through the nostrils as the *m* is enunciated) has become the one more commonly used among English speakers, and is the form we use. It should be remembered, however, that in the Blue Mong dialect the *m* is not aspirated. In both cases the *o* is pronounced as in the English word 'roam'.

Linguists classify the Hmong as a Miao-Yao language in the Sino-Tibetan family of languages. There are numerous borrowed words from Yunnanese, Laotian, and Thai. Most of the men learn other languages, such as Yunnanese, Northern Thai, and Karen, depending on where they live and what crops they plant.

The Blue and White Hmong dialects are markedly different, although some consider them to be mutually intelligible. The style of their clothing is sufficiently alike to be recognized as that of the same tribe.

Origin

Hmong legends tell how their ancestors lived in an icy land where the winters were severe and the nights long. This has led to speculation that they may have entered China through the high steppes of Tibet, Siberia and Mongolia, although this cannot be verified. Chinese records indicate that ancestors of the Hmong may have lived on the banks of the Yellow River some three thousand years ago.

Attempts by the Chinese to subjugate them over the centuries have engendered hostility in the Hmong and led to their periodic migration in the quest for freedom. There were three major periods in the 18th and 19th Centuries during which they engaged in protracted armed conflict with the Chinese, culminating about 1870 in the disappearance of the 'independent Hmong' as a fighting entity.

During World War II the Chinese Nationalist government attempted to prohibit the Hmong from speaking their own language and wearing their distinctive clothing, but with little success. Such oppressive measures have only sharpened their determination to remain independent. This resulted in their being the most widely dispersed tribal group to have come from China. Even so, there were over four million Miao living in China in mid-1983.

Although it is not known exactly when the Hmong first migrated into Laos, by 1850 they had established themselves in the mountains around Luang Prabang. By the end of the 19th century, according to their own reckoning, several Hmong villages had been established in Thailand.

Population

The total Hmong population in Thailand in mid-1983 was approximately 58,000, living in some 245 villages. (This does not include the Hmong from Laos living in refugee camps.)

Hmong are found in at least thirteen provinces of northern and central Thailand. Over 75% are located in the provinces of Phetchabun, Chiang Mai, Chiang Rai and Tak. They have spread over a larger geographical area than any other tribe except the Karen, due to their ceaseless quest for land, together with their desire for independence.

Blue Hmong women wear heavy silver neck rings and chains

White Hmong women dressing up for New Year

White Hmong women visiting neighbours

Blue Hmong man walking to his field with cross bow and gun

Blue Hmong boys in New Year garb

Clothing and Ornamentation

A tiny needle, strands of bright thread, lengths of vari-coloured cloth, and the genius of a Hmong woman – these are the ingredients of some of the most exquisite needlework to be found anywhere. Throughout their long history, Hmong women have devoted their artistic skill and industry to the development of an amazing variety of techniques using needle and thread. They adorn the clothing of every member of the family, from the smallest baby to the oldest grandparents. Even the corpses are richly endowed with embroideries to take to the next world.

Nowadays much of the cloth used is purchased from itinerant traders or in the marketplace, but traditionally it all had to be produced within the Hmong household. Even today many women prefer to weave their own homespun hemp or cotton cloth for much of the clothing worn by the family, using looms that combine back-strap and foot-treadle techniques. The weaver sits on a bench with one end of the loom attached to a belt. She controls the tension with her back, while shifting the warp threads with foot treadles.

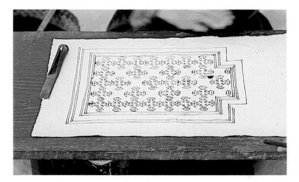

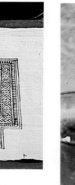

Blue Hmong woman weaving on foot-treadle/back-strap loom *(upper right)*

Steps in batiking cloth (Blue Hmong)

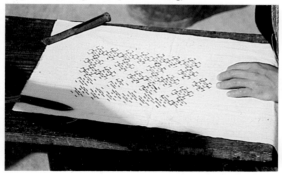

Hmong women doing needlework

How to use a Hmong baby-carrying cloth

Needlework for babies and children

Hmong mothers devote their finest skills in making carrying-cloths and caps for their babies. A carrying-cloth resembles a bibbed apron. It is made of two rectangular pieces of cloth, the smaller at the top, joined together at the borders. Long red straps attached to the top corners are used to tie the baby on the back. The Blue Hmong use batik material for the larger rectangle, accented with strips, squares, and triangles of bright red appliquéd pieces. The smaller top rectangle may be ornamented with a combination of cross-stitch embroidery, appliqué, and tiny shocking pink pompons. The White Hmong do not use batiking, but ornament their baby-carriers with a variety of embroidery stitching, appliqué, and reverse appliqué – the process of cutting a pattern into a cloth and stitching it onto another.

Many styles of caps are made for the babies, most of them very elaborate. All are ornamented with typical needlework of the respective branch of the tribe and many pink, red, or magenta pompons.

Children's clothing is mainly a miniature version of adult garb. For festive wear – especially New Year's – the mothers outdo themselves to ornament the clothing of even the smallest with their best needlework.

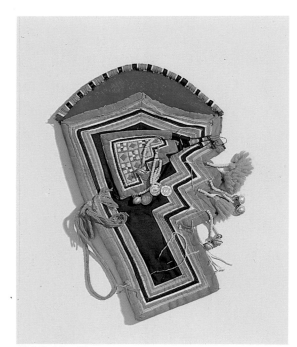

Child's New Year cap

Small boy's jacket

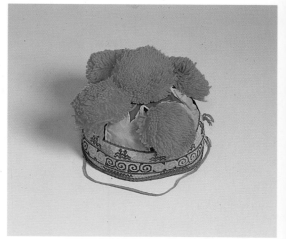

Children's caps

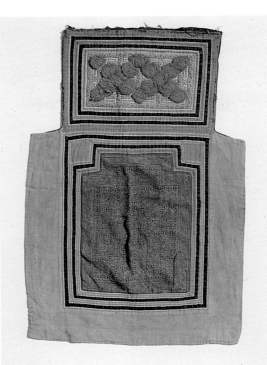

Baby-carrying cloths (Blue Hmong)

Front and back views of a small boy's jacket, particularly
richly embroidered

Women's clothing

Blue Hmong women wear knee-length pleated skirts of hand-woven hemp or cotton cloth, hemp being preferred. The central horizontal panel is 25 to 30 cm wide, and is covered with a batik pattern. The pattern is drawn with beeswax onto the cloth with a tool made by their blacksmiths. After the wax has been applied, the cloth is immersed in a cold indigo dye. When the dye has set, the wax is removed by boiling, then skimmed off to be used again. The Blue Hmong are apparently the only tribal people in mainland Southeast Asia skilled in batiking.

A 15 cm strip of plain cloth is attached to the top of the batiked panel, and a border with bright-coloured cross-stitch embroidery and appliqué of red and other bright colours is added to the bottom edge. The width of the border varies, with teen-age girls making their's wider than the adults. A strip of white is stitched to the bottom edge. The entire skirt, more than six metres for an adult, is accordion-pleated, anchored down with herringbone stitches. A thread is run through the pleats as they are made, holding them together in three or four places, and the skirt is stored that way until used.

Blue Hmong women's jackets are generally of black cotton; sometimes velvet is used. There are three types. The first has a five to six cm embroidered and appliquéd strip stitched to each edge in front. The second has a wide zigzag coming down in three steps from the right shoulder, crossing over to the left side. The third has a finer zigzag pattern. The jackets are unfinished at the lower edge, and are bound down with a black sash that is wound several times around the waist.

There are two types of collars: one is a simple rectangle about 12 by 16 cm; the other has a similar rectangle, with a wide border tapering to elongated points on the free edge. The collars are generally stitched to the jacket with the embroidered side down. There are many theories why the needlework is reversed, but the Hmong say they really do not know, only that it is the 'proper' way to do it.

Women wear an apron over the front of the skirt, which for everyday wear is black. Festive aprons, elaborately embroidered and appliquéd, tie on with a red, pink, or orange sash, and have long tassels hanging down the back. For full dress occasions extra red sashes are wound around the waist until a woman seems grossly overweight. Quite often a silver belt is worn over this. At New Year an unattached batiked bib is worn with the apron. Often silver coins and ornaments are stitched to it.

The costume is completed by leggings made of tapered pieces of black cloth. The wide end covers the leg from the knee to the ankle, and narrows as it is wound around the leg. At New Year they sometimes wear white leggings.

The Blue Hmong sweep their long hair forward and twist it around a horse's tail (or possibly a switch of human hair), then wind it into a large puffy bun which covers the crown of the head. (In Mae Hong Son area the bun is at the back of the head.) A black and white checkered or embroidered strip is tied around it. Some women wear a special type of headdress at New Year, consisting of 14 pieces of black and white cotton checked cloth. This is built up to a high point in front. (See picture upper right.)

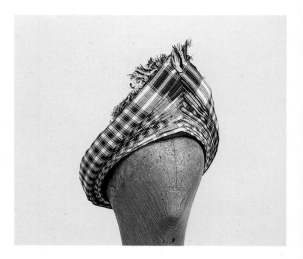

Blue Hmong woman's apron

Blue Hmong women's jackets

Blue Hmong skirts

White Hmong women's clothing varies from that of the Blue Hmong in several ways. The heavy pleated skirts are of white hemp cloth without adornment. These are reserved for special occasions; for everyday wear loose black pants are worn.

One type of jacket is black with edges and cuffs of bright blue. A jacket for special occasions has strips of embroidery and reverse appliqué down the front. Both types have a rectangular collar at the back, decorated with appliqué, reverse appliqué, and embroidery. Much of their time is spent making these collars in a great variety of patterns and techniques. They usually have a number of them stored away.

Black aprons, edged with blue, are worn front and back. For festive wear one with an elaborately embroidered central panel and a wide sash with embroidery and reverse appliqué is worn. A double bib with heavily adorned front and back pieces is added. Long tassels of magenta or shocking pink yarn hang in the back.

White Hmong women tie their hair in a knot at the top of the forehead. They do not like hair to show under their turbans, so they shave from above the ear to the forehead. Various kinds of turbans are worn in different areas. For one style the crown of the head is first covered with black cloth, then the remaining six metres are wound around to form a thick brim. Another style is a cloth folded to about a 12 cm width and wound around the head two or three times, with tiny red or pink pompons added to the embroidered front.

White Hmong apron

White Hmong turbans

White Hmong skirt

Blue Hmong apron

Hmong money bags

Striped Hmong woman's jacket from Laos

White Hmong women's jackets

The red X was sewn on after a curing ceremony

White Hmong collars show a wide variety of designs and
types of needlework

Men's clothing

Hmong men wear loose-fitting black pants folded across the waist, tucked in at the top, and often secured with a leather belt. Blue Hmong pants are extremely full, having narrow openings for the ankles with the very wide crotch falling mid-way between calves and ankles. White Hmong pants are less full, having a higher crotch.

Jackets are also made of black cloth – usually cotton, but sometimes velvet or satin. Both Blue and White Hmong wear short jackets leaving a bare midriff. Hmong in the Chiang Mai area commonly wear extremely short jackets. The collarless jacket buttons at the neck, crosses over the chest, and fastens on the left side with silver buttons. The piece across the chest is ornamented with the needlework customary for that branch of the tribe.

Many White Hmong men wear a longer jacket with a Chinese-style high collar, which, together with the cuffs and the front opening, are embroidered. Some Blue Hmong men now wear a similar jacket in cold season.

Men wear wide sashes up to six metres long. Some are folded on the bias so as to form pointed ends. The sash is carefully wrapped so that the heavily embroidered ends fall evenly together in front giving the appearance of an apron. White Hmong, and some Blue, wear red sashes which are squared-off at the ends and adorned with Mien-style embroidery.

Traditionally the men shaved their heads, except for the crown, where the hair was left long and sometimes braided into a queue. Blue Hmong in all areas and some White Hmong in Chiang Mai Province wear Chinese-style black satin skullcaps with a big fluffy magenta pompon on top. (See photo upper left.)

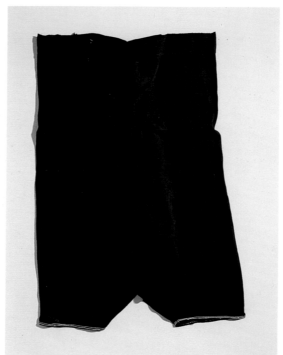

Blue Hmong man's pants

Blue Hmong men's sashes

Hmong men's jackets

Silver ornaments

The Hmong keep a great deal of their wealth in the form of silver jewellery. All Hmong – men, women, and children – wear silver neck rings, at least for special occasions. At the naming ceremony a silver neck ring is given to a Hmong baby to keep the soul in and signify that the baby belongs to the human world (Chindarsi 1976: 66). Silver has a special significance to the Hmong, symbolizing wealth and the essence of the good life.

Every household acquires as much silver as possible, and at New Year all the family silver jewellery is worn and displayed. Three styles of earrings are worn by Hmong women. One style is shaped like an arrow with the shaft bent around to form a circle. The second is an elongated S-shape, flat or round, with a pointed plug worn through the earlobe, and either hooked up into the back of the turban, or allowed to hang down in front. A more modern type is a small silver hook with a number of small dangles hanging from it. White Hmong, both men and women, wear heavy engraved round silver bracelets. Blue Hmong wear narrow flat engraved bracelets. These may be of brass or copper rather than silver. Neck rings, solid or hollow, are worn either singly or in sets of up to six tiers – five being standard. Frequently heavy silver chains with lock-shaped pendants are attached to the neck rings. These 'locks' are added during curing ceremonies to keep the soul in the body. At New Year they may wear heavy silver chains with pendants of fish, butterflies, wheels, bells, and miniature grooming tools, and young women may wear a pointed ring on every finger. The amount of silver displayed at the New Year festival in an affluent Hmong village is most impressive.

Hmong silversmith at work

Blue Hmong girls in New Year finery

White Hmong girl in New Year vest

Blue Hmong girl's necklace sports cloisonné pendants

Blue Hmong girls in full New Year garb

White Hmong girls share a joke

Blue and White Hmong girls in New Year garb

Blue Hmong couple

Blue Hmong young people playing catch at New Year's

The Village

Hmong like to locate their villages at high altitudes, especially if they grow opium poppies as their main crop. Now many live at lower elevations and are farming paddy fields.

Those who dwell in higher mountains favour a location in the lee of a hill rather than a ridge top. Even better, they like a site where they have the shelter of two or three hills to protect them from the monsoon storms.

When looking for a location they ask themselves questions such as: If this is a good site, why has no one built a village here before? Is there enough distance between the village and fields so that domestic animals will not destroy the crops? Is there sufficient land within a reasonable distance for relatives and friends who might come later? And, is there an appropriate site for burying the dead?

There is no set layout, although a 'horseshoe' pattern is common for a village. Every house must face downhill, and no two houses may be in direct line with each other, because spirits (good ones in this case) enter a house in a straight line and nothing must obstruct their path.

A typical village is made up of several clusters of houses with six to eight in a cluster. These usually centre around some influential person, and may be composed of families of a single clan. Some consist of families who arrived during the same season and started a new section of the village.

A Hmong village is not fenced, nor does it have gates like Akha villages. However, many ceremonial 'bridges' (*choj*), built for soul-calling rituals, can be seen along the trails leading into the village.

On the whole Hmong live separately from other ethnic groups. In villages relying heavily on opium production some Yunnanese traders may be found.

Hmong move their villages for a number of reasons, the principal one being exhausted soil. Other reasons include: a shaman's prediction that something evil will happen if they remain where they are; conflict with a government agency or another local group; a serious epidemic; a lack of eligible females nearby for their sons; and problems related to their Thai neighbours. One village moved after the following series of events: a tiger had killed two of their animals; the headman was injured in an explosion when preparing for New Year; another group had buried a body on the mountain above their village; and the man who was responsible for making the offering to the 'Lord of Land and Water' had moved away.

The move is carefully planned. First the 'patron figure', the most respected village elder, visits several areas looking for a possible site. He reports his findings, then a group of men from the village go together to scout out a likely location. After an area is chosen, four or five families go ahead to establish the new site. Some of these may be nuclear families from extended households. They build temporary shelters, then mark out fields for themselves as well as for those who will come later. They plant enough rice to meet the needs of the whole village for one year. Although the advance party has to put up with a number of hardships, there are compensations: they are assisted by those remaining behind in buying food while waiting for the first harvest, and they get first choice of land for making their fields and of girls for their sons to marry.

After the first rice harvest the remainder of the villagers move to the new site. Ponies are used to pack their goods, and it may be necessary for a party of men to go ahead to widen the trail. The people also carry all they can on their backs. Armed men go at the front and at the rear, women, children and animals in between. There is a distinct sense of relief when everyone has arrived.

The size of villages differs from region to region, the determining factor often being the amount of good land available for cultivation. In areas where the land has been overworked, as in Nan Province where the Hmong first settled in Thailand, the villages are now often quite small, most of them having only four to eight households. In areas more recently settled, however, there may be thirty or more houses per village. There is a great deal of movement in and out of poppy-growing villages, whereas those who make irrigated rice fields are the most stable.

Hmong boy playing Jew's harp

'Bridge' on path leading to Hmong village

Blue Hmong girl brings in potatoes from field

Bringing in leaves from jungle

White Hmong women in market town

Blue Hmong village

Houses

The site for a Hmong house is chosen with great care, as it is important that the site be acceptable to their ancestors. The family makes a tentative choice, then consults the ancestors through an offering of 'paper money' to determine whether the choice is acceptable. If no negative signs follow the offering, the family clears the site and levels it with mattocks and a tool made of wide wooden boards which is used to drag or push the soil. The ground should be as level as possible, as it forms the floor of the house. It is dampened and tamped down to make a hard surface.

Next the family must gather construction material. Posts are cut in the jungle, preferably of wood impervious to termites. Where wood is available the walls are made of planks. The wealthier Hmong hire Northern Thai or Karen to saw lumber for that purpose, but others hew the planks by hand. If wood is scarce split bamboo must serve instead. Thatch grass, rattan leaves, or wooden shingles are used for the roof.

On an auspicious day the family calls the neighbours and they build the house together. After the first two posts have been erected the head of the house announces, 'I am living here! From now on let all evil spirits stay away'. A fireplace is then installed and a temporary altar made, following which construction is resumed.

When the house is completed two chickens are sacrificed at the altar and the ancestors and other household spirits are invited to occupy the new dwelling. A rooster and hen are offered at the main entrance with an appeal to the 'door spirits' to provide protection to the family's domestic animals and crops, and to bring good fortune. A wooden sword is hung over the doorway to prevent evil spirits from entering.

The main room in a Hmong house, which is used for family activities and the entertainment of guests, is quite large. The guest sleeping platform is located off the main part of the house, and the bedrooms are partitioned with boards or bamboo mats. There is an attic for the storage of food, seeds and tools, which can be reached by climbing a ladder made of a notched log. Whatever is stored there is kept dry and free of vermin, but becomes darkened from the smoke of the open fire below it.

Most Blue Hmong houses have only one door, which is located in the middle of the front wall on the downslope side. White Hmong have a door at the side of the house as well, and maintain the front door for ceremonial purposes, much as the Mien do. The spirit altar is on the wall directly opposite the front door.

Tools used in house construction are: axe, machete, adze, posthole digger, hoe, and mallet with hardwood wedges. The latter are used for splitting wood for the walls, and in some areas the roof shingles as well.

There are two hearths, the fireplace being the focal point of the household where meals are cooked and guests are entertained. The fire is banked at night so it will not go out. The second is a large clay stove used primarily for cooking pig's food. It is also used during feasts when large quantities of food are needed. The foot-treadle rice pounder has always been an important feature in every Hmong house.

Stables for ponies and mules, as well as chicken coops are built against the house, but stone mills for grinding maize are separated from the house as are pig pens and granaries.

White Hmong man roofing house

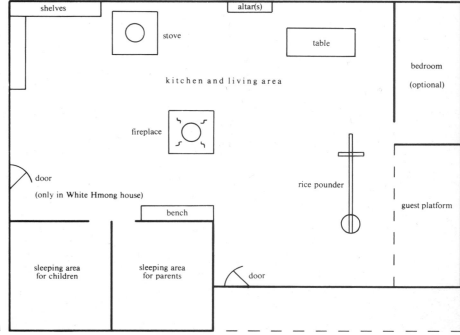

Hmong house plan

Interior of White Hmong house

Blue Hmong grinding maize

White Hmong women and children eating

Interior of White Hmong house showing attic.
(Note bamboo 'spirit ladders' under roof)

Family and Clan

The most important social units among Hmong are the family and the clan. The extended family household constitutes the basic cultural and political unit, with the eldest male having virtually unlimited authority over its members. All others in the household are subject to him as the chief decision-maker. He is responsible for the family's general welfare and must settle all disputes between family members.

Respect for age is of cardinal importance: children respect their parents; younger siblings respect older siblings; nieces and nephews respect aunts and uncles, varying in degree according to their relative age. The father-son link is especially important. The father's welfare in the afterworld depends largely on the sumptuousness of the funeral ceremony given for him by his sons, and a son's welfare in turn is thought to depend on the respect he bestows on his parents while they are alive and on the treatment he receives from his deceased ancestors.

When the head of a household dies, the married sons generally move off and start their own households. If all the sons are already married, the youngest son and his family will probably remain in the home with his mother, although it is not uncommon for one of the other sons to assume this responsibility.

Although the link between brothers is not as vital as between son and father, they assist one another both in work and ritual.

Overt expressions of conflict within the family are serious breaches of Hmong culture. Therefore, if unreconcilable disputes develop within a family, the household splits up. In any attempts to restore good relations, it is important that all factions be allowed to maintain their freedom.

Despite the fact that the Hmong move frequently, they regret leaving their house sites for two reasons: the placentas of their children are buried there, and the main hearth with its continual fire has a sacred significance. It is thought that when a person dies, his soul returns to its placenta, which is like his birth clothing. The problem regarding the fire is solved by carrying along to the new site some of the ashes from the hearth to represent the continuity of the home.

The patrilineal clan system of the Hmong ties together social, political, economic, and religious aspects of behaviour, and serves as a primary focus for their daily lives. Often the clan of the founding families tends to dominate the village numerically and politically.

There are reported to be twelve such clans, but not all are found in Thailand. According to Gary Lee the Chinese and Hmong names of the clans are (Hmong in parentheses): Lee (Lis), Taw (Thoj), Chung (Xjooj), Heu (Hawj), Ya (Yaj), Law (Lauj), Cha (Tsab), Wu (Vwj), Ha (Ham), Mua (Muas), Fa (Faj), and Wa (Vaj). Some of the clans are divided into sub-clans, for example the Taw has at least three subdivisions.

Each clan has its own way of doing things, such as healing. Therefore, a girl, who must marry into a clan different from her own, may be concerned that in case she falls ill, the healing methods used may not be as effective as those of her father's clan. Taboos also vary from clan to clan. For instance, some clans strictly forbid a daughter-in-law to climb up to the storage area above the fire, whereas others permit it.

Each person has certain obligations to others in the clan. For example, one shares with one's fellow clan members knowledge of good sites for making fields, and when called upon gives substantial aid so that they can exploit that opportunity. When a new family moves into a village, a fellow clansman acts as sponsor. Usually the new family lives close to the sponsoring family, and makes fields near theirs.

Hmong father and son

Old White Hmong couple

Grandfather and child (White Hmong)

White Hmong mother and son

Blue Hmong family

Blue Hmong mother with child wearing New Year cap

Courtship and Marriage

A Hmong man must marry a girl of another clan or sub-clan. Marriage between people of different generations is prohibited. That is, a man must not marry a woman old enough to be his mother, or young enough to be his daughter. Marriage of parallel cousins is also prohibited, although a family may encourage a young man to marry a cross-cousin (that is, his father's sister's daughter or his mother's brother's daughter) in order to retain the blood tie. In fact, there used to be a tradition of parents betrothing such children at an early age.

Most boys marry when they are about 17 or 18 years old, girls about the same age or somewhat younger. A Hmong young man looks for several things in a prospective bride: beauty, ability to work hard, suitability as a sex partner, and intelligence. The girl looks for a husband who is strong, rich, hardworking, and of a good family. If there are opium addicts in the family she may not want to marry him.

Courtship

The main courting period is during the New Year festival. The young people, dressed in their New Year finery, congregate in a level area in or near the village to play catch with black cloth balls the girls have made. They stand in two lines from six to 12 metres apart, the girls in one line and the boys in the other. Each girl throws her ball to the boy of her choice, or if she is shy she may give her ball to a married friend, asking her to pass it to a certain boy, suggesting that he should play catch with the girl. If he likes the girl he accepts the invitation.

Both boys and girls often wear white towels as a shawl or turban to partially hide their faces in a show of shyness. Whoever fails to catch the ball must give an item of clothing or jewellery to the partner. These forfeits may be redeemed while still playing catch, or in the evening by singing a love song – one song per item, drawing quite a crowd if the singing is good (Lee, private correspondence).

The courtship period continues until rice planting time. Young men often go to other villages in their search for wives. Villages come alive in the evenings with local boys as well as visitors calling girls out of their homes to sit and talk. They sing and play the Jew's harp to one another. There is sometimes a great deal of whispering through the planks of the girl's bedroom walls. The boy who is coaxing her out has a big red blanket which he promises will keep them warm that night (Lee 1981: 42–43). If the girl is interested she will go out with him, or in the case of the White Hmong she may invite him into her bedroom. It is taboo for a young man to sleep with an unmarried Blue Hmong girl in her house.

Marriage

If the girl agrees to marry the boy, he must first receive the permission of his parents, because they will pay the bride price and bear the cost of the wedding. The young man may then take the girl to live in his house. As soon as this takes place, the boy's father sends two representatives to the girl's father to tell him, 'Your daughter is now part of our family. Please do not be concerned about her. We would be grateful if you could set a date to celebrate the marriage'.

If the couple lives not too far from the girl's village, her mother may come and seek to retrieve her daughter, beating with sticks and berating the one who is 'stealing' her. There must be no retaliation or striking back (Lee 1981:44). This indicates how highly she values her daughter and hates to lose her – and incidentally may help to increase the bride price!

Sometimes the couple arranges for the young man to 'abduct' the girl, even though she is willing to marry him. The girl's mother hurls abuse at the young man for 'stealing' her daughter, while attempting to 'rescue' her. If the girl shows a desire to stay with the boy, the mother may beat her as well for such disloyalty to her own family.

Meanwhile, back at the girl's house, the representatives from the boy's father are quietly negotiating a wedding date for the couple with the girl's father or male relatives. The bride price is computed in silver ingots, and formerly depended on the relative wealth of the two families, the area in which they lived, and the girl's beauty and ability to work. Currently there is an attempt to standardize the bride price – five ingots being the amount established, or six ingots if there is no wedding feast.* The bride price is paid at the time of the wedding, which may take place within a few days of the time the girl goes to live in the boy's home. However, the wedding may be delayed for weeks or even years, depending on when the groom's family is able to pay.

If the groom's father cannot pay the bride price, the couple may live with the girl's family and work for her father, thus reducing the amount to be paid. Some couples have two or three children before the full price has been given. There are instances when a Hmong man's family never pays the bride price, so he must work off the entire

* One silver ingot weighs 378.5 grammes, the current value is between $115 and $130.

amount. This is a reproach on him and his family, however, and causes him to lose much standing in the community.

When the bride price has been paid in full, the woman belongs to the husband, his family and his clan. If a woman who has no children wants to leave her husband, she can do so only after the bride price has been repaid. If she has children, some of them may remain with the husband's family in lieu of repaying the bride price.

The wedding festivities start at the house of the groom, whose family must provide two pigs, two to four chickens, and ten bottles of Hmong liquor. A chicken is sacrificed to the house spirits and placed on a table, where the go-betweens are honoured with a drink of liquor, while the relatives of the groom stand before them to show their respect. Then the groom and his friend (who takes the role of best man) kowtow to the relatives in turn, beginning with the groom's paternal grandfather, his father, his paternal uncles in order of age, and finally to his brothers, again starting with the eldest. They conclude by kowtowing to the household spirits and ancestors.

Following this the groom, best man, bride, bridesmaid, and a helper plus the two go-betweens set out for the bride's house, taking with them two chickens, food, and liquor. The liquor is offered to mountain, forest and stream spirits on the way. On their arrival at the girl's parent's home, the go-betweens present two chickens to the bride's father to sacrifice to his household spirits. The groom and best man then kowtow to the bride's grandfather, father, uncles, and brothers in the same order as before.

After kowtowing to all the bride's male relatives, the groom must drink liquor with each one separately. As there are 20 to 30 of them, he would become very drunk if he drank a full cup with each one. To spare him this, some of his relatives stand by and finish off the drink in each case after he has taken a sip. After lengthy negotiations over the bride price and its payment, the groom and his party escort the bride back to his own home.

Geddes (1976: 82) describes the departure of a Hmong bride to become a part of her husband's household:

'For a girl who leaves her home to join her bridegroom in a distant place the breach is severe. She is losing the clan membership which has given her security, comfort, and companionship all the years of her life to become possessed by strangers. Many (Hmong) songs have as their theme the sadness of a girl at departing from her relatives and village, and her fear of the servitude and loneliness that may await her.'

After the return to the groom's house, more feasting follows in order to thank all who took part in the wedding process and to reward those who accompanied the bride to her village earlier to negotiate the bride price. Eating and drinking goes on late into the night.

Plural marriage

Some Hmong men take two or more wives, adding to their status, as indicated in their proverb, 'A man with two wives and ten horses is a very rich man'. A bride price must also be paid for other wives, unless a man marries the widow of his elder brother. In that case no bride price need be paid, as her parents already received it when she first married into the family. The man is supposed to secure the consent of his first wife before taking other wives. Some men may take three or more wives.

Birth

Each baby is said to be sent to this world by a 'Baby Goddess' (*Poor Dlang Por*). The first three days of its life it still belongs to the spirit world, and if it dies no funeral is held.

The third day after birth the father calls in an elder to hold a ceremony. Two chickens are sacrificed as an offering of thanks to Poor Dlang Por, and to invite the soul to take up permanent residence within the child's body and in the parental household. This serves to adopt the child into the world of human beings, and formally accept it into the parent's kinship group. The baby is then given a name and introduced to the household spirits, who are expected from that moment to give it protection. (Lee, personal communication).

The birth takes place in the couple's bedroom, and no one but the midwife or husband can be present to assist in her delivery. The woman sits on two stools on the sleeping platform with her body covered by a blanket, leaning on her husband for support. The child drops onto the springy bamboo, which cushions its fall and also, they say, helps the child to start breathing. The Hmong are known for their dexterity in turning the child in the womb if the position is not correct.

The father cuts the cord with a fresh sliver of bamboo. If a boy, he buries the placenta in the earthen floor of the house at the base of the main central post, to be close to the house spirits. A baby girl's placenta is buried under the place where she was born.

The mother lies near the fire of the main hearth for three days after giving birth, then may return to her bedroom. For 20 days she should eat nothing but chicken and rice, as it is believed that chicken will help her recover her strength quickly, and other food might poison her. After a month she returns to the fields to work and may resume sleeping with her husband.

Death

To have a proper funeral is of great importance to the Hmong, for as a result the soul will prosper in the afterworld. It is preferable to die in one's own home or, at least in the home of a clansman.

When death seems imminent, close relatives gather around the dying person for mutal comfort, and for sharing the many duties that arise when death occurs. The firing of a gun three times, and the wailing of family members announce to the village that death has come.

When an older person dies the children and grandchildren wash the body, then dress it in special burial clothing that will have been made and laid away for that purpose. Each wife makes burial clothing for her husband and herself which differs from that ordinarily worn. It is usually of hemp cloth, and in addition to the pants for the men and skirt for the women, there are three or more upper garments of varying lengths placed one on top of the other on the body, each richly embroidered, the outer one being the most elaborate. Strips of white cloth are wound around each leg and special shoes are placed on the feet. More affluent Hmong use ornamental Chinese shoes for this purpose, while others use simple hemp sandals. They are important because they are used to walk through the 'land of the giant furry caterpillars on the way to the other world'. (Lee, personal communication.) Until the time of burial the body rests upon a bier about one metre high, next to the family altar.

As prescribed by their oral traditions, special cloths must be presented to the corpse. These include richly embroidered 'pillows' (cloths 30 to 35 cm square) made by the sisters, daughters, and nieces of the deceased, and placed under the corpse's head. In addition they adorn a man's corpse with a sash, and a woman's with embroidered collars.

The fingers of the dead person are often tied with red thread so if on his journey in the afterlife he is detained by spirits wanting him to 'help peel onions and garlic', he can say his hands are injured and he cannot help. A small red cloth is placed over the forehead or face so the deceased will 'not be ashamed in front of other people'.

Soon after death a chicken is sacrificed and laid above the head of the dead person. The presiding elder says a prayer for the dead and tells him that he can live under the chicken's wings if it is hot, or under its tail if it rains, thus revealing to the deceased that he is dead. He is further instructed to take the middle path to reach the land of the ancestors with the chicken as his guide.

The many tasks related to the funeral are assigned by two men who are in charge of the rites. One man is assigned to blow the Hmong mouth organ (*qeej*), and another to beat the ceremonial death drum, which is used only for funerals. When these two instruments are heard together in a Hmong village, one can be sure there has been a death.

Others are assigned to 'feed the corpse', and to fire three shots each time food is offered. Another person is chosen to settle the dead man's accounts, for the ledger must be closed and all brought back to zero before burial can take place. Consequently the deceased will be happy, prosperous, and free of debts in the next life. Others are assigned to make the coffin, cut firewood, cook, and so on.

All family members must be present for the burial. If some of the married children have moved to other areas, the burial is delayed until their arrival. The coffin must be completed, and all the sacrificial animals in readiness. Only on a day which is auspicious for the family can the burial take place. The corpse, meanwhile, must be kept in the house, even though it may already have begun to decay.

When all is ready the corpse is carried out of the house on the bier on which it has lain since death, and placed on a wooden carrying frame. The oxen which have been given by the dead person's spouse and relatives are then sacrificed.

In the afternoon the funeral procession gets under way, timed so the burial can take place around four o'clock. The leader of the procession, blowing a mouth organ, is followed by a girl who carries a burning brand for the deceased to 'see the way'. Those carrying the body follow.

After they have gone part of the way the girl throws the brand on the path and runs back home, thereby confusing the soul of the dead man. Various stops are made along the way to instruct the dead person, and to ensure that his soul will not return to the village.

When the procession reaches the burial site, the coffin is placed in the grave, the body lowered into it, and the lid put in place. The grave is then filled with earth and a cairn of stones built over it, with branches placed on top, to prevent wild animals from unearthing the body. The two poles used to carry the corpse are cut in two so that they cannot 'return home and bring other people to the afterworld'.

If a Hmong dies a 'bad death' a number of food and drink offerings are placed at increasingly greater distances from the house, while saying to the soul, 'Come, eat and drink. Do not return, but come further. There will be plenty for you to eat and drink in the next life'.

Blue Hmong woman dressed in her burial clothes which she sold as she converted to Christianity

Woman's and man's burial clothes (Blue Hmong)

Scenes of a Blue Hmong boy's funeral:

1) Leaving house with corpse. Note man with mouth organ followed by girl with burning torch

2) Killing sacrificial ox, who follows the dead to the ancestor village

3) Corpse on bier at the edge of the village

4) Playing death drum and mouth organ, while loved ones wail at bier

5) Opening the way to the beyond through firing of a crossbow

6) Last questioning of the dead by means of the divining sticks

7) Cleansing ceremony at the edge of the village on the way back from the burial site

Religion

Supernatural beings are involved in every aspect of Hmong life. There are a number of household spirits in each home which they believe protect them from attacks by the spirits of disease and death. They also protect the souls of crops, money, and livestock in order that the household will prosper and be healthy.

The 'door spirit' is especially important. When a Hmong dies his souls must seek permission from the door spirit to leave the house and cross into the afterlife. There is also an annual ceremony to the door spirit. A pig is killed, offerings are made, and the family eats the meat. The head of the household then takes a piece of burning firewood in one hand, and opens the door with the other declaring, 'I open the door, not to let diseases come into the house, or to let the souls of money, silver and gold leave the house, but to let the souls of money, silver, and gold, and good fortune, come in'. Some hold a similar ceremony to the main central post once a year.

Every Hmong house has at least one altar, while those of shamans have more. The focus of the main altar in a Blue Hmong house is a piece of white paper about one hand-span square put on the wall opposite the doorway. At this altar protection is sought for all of the people and animals of the household. Here at each New Year festival a cock is sacrificed and some of its feathers are stuck on the paper with its blood.

The household spirits have names, and are graded in order of seniority. According to some White Hmong informants the six most important spirits in a household are: 1. spirits of the ancestral altar, 2. spirit of the central post, 3. spirit of the fireplace, 4. spirit of the stove, 5. spirit of the door, and 6. spirit of the bedroom. All are 'tame' spirits, as distinct from the 'wild' spirits which live outside the village.

During heavy winds and rains the household head may call on spirits for protection. If this does not suffice, he may fire a gun to drive the storm away. If it abates shortly after, he may shout victoriously, 'The rain has given in to me!'

Some Hmong believe there is a 'Lord of the Land' dwelling in each locality. The villagers jointly construct a spirit shelf on the trunk of one big tree in a grove above the village. During the New Year festival elders make offerings to the 'Lord of the Land', so that their village will be protected from wild animals, robbers, fire, enemies and outside evil spirits. Representatives of all households attend these rites, which help to sustain unity.

Hmong believe that some of them have the power to 'send spirits' (*tso daab*) to harm other people. Once a person is suspected of having this ability, people are afraid to bring any charges against him for fear of his malevolent power.

Religious Practitioners

Most household heads are able to perform the common rituals. However, to contact the spiritual world in emergencies shamans are consulted.

Shamans may be either male or female and every village must have at least one. In a village in southwestern Chiang Mai Province, Chindarsi (1974) found six resident shamans, three men and three women. A person is 'chosen' by the spirits to be a shaman, and he or she usually learns of this calling through a long illness, which is cured only when the person consents to become a shaman. Each shaman has 'teacher spirits' who instruct him or her how to perform.

When a shaman is called in to cure a sick person, he usually goes into a trance to be in direct communication with the unseen powers. He veils his eyes with a black cloth 'so as to see the spirits', and sits on a bench facing the shaman's altar, with his ceremonial rattle in his hand. He then calls his 'teacher spirits' to come cure the patient.

Tension builds up as the shaman shakes his rattle with one hand and slaps the other on his thigh, his helper beating a gong in time with the chanting. He bounces up and down on the bench as if riding a horse, and begins to tremble. While in a trance he calls out that a pig or a chicken must be sacrificed to soothe a spirit which has been angered. When this is done, some of the blood is wiped on the clothing of the patient or on the soles of his feet, depending on the instructions of the shaman. Paper spirit money is then burned as an offering following the practice of the Chinese.

The shaman may jump up from the bench and declare that wicked spirits have come; he must fight them off. He may jump up backwards from the floor onto the bench as part of the struggle with the forces of evil. The battle may grow so intense he falls to the floor and rolls around

groaning and shouting. The family watches to see whether the shaman will emerge victorious.

Finally the shaman becomes still and doubles over, face downward. His helper raps him gently on the back to bring him out of his trance. Now recovered, the shaman removes the black cloth from his eyes and throws the divining sticks to see what the outcome of the struggle will be. He then ceremoniously thanks his 'teacher spirits', after which the family does obeisance to him and to the spirits in turn, expressing gratitude for their help. The meat of the sacrifice is then cooked, and all present eat a meal. The shaman is paid for his services, and given some of the meat to take home.

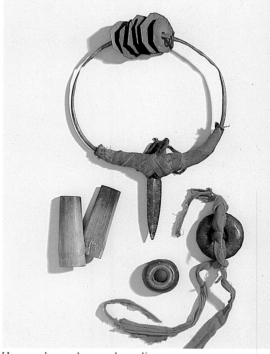

Hmong shaman's paraphernalia

Hmong shaman in trance

White Hmong house altar

Sickness and Treatment

In every village there are some adults, both men and women, who have learned one or more curing rites that have been passed down from generation to generation. Unlike shamans, they do not go into a trance and are not spirit mediums, but know how to perform certain rites and sacrifices for curing illnesses and exorcising evil spirits.

Most Hmong ritual activity is concerned with determining the cause of illness, and then curing it. If a Hmong falls ill and the family believes an offended spirit may be the cause, a shaman is called in to perform a curing rite. They believe that spirits who have been disturbed or insulted seek revenge, and may thus capture the souls of the offenders or block their path. Supernatural cures are needed for supernatural illnesses.

If a person is sick and the shaman determines that the cause is due to the souls leaving his body and wandering around in the forest, a 'silver and golden bridge' ceremony may be held to show the souls the way home. There are five types of ceremonies in which a 'bridge' is made either along a trail or over a small stream and an animal is sacrificed. On completion, the sick person is led across the bridge and returns home; then all present tie strings around his wrist. The sacrificed animal is cooked and all participate in a meal.

In various curing ceremonies Hmong tie hemp or cotton string on the wrists of the patient. If the patient does not improve, another ceremony is held and a metal neck ring, bracelet, or anklet is used instead of string. In case of serious illness two or three kinds of metal are twisted together, silver, brass and iron being the metals used.

In their quest for health Hmong do not become discouraged if one ritual does not result in a cure, but try one after another until the right one is found. Sometimes they may make a contract with the spirits, 'If you will effect a cure now, I will sacrifice such-and-such an animal to you at the New Year'.

Curing is not limited to such ceremonies. Many Hmong men and women have a knowledge of herbal medicines widely used for common ailments. Increasingly they are also turning to modern medicine. In many cases they first perform ritual healing ceremonies, then seek the help of modern medical practitioners.

Relationships

Hmong are hospitable, always ready to welcome strangers and give them the best food they have. When it comes to competing for land, however, another side of their character can be revealed. This is especially true of opium-growing Hmong, who may take as much as 30 *rai* (4.8 hectares) of land per family for their poppy fields. Although this is small by Western standards, it may be disproportionate when the needs of their tribal neighbours are considered. Their hunger for land even leads to disputes among themselves, the severity of which may tax the ability of the village headman to arbitrate. More significantly, it may lead them into rivalry with other tribal groups for land they wish to possess.

Hmong see themselves as being inferior to no other tribal group, but have high regard for the Mien. These two peoples appear to have a common origin, which may account for this affinity. They both have close ties to the Chinese, and the older men of the two tribes generally converse with one another in Yunnanese, a language in which they feel more at home than Thai.

The relationship of Hmong with Yunnanese has developed over hundreds of years, during the time that both groups were making their way southward. Ordinarily the Hmong do not form close friendships with them, but opium growers accept them in their role as traders in the drug.

In the past, Hmong contacts with Thai have not been as significant as those with Yunnanese and tribal groups, but this has changed over the last 20 years. The Thai Government has come to realize that it must become involved in the affairs of the tribal people, and the Hmong are becoming aware of their responsibilities to the country in which they live. There has been mutual distrust between Thai and Hmong, but this situation may be changing due to the interest shown in the Hmong people by the King and Queen, better understanding on the part of certain Government officials, and some Hmong being brought more into the mainstream of the life of the country by means of education and development projects.

Conclusion

Hmong see themselves as a people born to the open spaces of the mountains, without physical or temporal limits. Hundreds of years of adversity have bred a spirit of independence; they value liberty and dignity above easy living. The independence they seek, however, is not for the individual, but for the kin group, and the liberty they cherish is group liberty.

The image of sturdy Hmong people, master poppy-growers, living high on mountain slopes, breeding superior dogs and ponies and amassing large amounts of silver ingots and jewellery is changing as the realities of the late 20th century press in on them. The trend is toward moving to lower elevations. While some climb back up the slopes to continue cultivating their poppies, growing numbers are making irrigated fields and are turning to other cash crops, such as coffee, soy or kidney beans, and fruit trees. Some who live near population centres are building car ports for their pick-up trucks alongside the pony stables. With their instinct for finding ways of gaining wealth, a growing number are prospering as entrepreneurs. While most villages still practice shifting cultivation, more and more are settling into permanancy.

Children are being educated in Thai schools and many youth are attending vocational schools – a few even university. Young people, once they have completed their education, may serve brief periods as teachers or in some other profession, but many return eventually to farming or trading along with their parents and grandparents.

In all of this the changes in Hmong life-style are largely superficial. Their ancient culture remains deeply woven in the very fabric of their beings – independence is still their ultimate goal. While the environment has changed for many and their major means of livelihood is different from that of their forefathers, they remain profoundly *Hmong*. Women continue wearing their distinctive Hmong dress, though it may be of imitation printed batik and stitched on a sewing machine. Hmong men, unlike many of the other tribes, proudly wear their Hmong clothing when going to town just as they do in their villages. There is little breakdown of the Hmong family and the Hmong way of life. That culture which has preserved their integrity as a people throughout past generations continues to give them identity in the late 20th century.

Mien village scene

Chapter 5

MIEN (Yao)

Desire for Propriety

Kwei Lin was quite sure his father still had a copy of the letter written several years ago by the Mien leader, Chao La. The letter, written in Chinese characters, was a request for Mien to stop spending so much money on bride price and the purchase of pigs for marriage ceremonies. Most Mien realized Chao La was right, but they were not willing to suggest anything which might not seem proper to other Mien.

The father found the letter, and after adjusting his glasses read it aloud to his son. He was proud to be able to read and only wished his sons showed more interest in learning to read Chinese, which in his eyes was the proper script. What the letter said was true; far too much was being spent by Mien people on pigs in order to feast guests for three days of wedding celebrations, and bride prices had escalated to the point where families with several sons suffered severe economic problems.

Kwei Lin's youngest brother was 20, and really should get married so that they could have another worker in their household. But where would the pigs come from for the wedding celebration? They would have had more pigs if the family had not held 'bridge ceremonies' for their parents, and observed other healing rituals. Kwei Lin did not mention this to his father, as that would cause him to lose face. Instead he said, 'I know, father, that you want to perform the *kwa tang* merit-making ceremony, but perhaps that will have to wait'.

Both men, proud to be Mien, knew there was a proper way, a *right* way, to live one's life, and they were determined to do so with dignity. It weighed heavily on the father, however, that he never had the *kwa tang* ceremony, especially as death could not be far off. At the same time Kwei Lin was well aware of the fact that there would not be enough pigs for a wedding, an initiation ceremony, and a funeral (he was not blind to his father's condition).

'It will be all right, father', Kwei Lin said. 'Let's concentrate first on youngest brother getting married. When we have more workers in the household we can increase the size of our fields and raise more pigs, so that in the future, well. . .' his voice trailed off. Surely, on the basis of all the family had done for the ancestors and all the offerings made to the spirits, doing everything in the proper manner, things would improve.

Baby boy peaks over mother's shoulder

Name and Language

The ethnic group which calls itself 'Mien' is referred to as 'Yao' by other groups. In its full form the term they call themselves is 'Iu Mien'. The first part of the name is written either as 'Iu' or 'Yu', but is pronounced 'Ee-yu'. Some think that 'Yao' may be a corruption of this term. In Vietnam they are often referred to as 'Man', which comes from the Chinese term for 'barbarian'.

The Mien speak a Miao-Yao language, considered by some to be related to the Sino-Tibetan family of languages. Influences from Chinese, Lao, and Thai can be detected; most borrowed words coming from Chinese.

Mien are unique among tribal people, having a tradition of writing which dates back several centuries. The men use Chinese characters to record their rituals, keep family records, and write contracts and letters. Boys have been taught to read and write either by their fathers or by Chinese teachers hired by the village. This tradition is beginning to break down, however, and Mien elders are deeply concerned about the future of their culture if it is not possible for the boys to study Chinese as well as Thai.

In addition to the script in Chinese characters, both a Romanized and a Thai-based script have been devised for the Mien by western missionaries.

The Mien of Thailand are a homogeneous group, all speaking the same dialect, wearing the same style of clothing, and following the same traditions, with only minor regional variations.

Origin

Mien probably originated in southern China about 2,000 years ago. Their early history is uncertain, as most of the non-Han ethnic groups were simply referred to as 'barbarians'. The Mien have a legend that their ancestors 'crossed the sea' during the latter part of the 14th Century. One fact which lends credence to such a migration is that the *She* (a group closely related to the Mien) are found along the southeastern coast of China from which the migration by sea may have taken place. This would have brought them to Hainan, Guangxi (Kwangsi), and the adjoining provinces where they are now found.

Population

Apart from the *She*, there were about 1.3 million Mien-Yao in China in mid-1983. Mien living in Vietnam may number over 200,000. It is difficult to estimate the number remaining in Laos after large numbers of them fled to Thailand, but since 1975 the total may be 20,000 or so. Possibly 15,000 'Hainan Miao' live on the island of Hainan. They should probably be classified as Mien, as they speak a dialect more closely related to Mien than to Hmong.

There were about 30,000 Mien in Thailand in mid-1983, excluding those in refugee camps. The largest concentrations of Mien reside in Mae Chan District of Chiang Rai Province and Chiang Kham District of Phayao Province. Considerable numbers live in the provinces of Nan and Lampang, and the remainder are located in Chiang Mai, Phitsanulok, and Kamphaeng Phet provinces.

The first Mien to migrate into Thailand probably came around the middle of the 19th Century. Their migration was almost totally from Laos, although a few villages have been located near the Thai border in Burma from time to time.

Legends

The legend of the dog, Phan Hu, figures widely in Chinese and Yao literature, although many Mien disclaim any knowledge of this myth. Those who do know it give different versions. We recorded the legend from a knowledgeable Mien elder who still owns a 'Mien Passport' (see next section). The Emperor Pien Hung of China, was attacked by the very powerful Emperor Kao Wang, and faced defeat. The dog, Phan Hu, was able to get through the lines, kill the agressor, and bring Kao Wang's head back to Emperor Pien Hung. Phan Hu was rewarded with one of Pien Hung's daughters as a wife, whom he took up to the mountains to live with him. They produced 12 children, six boys and six girls, from whom sprung the 12 clans of the Mien.

Literature

In Mien homes it is not unusual to find several pamphlets hand-written in Chinese characters. One deals with sickness (*mang paeng so*), explaining the proper treatment for various types of illness, another (*fat so*) explains how to deal with fractures, bone displacements, tendon problems, and the like.

Very important is the 'Book of Days' (*thong so*). This book must be examined before a couple is betrothed, for by comparing the months and years of their births, it can be determined whether the union will be harmonious or not. One section indicates the location of the soul of the fetus of an unborn infant during each month of the year (see section on birth).

Another pamphlet is often called the 'Ancestor Book' (*ca fin tan*), as it contains the ceremonial names of the ancestors going back at least nine generations. There are three other sections: 'The Flowering of Children', 'How the Stars Care for Us', and 'Helps for Hunters'.

A most unique document, but now very rare, has often been called the 'Mien Passport' (*cia sen pawng*). It includes a copy of the Imperial Edict issued by Pien Hung (see the legend above) to the Mien living in China, permitting them to migrate and engage in cultivation anywhere in the mountainous areas. Furthermore, they were to be accorded certain rights as 'children of Emporer Pien Hung'.

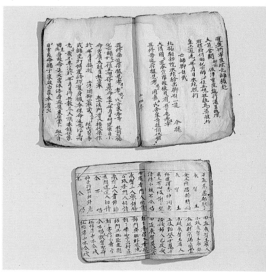

Pages of two Mien books

Wooden figures used in Mien ritual

Enthroned figures represent ancestors, the figure
on horseback is the 'Leader of the Mediums'

Clothing and Ornamentation

Groups of black-turbaned, red-ruffed women on low stools bending over their embroidery are sufficient to identify a village as being Mien. Needles fly while tongues keep pace with the village gossip as these highly-skilled embroiderers produce ornate caps for their children and sumptuously-patterned pants for themselves. Surprisingly they work from the back of the cloth, and cannot 'see' the pattern until it is turned over.

The costume of a woman consists of loose-fitting pants, ankle-length tunic, sash, and turban. All garments are black or indigo, and are made of cotton homespun cloth, with the possible exception of the tunic, which may be of machine-made material.

Elderly Mien have childhood memories of their mothers weaving all the cloth needed for the family. They grew their own cotton, and spun it into thread either with hand spindles or spinning wheels. Eventually they turned to the use of cloth purchased from the Tai in Laos. Today most of the cloth used for Mien embroideries in Thailand comes from the Shan in Kengtung State, or Northern Thai weavers in Chiang Kham District. Many Mien women prefer to dye their own cloth, using either chemical dyes or their own home-processed indigo dye.

Every Mien woman devotes her finest skills to embroidering the two matching panels forming the main part of her pants. Five standard designs used at the bottom of the pant legs form the border. Four of those designs use the weaving stitch, and the fifth the horizontal/vertical stitch. The weaving stitch, so called because it consists of all vertical lines that resemble weaving, was originally the only type of embroidery used. The horizontal/vertical stitch, which follows the warp and weft of the cloth with a lacy effect, was introduced later, but is also an old technique. At one time only the borders of the pantlegs were embroidered.

Women found that cloth woven by the Tai was quite satisfactory and gradually discontinued weaving. Having more time, they added more and more rows of embroidery to their pants. Today the entire garment, except for the waistband and crotch, is covered with embroidery.

Diagonal cross-stitch embroidery has come into use during the past 40 to 50 years. There may still be a few elderly women who never learned the technique. We met one such old woman (now deceased) who had gone as a refugee with her family to the United States in 1979.

Apart from the five standard patterns, the embroidery on the pants is the expression of each individual. She may draw from a great repertoire of Mien designs, or she may innovate as she wishes. Many of the designs have been given names, but the same design may be given different names by different people. As far as can be ascertained, there is no mythical or religious significance to the patterns.

Formerly silk thread was used for embroidery floss, and many Mien produced their own. As they used natural dyes the number of colours was limited. Today Mien women in Thailand use pearl cotton crochet thread, embroidery floss, weaving thread with a sheen, or wool-like acrylic yarn. These market threads bring a wide range of bright colours to modern Mien embroidery.

Mien recently come from Laos, or who consider themselves to be 'Lao-Mien', use a great deal of pale blue in their embroidery. Those called the 'Chiang Kham-Mien', however, use red hues (magenta, and various shades of pink and golden orange) as the dominant colours. There is no prescribed number or set of colours, although some women favour using five.

Girls are taught to embroider from the age of five or six. They start with the five original patterns, and gradually add to their repertoire as they gain in skill. A mother may make pants and tunic for her daughter when the child is four or five. Girls wear caps until they are nine or ten, although on festive occasions even small girls may wear turbans. By the age of ten a girl should be able to embroider her own pants, and from then on she spends countless hours creating beauty with her embroidery needle.

Mien women at their favourite occupation

Girls learn to embroider at an early age

Women embroider from the back of the cloth

Woman's outfit

Women's richly embroidered pants

Both the sash and turban have 20 cm or more of embroidery at each end, using mostly the weaving stitch and horizontal/vertical stitch. Mien in the Chiang Kham area use seven metres of cloth for both turbans and sashes, while the Lao-Mien use only half that length. In both cases the cloth is about 50 cm wide. The sash is folded in half lengthwise, wound around the waist over the tunic, and looped in the back so that the embroidered ends hang evenly.

Women's turbans are wrapped in different ways according to the area. Lao-Mien women, using the shorter length of cloth, wrap their turbans very neatly, criss-crossing them front and back, with embroidered patches showing around the rim or across the crown. The Chiang Kham-Mien cover the crown of the head with red cloth, then wind the turban around many times, leaving the embroidered ends to stick up inside the roll on either side. Others wrap it loosely into a massive headpiece, being careful, of course, that the embroidery shows. Women consider it untidy for hair to show under the turban, so they pluck out any hair that might be exposed.

The ankle-length tunic is made of one straight piece in the back and two in the front. It is split nearly to the waist on the sides. The front edges of the Lao-Mien tunics have a 3 cm wide embroidered border to the waist, while the Chiang Kham-Mien often sew on a strip of cotton print material. Along the inside edge of the border is a ruff of red wool yarn, short and thick on the Lao-Mien style, longer and looser on the Chiang Kham style. The two strips of cloth forming the front of the tunic from the waist down are folded together and tucked up into the sash on one side, exposing the embroidered pants. A fine tunic has silk and bead tassels hanging at the tops of the split sides, a row of rectangular-shaped engraved or repoussé silver buckles down the front to the waist, and burgundy-coloured braid with fine silver wire twisted around it attached to the edges of the garment.

Articles of clothing and ornaments worn by Mien bride.
(Boots now rare)

Two women's turbans or sashes (above), bridegroom's sash (below)

Antique bridal head coverings

Embroidered end of bride's turban

An ornate apron/cape is worn for weddings and other special occasions. The band at the top is decorated with red, white, and black strips of cloth edged with saw-toothed red appliqué. The body of the garment is adorned with patches of cross-stitched embroidery and bold appliqué patterns of symmetrical shapes with many lobes and curlicues. It can be worn either as a cape or an apron and is embellished with silver buttons, coins, dangles, and chains. The ends of the sashes have long tassels of beads and burgundy or red silk thread. A simpler version is used as a baby-carrying cloth.

A man's suit consists of a loose-fitting jacket that crosses over the chest and is closed by eight to ten silver ball-shaped buttons down the right side, worn with Chinese-style pants. Both garments are made of black or indigo homespun cloth, although some older men wear satin jackets for festive occasions. The jackets of younger men are embellished with red, black, and white piping around the edges and have patches of embroidery, sometimes forming pockets. As men grow older, the decorative features are gradually reduced until they are devoid of colour. The finer jackets are edged with silver-wound braid, as are women's tunics. Turbans are only occasionally worn for ceremonies.

Mothers make delightful caps for their babies and small children. Little girls wear close-fitting caps of black or indigo homespun cloth, covered with fine embroidery. A large red woolen pompon encircles the top, and ball-shaped ones may be added over the ears.

Small boys' caps are made of red and black cloth, with bold appliquéd patterns, edged with white braiding. A large red pompon is attached to the top, and others to the embroidered band around the edge.

Large shoulder bags made from black and white striped Tai cloth are embellished with bands of embroidery, thick tufts of red and white wool yarn down the front, and pompons across the bottom. Other bags are made of black cloth with appliqué. Square embroidered or appliquéd bags without straps are used to store silver jewellery and money.

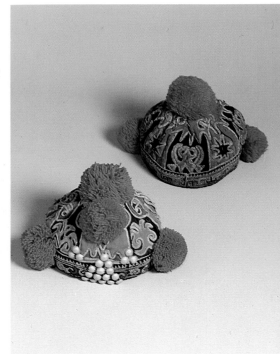

Caps for boys

Girl's cap *(upper)* and boy's cap *(lower)*

Caps for girls

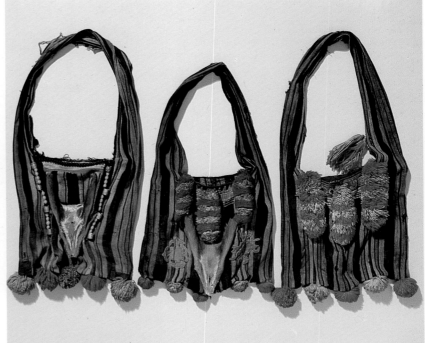

Two hunter's bags have trophies from the kill attached

Square embroidered bags for storing silver or carrying money

Embroidered saddle covering – blanket is carried inside

Ornaments

On festive occasions women and children wear silver neck rings, occasionally multi-tiered. From the hooked ends at the back women may suspend silver chains to which bells, balls, dangles, and tiny grooming tools are attached, some of them brightened with cloisonné enamel. A few women have ornamental pieces made of a network of chains, bells, and dangles which cover the back from the neck to the waist, but most have silver only at the top with long silk burgundy tassels hanging to the waist.

Mien women, like the Hmong, wear arrow-shaped earrings with the shafts bent into circles. They also wear a variety of silver rings. A pair of heavy silver bracelets is worn by the women on their left wrists above a long silver chain, wrapped around the lower wrist. They do not wear the bracelets on the right wrist as it would interfere with their work.

Exquisite silver butterflies, birds, flowers, and geometric designs, as well as bells, balls, and tiny grooming tools come from the forges of the highly skilled Mien silversmiths.

Mien women and girls dressed for wedding

Village

The structure and location of the village (*laang*) is of less importance to the Mien than the individual household (*pyao tsong mien*). There is no village gate, ceremonial building, or dancing ground – sometimes not even a very well-defined village area.

Mien favour a site on a gradual slope, with steeper slopes above and below. The site must also have a forest area with a stream nearby.

While most villages consist of only 10–25 houses, at least one in the Kamphaeng Phet area has over 200. Each village is made up of two or more clans, that of the founding headman tending to predominate.

Headman

The main tasks of a Mien headman are: to direct village celebrations; maintain security; and preside at meetings of the elders. Decorum and politeness are stressed when elders meet to discuss the affairs of the village. In cases of disputes between villagers, the headman does not serve so much as judge as one who suggests alternatives for resolving the issue quickly and in a mutually acceptable way.

The headman is also responsible for the welfare of the villagers. Some years ago an anthropologist recorded the ceremonial names of the ancestors in a certain village during the absence of the headman. On his return the headman, who was most upset about this, politely explained to the anthropologist that if someone learned the ceremonial names of their ancestors he could use that knowledge in black magic against the villagers. The headman then asked for the list of names, which he promptly burned.

Houses

Mien houses are built on the ground. Walls are preferably of wood, but if not available, bamboo is used. The roof is commonly made of thatch grass, but sometimes of wooden shingles or large leaves.

There is a door at each end of the house. The 'men's door' leads into the area where guests are welcomed, while the 'women's door' leads into the kitchen. A third door is called the 'Big Door' (*top keng*), not because of its size, but because of its importance in special ceremonies. Directly opposite the Big Door is the ancestral altar.

The number of bedrooms depends on the number and ages of the people living in that household. A girl of marriageable age is given a private bedroom next to the women's door, allowing easy access to suitors.

The house is a sacred structure, for to construct it the earth must be disturbed and material from the jungle used. Various omens and dreams are taken into account in order to avoid offending the spirits or constructing a building in their path. After the house has been built, the ancestral altar (*mien pai*) is installed on an auspicious day. A small structure in the shape of a house (*mien tia*) may be placed on it. If everything is done properly the spirits and ancestors will ensure health and prosperity for the household.

There are two main stoves: one where food is cooked for the family, and another for cooking pig's food. As a spirit is said to live in the stoves, it is forbidden to put one's feet on them or to sit with one's back against them.

Houses should not be built in a way which prevents free entry of the spirits through the Big Door to the altar. Pens for animals or other structures are not built behind the house, as this area is kept clear of buildings and big trees allowing freedom to the 'water dragon spirits', who bring good luck to the household.

Mien house plan

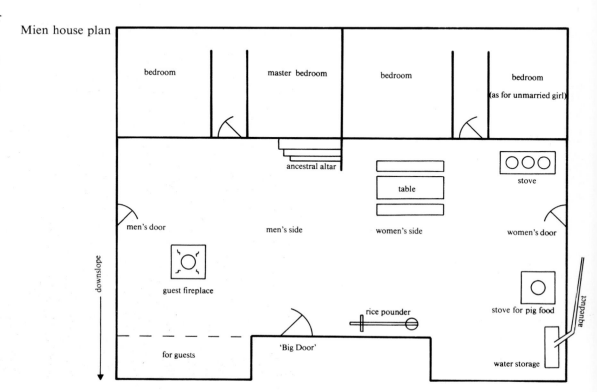

Family and Household

The extended family, comprising a husband and wife, one or more married sons and families, and the unmarried children, is the basic unit of Mien social organization. There may be from two to 60 people living in a household, with 20 not being unusual. If several nuclear families dwell together, each tills its own fields and contributes its share to the household larder. The head of the household keeps the income derived from the animals, but that realized from the sale of opium and other cash crops is retained by the individual families.

Larger households may become so crowded that some of the nuclear families have to take turns staying out in field huts rather than in the main house. However, in most cases before a household reaches this stage of congestion, one or more of the nuclear families will probably have left to establish their own households.

Parents are quick to put an end to strife among children, for the Mien do not tolerate quarrels. Should there be a serious clash between married sons living in the household, their father will suggest politely but firmly that it is time for one of them to move out.

The men in a Mien household are accorded special status. Food is served to the men first, then women and children eat. A wife is subservient to her husband and is expected to defer to him. The women are expected to rise early to perform their chores, and work very hard indeed. Men and women share the field work; the men performing the heavier tasks, like cutting trees and building fences.

The elders are accorded special respect. It is felt that as they know a great deal about life and ritual, the younger generation should listen to them.

Chickens are essential for ritual use

Steaming rice

Children enjoy the wedding feast

Clan and Kin

Clan (*fing*) membership is inherited from one's father for life. Women do not take on the clan of their husbands.

The 12 clan names are written in Chinese characters in the Mien Passport. There are various versions of this list. Walker (1974:57) gives the following: Pieun, Ch'in, Yieun, Le, Tang, Chiuh, Chiu, Ho, Tong, Pum, Lwi, and Chiang. The clans are not organized, nor is their geographical location demarcated.

Each clan maintains a particular style of ritual behaviour, and even among some sub-clans there are distinctive ways of carrying on Mien rites. One clan, for example, uses ropes when capturing a pig for ritual sacrifice, while another uses a basket.

Adoption

Mien adopt children from the Lahu, Akha, Shan, Khamu, Lao, and Thai, as well as from within their own tribe. Kandre discovered that at least 10% of the present Mien population has been adopted from other ethnic groups (in Kunstadter 1967:594). Miles states that if adopted Mien are included, over 20% of the population under the age of 20 is made up of adoptees (in Ho and Chapman 1973:258). We know one older Mien couple with eight children of their own, who has through the years adopted 10 children from several ethnic groups.

When Mien adopt from outside their tribe, they feel that either money or goods must be given in exchange. Payment may be made in opium, especially if one of the natural parents is an addict. Sometimes a child is received in payment of a debt. A Mien child may be adopted, especially that of a close relative who cannot care for the child properly. Mien will never adopt out or sell their children to non-Mien – something as bad as allowing young Mien girls to become prostitutes.

Courtship and Marriage

Choice

Young people are free to choose their marriage partners. The young man may come to the girl's bedroom for a night, or indefinitely – if the girl consents. One or two children may have been born before the marriage ceremony is held.

The freedom of choice of the couple is conditioned by two factors: they should be from different clans, and there should be affinity of their birth dates. Generally older siblings marry before the younger. If a younger sibling marries first, money must be given to the older to 'take away his/her shame'.

Betrothal

Betrothal usually takes place soon after New Year, and the wedding shortly before the next New Year.

When a young man becomes interested in marrying a girl, he must send someone to find out her birthdate. His family then examines its 'Book of Days' to make sure the union will be auspicious. For example, if a boy born in the year of the tiger marries a girl born in the year of the pig, the union will be an auspicious one. However, if a boy born in the year of the horse marries a girl born in the year of the rat, calamities will ensue. If the relative times of their births indicate that it would be a good marriage, the boy's parents consent.

Word is then sent to the girl's parents that the following evening family representatives will come to propose the betrothal of the couple. They are served a meal by the girl's parents, and as they sit down to eat, the go-between places a pair of silver bracelets on the table. When the dishes are cleared away the girl picks up the bracelets. If she does not want to marry the boy, the bracelets will be returned in a day or two. If they are not returned, the go-between sets a date for the discussion of wedding arrangements.

On that date at least two members of the boy's family go to the girl's house, taking a rooster with them. Her parents call in two or three relatives as witnesses. The rooster is cooked, the girl's family providing rice, and during the meal they begin to discuss the bride price. They must reach agreement on all details: the amount to be paid in

silver ingots, silver coins, and paper money; when and how payments must be made; the number of pigs and bottles of liquor to be provided; the number of guests to be invited; and the amount of cloth and thread to be given to the bride. All of this has to be provided by the groom's family. Once an agreement is reached, it is written down in duplicate by one of the witnesses, and signed by both fathers, each retaining a copy.

The bride price is determined by several factors. The price will be slightly higher if a girl has a child, because there will be an extra person joining the family. The amount often depends on how much was paid for the boy's mother by his father. Traditionally the bride price is calculated in silver ingots. Miles (1974:104) found in a study of 15 marriages that between three and 16 ingots were paid, the average being about eight, which was worth $1,120 in mid-1983.

Children born before the total bride price has been paid belong to the family of the bride. On some occasions the groom's family gives them a child in lieu of silver.

On the morning after the betrothal, a ceremony is held to inform the ancestral spirits of the girl's family that the couple is going to be married. The girl begins embroidering the wedding garments on an auspicious day. These include an entire outfit for herself, possibly a wedding head covering, an embroidered sash for her fiancé, white embroidered scarves for each of them, and in some cases a pair of embroidered pants for her fiancé's mother. During that time the bride-to-be is excused from all field work.

If the young man breaks the engagement, his family forfeits everything which has been paid. If it is broken by the girl, her family must pay back two-fold whatever has been received.

After the betrothal the couple may live together if they wish, staying in the home of either, in accordance with the agreement.

Residence

The bride usually moves into her husband's house. Before leaving her home she pays obeisance to the spirit of the household fireplaces and to the ancestral altar, thus breaking off relations with the guardian spirits and ancestors of her natal family. In her new home she has obligations to the spirits and ancestors of her husband's family, and will be under their protection as long as she lives there. Should her husband die and she remarry, her new husband will pay a bride price to the family of her late husband, roughly equivalent to the original amount paid for her.

'Major wedding'

At least ten days before a 'major wedding' (*tom ching ca*) the groom's parents give a large packet of salt to the bride's parents. From this they make small packets which serve as invitations for those who are to participate in the bridal procession and are to receive gifts of meat and money at the close of the ceremony.

Before the bride is led in procession to the home of the groom, an elaborate structure is placed on her head. Traditionally the girl's hair was coated with beeswax, then pulled through a tube projecting from a board which is cut straight across the front and rounded in the back. The hair was then fanned out over the board and plastered down with beeswax.

At a wedding we attended this procedure was modified by placing a cap made from a gourd on the girl's head, and her hair pulled up through the neck of the gourd, which was in turn attached to the board. Wooden braces angled up to a high-vaulted point, rather like a roof truss. A framework made of bamboo sticks was attached to the rounded portion of the board and rose to a peak in back. Then a red cloth with tasseled corners was placed over the framework, and a chain of beads and silver ornaments with a long burgundy-coloured fringe tied around. The shoulder-length fringe almost covered the bride's face. Then embroidered rectangular cloths were used to cover the structure and stitched in place, and a red strip of cloth draped over the sloping edges at the back. Silver flowers were pinned at the peaks both front and back. These embroidered cloths are family heirlooms, and a number may be placed on the framework.

The bride wears the headpiece from the time of the procession to the groom's house until the festivities are over, although the coverings are removed between ceremonies to lighten the weight. In order to sleep she must rest her neck on a high pillow or wooden block.

If the bridal party, en route to the groom's village, passes another village, the bride must go around it on the lower slope, so as not to disturb the protective spirit that dwells above the village.

The day before the wedding, the bridal party proceeds to the groom's village, and the bride is led to the place she will spend the night. That evening a contractual meal is held at the groom's home, where the bride price, or the agreed portion of it, is paid by the groom's father to the father of the bride in the presence of witnesses.

The next morning before dawn the officiating priest (*ching sui*) starts to explain to the ancestors that a new person is coming to live in the house. Half-way through this ceremony word is sent for the bridal party to proceed to the groom's house. The priest ceremonially purifies the house before the entry of the bride.

The bride in the meantime has left the house where she spent the night, and has been met by the orchestra consisting of an oboe, a drum, a bronze gong and cymbals. Arriving at the groom's house, the procession enters a square area where they are served tobacco and tea. The orchestra walks around the bridal procession three times, then leads the bride to the Big Door. Upon entering she kneels before the altar and pays obeisance to the spirits and ancestors, then is led to the bridal chamber where she remains until evening. Throughout the day there is a great deal of feasting, guests being fed in shifts.

The high point of the wedding is the kowtow ceremony which begins about 8 PM. The bride and groom, appearing in full wedding garb, first pay obeisance to the ancestors, then to the two wedding officiates, followed by the parents of the couple, older relatives, and finally the guests. One act of obeisance consists of the groom bowing three times from the waist and kowtowing three times from a kneeling position. Due to the large structure on her head the bride simply kneels when the groom drops to his knees. The couple performs twelve acts of obeisance to the ancestors, six to each of the two wedding officiates, six to each of the parents, and three each to all others. They conclude it by repeating obeisance three times each to the wedding officiates. If the kowtowing goes on until daybreak it is considered a good omen, since it shows that there were many people present to honour the occasion.

When this is completed, the priest takes two cups and pours liquor back and forth while chanting. He then crosses his arms, and gives the cups to the attendants. They in turn hand them to the bride and groom, who drink the liquor in front of the altar. This is done three times.

Then an elder instructs the couple on their duties as husband and wife, and urges them to create a strong family bond. Afterwards the bride and groom circulate among the guests serving them tobacco, tea, and liquor.

Later in the morning there is a final feast for all, after which the bride takes off her headdress. She is now considered to be a full member of that household.

'Minor wedding'

For those who cannot afford the expense of a 'major wedding', a 'minor wedding' (*ching ca ton*) is held in the bride's home, lasting for only one day. The bride and groom wear new clothing, but there is no special headgear or ritual garb. While all the guests are being feasted the groom distributes cigarettes and the bride serves liquor and tea. The couple does not perform obeisance.

'Major wedding'

1 and 2) Great pains are taken in the construction of the bridal headdress

3 and 4) Bridal procession to groom's house

5) Bride kneels before ancestral altar in groom's home

6) Weary newly-weds at the end of the kowtow ceremony

7) Bridal procession is received by groom's family

8) Bride and groom paying obeisance to wedding guests

9) Kowtowing to parents

10) Weighing silver for the bride price at the contractual meal

11) Sacrificial pig before ancestral altar

Birth

Pregnancy

Mien believe that during a woman's pregnancy the souls of the unborn baby do not yet reside in the fetus, but in various locations, depending on the month of the year. During the first and seventh months, the souls reside in the door of the house. The second and eighth months they live in the stoves. The third and ninth months find them in the rice pounder and the maize mill, and during the fourth and tenth in the floor near the altar. During the fifth and eleventh months the souls live in the mother's body, and during the sixth and twelfth in the mother's bed.

Precautions must be taken to prevent miscarriage and deformity. For example, Mien will not strike the door or rice pounder with a knife of any kind. They are careful not to spill water on the fireplace, nor will they enter the bedroom of a pregnant woman for fear the souls of the unborn infant might be frightened away.

Delivery

If an unmarried Mien girl has a baby, she must not give birth in her home, but in a hut built for that purpose at the side or front of the house.

A married woman gives birth to her child in her bedroom, usually assisted by her mother or mother-in-law. On an auspicious day the baby's birth is recorded in the 'spirit register' so the spirits know another person has arrived. The baby is then carried outside to 'see the sky', indicating that baby and mother are now ritually clean. Bamboo taboo signs are hung at the doors of the house to prevent strangers from entering, as they might 'step on' the child, causing it to cry.

After giving birth the mother stays near the fire to keep warm because her body is 'raw'. She must eat only hot, cooked food, chicken and fermented rice being preferred. Even cooked vegetables are not allowed the first ten days. She must do no heavy work or enter other houses for 30 days. An opening is made in the wall of her bedroom so she will not pass through doors in the house until after the 'cleansing ceremony'.

Naming

Each male has a childhood name which is given in accordance with the birth order following the Chinese system. Lao Ta is the first son, Lao Le the second, Lao San the third, and so on.

A Mien may also be given a nickname which either indicates a certain circumstance of the birth, or is a term of endearment. If the baby is often ill the name may be changed, because they think the wrong name was given.

There is also a 'small name' which uses the second part of the father's name for the second part of each child's name. If it is a first son, the first syllable will be Kao, Nai for the second son, San for the third, Su for the fourth, and U for the fifth. Girl's names use the prefix May for the first daughter, Nai for the second, Fam for the third, Fay for the fourth, and Man for the fifth, followed by the second name of the father.

A ceremonial name is given to each male over the age of 12. The name is chosen by the father, who first obtains the approval of the spirits by using his divining sticks. It is used by the man's children after his death when they make offerings or pray to him.

Religion

The Mien religion is composed of two interrelated systems: first, the belief in spirits and ancestors; and second, the belief in the Taoist religion as they learned it in China five or six centuries ago. The two systems have bonded together, resulting in a religion unique to the Mien.

Souls

Every human being has many souls (*wuan*) which are located in different parts of the body. It is not clear how many there are altogether, but texts used by the spirit priests (*sip mien mien*) indicate there are three in the head and seven in the legs. If one of the souls in the head leaves, the person falls sick, and if they all leave, the person dies.

Souls of children are easily frightened, so nothing should be done to startle them. Some parents are afraid that taking a photograph of their child might frighten the soul away.

Mien liken the souls of children to 'flowers' (*piang*). When a child reaches the age of 12 or 13 a ceremony is held to tell the flower spirits that they may leave. The ancestors are then told that this person is now an adult.

At death a person becomes a 'spirit' (*mien*, spoken on a different tone than the name of their ethnic group). However, one of the person's souls goes to a special place where it waits to be reincarnated. The blue mark on a baby's buttocks (commonly called the Mongolian spot) is believed to be the result of the soul having been slapped and told to be on its way as a child was about to be born. If a child dies at birth or when only a few days old, it is not considered to be a real child ('flower'), but has come to deceive the parents. A red mark is put on its forehead so it will be recognized if it returns in another baby's body.

If a person dies owing a large debt, he or she may be reincarnated to pay it back. If a young person has a premonition of death and speaks of another place and time, he/she obviously was reincarnated to settle an old debt.

We were told of a 12-year old girl who had lived twice before and could give the dates of her other births, the names of the parents, and some details of her previous lives. She requested a special ceremony on a certain date, saying if it was not done she would die. The parents paid no heed, and she died as predicted.

Spirits

The many spirits in the world of the Mien are proprietors of such things as streams, trees, and regions; it is important to maintain orderly relations with them. Mien recognize them as beings who live in a world opposite to that of people; they work at night, while humans work in the day; they are stupid, while people are clever; and they are strong, while humans are weak.

The fear of spirits constricts Mien activity. For example, they do not bathe in still water as it would make it dirty, thus angering the spirit of the water, resulting in illness.

Ancestors

Ancestors (ca fin), especially those of the last four generations, are important to the Mien. Consequently they are informed of all new members of the household; the new born, the adopted, and those marrying into the family. A priest performs rituals to ensure that the ancestors protect everyone in the household. When a certain ancestor is honoured, the family provides liquor, a pig or chicken offering, paper money, and joss sticks. The priest first chants a liturgy in which he informs the ancestor that an offering is being made and invites him to come and eat it. By throwing divining sticks the priest determines when the ancestor arrives and accepts the offering.

Next the priest reads the names of the ancestors written in the 'ancestor book' (ca fin tan) starting with the one who has been dead the longest. They are requested to protect the family members from harm and illness. Various questions are asked of ancestors, so worded that they can be answered 'yes' or 'no', as the divining sticks are only capable of handling such questions.

Taoism

The Mien in Thailand today follow Taoism as it was practiced in China in the 13th and 14th Centuries, which differs considerably from 20th Century Chinese Taoism. (Lemoine 1982.)

The rituals are expensive and time-consuming, requiring specialists who can read the texts and are proficient in the ceremonies. Much of their daily activity revolves around amassing money, livestock, and goods required for such rituals, as it is essential that they be carried out in the proper way.

Mien who are literate in Chinese write petitions and memorials to the ancestors and spirits to be used in Taoist rituals. Blessings are written on red paper banners for weddings, initiations, and funerals.

Taoist pantheon

Mien believe in a celestial hierarchy made up of many supreme functionaries. Paintings of this Taoist pantheon are displayed during the most important rituals.

The set of pantheon pictures in this book was painted in China about 1880 and later taken to Laos and Thailand. The three most important gods portrayed depict the 'Three Stars', and are always hung in the centre of the display. Each painting has its proper position and a certain role to play in the rituals.

The painter must work in an atmosphere of religious devotion and ceremonial purity. During the two or more months that it takes, both client and artist must remain celibate. Upon completion of the set, the pictures are consecrated and the gods invited to 'don' the pictures – in much the same way as a man wears a shirt. If after many years the pictures wear out, or for some reason the family decides not to use them any more, a priest presides at a ceremony in which he politely invites the gods to depart from the pictures and 'go visit somewhere else'.

On the back of the paintings are written the names of the gods depicted; the name of the artist; the owner; the day, month, and year of completion; and the hour the gods came into them. The ideal time to have such pictures painted is when a man has at least three married sons, one of whom in turn has three sons.

The set includes 17 pictures and a long scroll called 'The Dragon Bridge of the Great Tao'. This symbolic 'bridge', often 2.5 metres or more in length, is displayed above the pictures during certain ceremonies. In one important ceremony, held about three months after the death of a high-ranking priest, the scroll is suspended from the top of the Big Door to the floor in the middle of the room. It points towards heaven, to guide the dead priest's divine soldiers who are being sent home (Lemoine 1982:138). The figures on the scroll represent both those who escort the priest, and those who welcome him to his new abode.

Four or five small paintings accompany each set. Each of the acolytes wears one on his head at various points in the ceremonies. A ceremonial 'crown' worn by the officiating priest is divided into seven sections, with the pictures of the 'Three Stars' in the centre.

Complete set of paintings depicting the Taoist pantheon

Special ceremonies

Unique among the Mien are their merit-making ceremonies, called by some 'ordination'. The first-grade rite, called 'Hanging the Lanterns' (*kwa tang*), is usually performed for a boy before the age of 20. Lasting two days, the ceremony introduces him to the Taoist pantheon and guarantees him entry into the realm of the ancestors when he dies. It also marks him as a true Mien, one who can fully take part in all ceremonies and rituals.

The second-grade rite, called *tou sai*, lasts for seven days. It is much more complex than the first rite, and requires the assistance of several high-ranking Mien priests. During the ceremony it is forbidden for those being initiated to eat certain types of food, especially meat and fat, or to have sexual relations. Part of this complicated ceremony calls for the initiates to climb a 'sword ladder', the rungs of which are made of wooden swords. The 'master priest' leads the way and the postulants follow. Often, many men, up to forty in some instances, hold the ceremony at the same time to save expenses (see Lemoine for pictures and description).

Women attend the ceremonies dressed in all their finery, and share in their husband's promotion. They are included in a special feast at the conclusion of the rite, and receive a new name which bestows a higher status on them.

There are two ceremonies in which the entire village participates. The first is held in honour of the guardian spirits of the area. Everyone must contribute towards the purchase of pigs, chickens, paper money and liquor used as offerings. It is a one-day ceremony, following which no one may enter or leave the village for three days. Tree branches are placed on the paths at each entrance to the village to keep visitors out.

The second one-day ceremony is not closed to outsiders. The purpose is to beg forgiveness of the guardian spirit of the mountain for allowing domestic animals to search for food in his territory. It is held at times when problems arise, such as: death of livestock, women having difficulty dyeing cloth, or liquor not turning out well.

Scenes from the *tou sai* ceremony

Religious Practitioners

Priests

Priests (*sip mien mien*) acquire their ability to perform ceremonies and rituals by studying with older priests and serving as their acolytes for a number of years. Certain powers are passed on from one priest to another. Higher level priests are capable of dealing with the 'big spirits above the sky'. It is essential to employ such a priest for any ceremony involving the Taoist pantheon, and his participation is preferred even for smaller ceremonies. Lesser priests deal only with the 'small spirits under the sky', the evil and often malicious spirits which need to be controlled in order to avoid sickness and misfortune.

Mien priests perform ceremonies for anyone who can pay the fee. Wealthy families use priests of high reputation, both to ensure the efficacy of the rite and to maintain their social standing.

Each priest has a set of ritual texts which he has copied from his mentor. Those portions of the texts most often used are committed to memory, but in some of the more intricate ceremonies the priest reads his text carefully, because a proper execution is important for the efficacy of the ceremony.

Shamans

The shaman (*bokwa mien*) differs markedly from the priest. He has either inherited a capacity for possession by supernatural beings, or has been chosen by those beings to serve as a medium. His main task is to help in curing ceremonies.

A priest's robes and paraphernalia used in ceremonies

Sickness and Curing

A shaman asked to perform a curing ceremony goes to the house of the sick person, and calls the ancestral spirits. He then invites his own mentor spirit to possess him. He sits on a bench in front of the ancestral altar, and when he becomes possessed, shakes all over. After he has quieted down he takes a handful of uncooked rice and hops back and forth from the middle of the room to the altar and from the middle of the room to the Big Door a prescribed number of times.

Then he presses his palms to the 'Big Table' (which is specially set up for the ceremony) and asks, 'What have you called me for?' The household head explains about the sick person and asks the shaman to have his mentor spirit go to the spirit world and find the cause of the illness.

The shaman then takes rice in both hands and slaps them together, spraying rice grains in every direction. This represents his spirit soldiers being sent to find the sick person's soul. Using his divining sticks he questions the ancestors and the spirits, such as the grandfather and grandmother who have died but are not yet considered to be ancestors. If he does not get an answer, he asks spirits who are not connected with the household.

Once it is ascertained which spirit has caused the illness, a date and an hour are set as a deadline, stating that if the person is cured by that time, the family will 'worship' the spirit. Still using the divining sticks, the shaman determines whether the spirit wants a pig or a chicken. Paper money is burned and the ceremony is ended. If the person is well by the date set, the sacrifice is made as promised. If still ill, the family tries another procedure.

Ritual therapy is also effected by building a 'bridge' so the soul of the sick person can return to the body. This one-day ceremony is usually held just outside the village. A plank freshly hacked from a tree is prepared, with a knob of wood projecting from it for each time such a ceremony has been performed for that person. This is laid across a stream or on the ground parallel to a path which enters the village.

Before the ceremony, the priest in charge writes several letters: one to the ancestors, one to Nyut Tai (the spirit of the sky), and one to the soul which has departed. The Chinese word for 'horse' is stamped on each letter to prove its authenticity and to speed it to the realm of the ancestors.

A pig is slaughtered, cut into five pieces and put back together at the end of the bridge on the village side. Offerings for Nyut Tai are placed near or on the carcass of the pig. Similar offerings are placed upon a small table at the other end of the bridge. The priest propitiates his mentor spirit, and burns the letters in order to send their contents to the spirit forces.

The patient first sits at the end of the bridge nearest the village with a cloth spread across the knees. While repeating the liturgy the priest throws uncooked rice from the opposite end, which the patient catches in the cloth and then takes to the far end of the bridge, where the priest presents him or her with a live chicken and a wooden rod. Following more liturgy the patient, carrying the rice, chicken, and rod, walks across the bridge to his or her home without looking back. If all has been done properly, the soul will again be safely dwelling in the person, thus ensuring recovery.

Preparing for bridge ceremony:

1) Paper money production

2) Wrapping sticky-rice sweets for sacrifice

3) Collecting the blood from the sacrificed pig

Bridge ceremony:

4) Wooden plank (bridge) and offerings

5) Priest reciting ritual text

6) Patient for whom ceremony is held

7) Burning of letters over bowl of water

8) Burning of paper money towards the end of the ceremony

Death and Burial

Death

Before an elderly Mien dies the sons take turns lifting the parent's head three times each, while saying, 'Go well'. This helps the person to die peacefully.

Immediately after death the oldest son closes the eyes, and puts a tiny piece of silver into the mouth. This gives the deceased an 'expensive mouth', so that he or she 'will say only good things and not tell lies'. Family members wash the body, cut the hair, and remove gold caps from the teeth. The body is clothed and laid on a bamboo mat on a shelf in front of the ancestral altar, the feet pointed toward the Big Door.

The family and friends gather to start preparations for the funeral. Paper money is made, pigs slaughtered, and an abundance of rice and liquor provided for the three days and nights of the ceremony.

The presiding priest chooses six men to make the coffin. Before leaving the house they inform the dead person of their mission, and ask him to help them choose the wood and make the coffin.

When they bring the coffin back to the village the men call out, 'Is there someone here who needs a house?' Those inside respond, 'There is indeed someone who needs a house. What will you sell it for?' Even though no money is actually paid for the coffin, they go through a pretense of bargaining.

Next they bring it in through the Big Door, and the priest knocks on the coffin several times with his ceremonial knife and sprinkles it with water to drive out any evil which may be lurking in the wood. The corpse is then laid in the coffin and the lid put on. At each stage there is a running commentary by the priest explaining to the deceased what is being done.

Death ceremony

The presiding priest, his assistant, and two acolytes for each, begin the task of chanting their way through the liturgical books for the dead, which must be followed through to the end before the ceremony can be complete.

Before the main part of the ritual begins, the presiding priest and his acolytes put on their special garb. The relatives show respect for the departed by wearing white cloth on their heads, following a Chinese tradition.

At a certain point the presiding priest runs out of the house and comes hopping back on one foot. Several paper figures are held to the sole of his raised foot by using a rope of rice stalks he holds in his hand. Each figure has the name of a body part written on it, representing the 'soul force' of that particular part of the deceased's body. The priest throws the divining sticks three times for each paper figure to discover which spirits are evil. He jabs the evil spirits with a wooden sword, and then turns them over to an assistant who, acting as the 'head jailer', beats them.

Any evil spirits present are induced to enter a human effigy made of straw. This is also handed over to the 'jailer' to be beaten. Some Mien once told us, 'We lie to induce them to come into the figure – but remember they are evil! We can then trap and beat them'.

A 'boat' made of banana leaves is placed between the altar and the Big Door. From time to time various symbolic items are put into it, including the straw figure. A bundle of green reeds is broken by the priest over the edge of a bench to show the deceased that he/she has 'broken' away from the land of the living, and is now in the land of the dead. These are then cast into the boat, which is later pulled out of the Big Door and 'shoved into the sea' (a jungle area away from the house), and burned. Spirits might well come back over land, but it is impossible for them to return over water.

The request that the deceased be granted entry into the land of the ancestors is implicit in the liturgy. The long scroll hanging over the pantheon pictures is taken down and used as a bridge. It is draped on a ladder, one end attached to the coffin, the other to a long blue cloth which goes through the roof and is tied to a tall bamboo pole. The priest climbs up onto the roof and instructs the souls how to make the needed transition.

Priest chanting at 'Big Door'

Sacrifice of rooster

'Boat' to send spirits away

The presiding priest

Evil spirits are induced to enter human effigy made of straw

Relatives wear white pieces of cloth on their heads

The buffalo horn is played many times

Relatives of the deceased burning paper money

Performing of a ceremony under the roof

Priest resting and smoking waterpipe

Performing various ceremonies in front of the coffin

The soul of the deceased leaves the body over the scroll and a long piece of blue cloth through the roof, following the instructions of the presiding priest on how to reach the land of the ancestors

Women in funeral procession

Cremation

After the rituals in the house have been concluded, the priest checks by means of his divining sticks, to see whether the time has come for the deceased to join the ancestors. Upon an affirmative answer the coffin is taken out through the Big Door as many guns are fired.

The priest and orchestra lead the way to the cremation site, followed by the coffin carried by male relatives. Female relatives, children and other mourners are at the rear.

After the coffin has been placed on the funeral pyre, a close female relative, who has brought a rooster to the site, carries it around the coffin three times. The rooster, which now possesses the souls of the deceased, is taken back to the village where it will be set free after three days.

When the priest has made the final incantations, he lights a torch and stands on top of the coffin, while his assistant and acolytes dance around it. He then comes down, and with his back to the coffin, starts the pyre burning at each of the four corners.

When the fire is burning well, everyone returns to the village. The priest follows behind, praying that the door of the village will be closed to keep the spirits of the dead from entering. There is great concern lest the souls of those who have died return at night to appear in dreams, indicating that there has been an error in the ceremony or that the souls are hungry. In either case, more offerings must be made to appease the souls.

Some 24 hours later, the priest and male relatives of the deceased go to the cremation site. Using bamboo chopsticks they 'pick up some bones', which are carefully placed in a container and then buried in a spot located by means of the divining sticks.

Woman circles coffin three times with rooster

Women relatives return to village under white cloth

Priest prepares to set fire to pyre

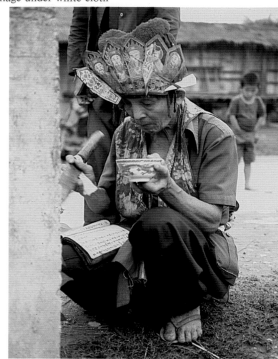

Priest 'closing door' of the village

Burning coffin

Conclusion

The Mien have a concept of a well-ordered cosmos. Each person must cultivate proper relationships within the human realm as well as with the spirit world.

There is a studied politeness and an effort to avoid causing another to lose face. Harmony within the household and village is of great importance. Efforts are made to adjust to local government requirements and to live acceptably within the prevailing social system.

Harmony with the spirit world is sought through meticulous observation of the rituals and ceremonies. They are careful to pay proper respect to the ancestors, and behave in a way acceptable to the household spirits, always instructing their children to do the same.

In their desire for propriety they make numerous contracts. In the human realm these relate to marriage, adoption, and business. In the spirit world they are made within a ritual context to ensure health, wealth, and security in the life to come. The Mien have a perpetual desire for propriety in all relationships in every area of life.

Ceremonial knives used by Mien priests

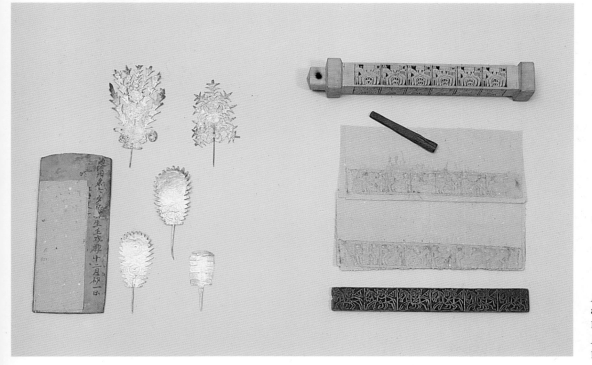

Left: Silver 'flowers' worn by bride and groom. They are kept between small wooden boards and pieces of paper

Right: Wooden printing blocks and chop used in the production of paper money

Lahu Sheh Leh village

Chapter 6

LAHU (Mussur)

Desire for Blessing

It was the final day of the Lahu New Year. The giving of gifts, ceremonial washing of hands, dancing, top spinning, ball throwing, firing of guns, shooting of firecrackers, and feasting had finished. Ca Fa called his son-in-law, Ca Leh, into the house. Together they knelt before the altar which had held offerings of rice cakes, pork, bananas, and beeswax candles. Ca Fa said the final prayer of the New Year ceremony:

Oh Lord of the year, and Lord of the months,
In Majesty far superior to us,
This morning we remove the rice cake altar.
Bestow on us the blessing of one year's work in the field providing food sufficient for ten years.
Grant us the blessing of one day's work providing food for ten days.
Open to us the blessing of having many people in the house, and much livestock under the house.
Clothe us with the blessing of an untroubled heart, and grant us an undisturbed mind.
Next year at the New Year festival we will again bring offerings and sacrifices to you.

The Lahu are a people permeated with the desire for blessing. They long for the blessings of good health, enough to eat, security for their families, and peace in their hearts. Their term for blessing is *bon*, or *aw bon*, which is borrowed from the Tai term *boon* (merit). The area of meaning of the Lahu term *bon* is broader than the Tai *boon*. For instance, *aw bon caw* means 'to have value'; *bon te* 'blessing/merit ceremony'; *bon law* or *bon ku* 'to pray'; *bon na* 'to bless'; *bon ma da* 'bad luck'; *bon ma* 'to preach'.

The Lahu often refer to themselves as *bon ya*, which literally means 'children of blessing'. In their prayers they speak of *bon ca* 'seek blessing'. All Lahu – regardless of their sub-group or religion – are deeply concerned with and constantly striving for blessing.

Lahu Sheh Leh girl making an offering

Name and language

This tribal group calls itself 'Lahu' (the first syllable pronounced on a high tone, the second on a low tone). The Tai refer to them as 'Mussur' ('Museur'), which comes from Burmese via Shan, and means 'hunter'.

The Lahu language is in the Yi (Lolo) branch of the Tibeto-Burman family. The five dialects spoken in Thailand fall into two main sub-divisions: *Lahu Na* (Black Lahu), and *Lahu Shi* (Yellow Lahu). Lahu Na is considered to be the standard dialect wherever Lahu speakers are found: Yunnan, Burma, Laos, and Thailand. In areas of these countries where Lahu live, Lahu Na has become an important lingua franca for highland people, including the Yunnanese.

Origin

The earliest documents known to us regarding Lahu people locate them in southwestern China. They have been migrating southward for many generations. By about 1840 Lahu had villages in Kengtung State, Burma, and by the early 1880s some were living in the Fang area of northern Thailand near the Burma border. Other Lahu found their way into Laos, some directly from China, and others by migrating eastward from Burma.

Population

The approximate Lahu population in mid-1983 was:

China	250,000
Burma	150,000
Thailand	40,000
Laos	10,000
Total	450,000

About 85% of the Lahu in Thailand live in the provinces of Chiang Mai and Chiang Rai in almost equal numbers. The other 15% live in the provinces of Mae Hong Son, Tak, and Kamphaeng Phet.

Sub-Groups

The main Lahu groups currently living in Thailand can be classified as follows:

English name	Their own term	Thai term
1. Black Lahu	*Lahu/Laho Na*	*Mussur*
Lahu Nyi (Red)	Lahu (peh tu pa[1])	Mussur Daeng[2]
Lahu Na (Black)	Lahu/Laho Na	Mussur Khrit[3]
Lahu Sheh Leh	Lahu/Laho Na	Mussur Dam
2. Yellow Lahu	*Lahu Shi*	*Mussur Kwi[4]*
Ba Lan	Lahu Shi Ba Lan	Mussur Kwi
Ba Keo	Lahu Ba Keo	Mussur Kwi

There are a few other Lahu groups with small populations, such as the Ku Lao (referred to as Lahu Hpu, or 'White Lahu', in Laos), the A Ga (called Abele by the Lahu Shi), and the La Ba.

The comparative populations of the Lahu sub-groups in mid-1983 were:

1. Black Lahu	
Lahu Nyi	46%
Lahu Na	18%
Lahu Sheh Leh	13%
2. Yellow Lahu	
Ba Lan	17%
Ba Keo	3%
3. Other	
(Ku Lao, La Ba, etc.)	3%

The Lahu Nyi arrived in Thailand first, followed by Sheh Leh and a few households of Ba Keo. The first major incursion of Lahu Na from Burma occurred in 1954. This was followed in the 1960s and early 1970s by a surge of Lahu Na and Lahu Shi Ba Lan, with a few Ba Keo, who fled from what they considered an oppressive situation on the Burma side. In the dry season of 1982–83 there was another influx of Lahu from Burma.

[1] Literally, 'the Lahu who burn beeswax candles'.

[2] The term 'Red Lahu' has led some Thai to believe that the Lahu Nyi are Communists, since Thai call the Hmong who follow Communist leaders 'Meo Daeng' (Red Meo). This is deeply resented by the Lahu.

[3] Literally 'Christian Lahu', since virtually all of them are Christian.

[4] Kwi has no meaning that we know of.

Lahu headman

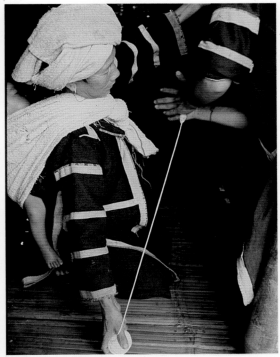

~Lahu Sheh Leh women make beeswax candles

Lahu Na girls pound and winnow rice

Lahu Nyi man leads pony to field

Lahu Sheh Leh man aims crossbow

Lahu Nyi woman climbs up to storage house

Clothing and Ornamentation

If at New Year time one could visit in sequence Lahu Nyi, Lahu Sheh Leh, Lahu Na, and Lahu Shi villages, one would experience the full impact of the diversity of these groups, and yet recognize a common Lahuness. Some Lahu have discarded the use of traditional clothing except at festival times. Lahu Nyi and Sheh Leh, however, still generally wear their own style of clothing, as do the Lahu Shi recently arrived from Laos. Lahu Shi Christians had completely abandoned the use of traditional dress until the coming of their kinsmen from Laos. Now some are beginning to wear Lahu Shi clothing for special occasions. Most Lahu Na in Thailand dress like their lowland neighbours for daily wear, but on festive occasions many of them wear traditional clothing.

Formerly Lahu wove their own cloth on foot-treadle looms. Most of them have lost that art, but a few Lahu Na women still weave cloth. The women of all Lahu sub-tribes use the back-strap loom to weave shoulder bags, or at least straps for their bags.

All the groups embroider, but have distinct techniques. Lahu Na and Lahu Shi do patch-work appliqué, and all groups use bands of cloth for decorative purposes – the Sheh Leh being masters of that art.

Stitching Lahu Na appliqué

Steps in making strap for a Lahu Sheh Leh shoulder bag

Scenes of Lahu Shi Ba Lan

Lahu Hpu – or 'White Lahu'

Lahu Nyi

Lahu Nyi

Lahu Nyi women wear short lined jackets, sarong-type skirts, and leggings, usually made of black cotton cloth. For festive wear velvet or satin may be used in black, blue, or green colours. Jackets are edged with red down the front and around the bottom, with added strips of red around the upper arms. It is the predominance of red in their clothing which has earned them the name 'Lahu Nyi' (Red Lahu), although bands of blue, white, and printed material are also used. Jackets are closed in front with one or more engraved round silver buckles, some of which are very large.

Skirts are made of three horizontal panels. The top panel is basically red with woven stripes in other colours. The bottom panel is sometimes simply a six cm strip of plain white cloth stitched over the skirt, but the festive skirts have broad borders up to 15 cm wide of red cloth with many lines of coloured thread stitched on it. This is done by couching (laying a strand of thread in a straight line and tacking it down with tiny evenly-spaced stitches.) The same technique is used for accent around the edges, using a cord made by twisting many threads together. The central panel of the skirt is often left plain, but is sometimes decorated with evenly-spaced bands of red cloth embellished with couched thread as in the border. Skirts are worn folded in front and secured with a sash or metal belt. For dress-up occasions silver belts are worn – often of silver rupee coins. Leggings are black or blue, with red and white trim.

Recently some of the more affluent Lahu Nyi women have discovered the sewing machine. They have attachments for fancy stitches, and now lavishly decorate jackets and skirts, replacing laborious hand-stitching. Many women who do not own machines buy clothing from those who do.

Silver ornaments worn by women include wide bracelets, neck rings, finger rings, and earrings. One type of earring is in the form of a circle which hooks into the ear, with a tightly-wound coil or leaf-shape at the bottom; the other has a decorative crown with club-shaped dangles attached.

Lahu Nyi men wear loose black jackets that fasten on the side, and three-quarter length Chinese-style pants. In some cases the pants and jackets have an embroidered trim. Young men prefer blue or green pants, elders wear black, sometimes lined with white cloth. Leggings are black or white with blue trim.

On festive occasions the jackets of both young men and women are studded with silver buttons and coins. Traditionally the men have worn New Year's turbans made of two yards each of red, black, and white cloth.

The standard Lahu Nyi shoulder bag is predominantly red, embellished with a variety of embroidered designs. Festive bags are ornamented with silver buttons and coins and have a long fringe across the bottom. The strap is handwoven, mostly in red.

Women's outfits

Women's outfits

Woman's outfit

Man's outfit

Bags

Lahu Sheh Leh

Lahu Sheh Leh clothing is preferably made of fairly heavy black cotton cloth with a sheen. Women wear three-quarter-length tunics which open down the front. All edges of the tunic are set off by narrow bands of white and pale yellow with touches of red and blue for accent. Strips of banding are also added across the shoulders, just below the waist, and on the sleeves. Some of the young women, however, are now sewing wide bands of red, white, and blue or gaily printed cloth on their sleeves.

Older women and young girls have only narrow strips of the banding at the back hemline, while young unmarried women make wide borders of exquisitely stitched bands and scallops. Tunics for festive wear are embellished with half-sphere silver buttons and coins, and are closed with a row of repoussé or engraved buckles to the waist.

Women's pants, resembling culottes, are trimmed with red and yellow stitching and reach to just below the knees. Black leggings with white and yellow banding have cuffs which turn down at the top.

Sheh Leh women wear quantities of small white beads wound closely around their throats, which consist of a single strand several metres in length. Wide silver bracelets adorn their wrists and silver neck rings are worn on festive occasions.

Men dress in black jackets, knee-length loose pants, and leggings with blue trim, all lined with white. A hand-woven sash is used as a belt.

Traditionally men and women wore black turbans, but turkish towels now serve that purpose – bright flowered ones for women and white for men.

Their black shoulder bags have the same type of trim as the women's tunics, young women's bags being the most lavish. The hand-woven straps are pale yellow with narrow stripes of other colours. Long fringe hangs down from the sides, and tassels of thread and torn cloth extend from the lower corners. Less elaborate bags of similar design are in everyday use.

Young woman's festive outfit

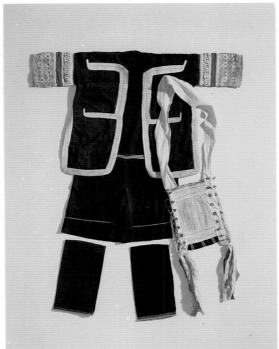

Girl's outfit

Man's outfit

Women's clothing

Back view of woman's tunic

Boy's outfit

Lahu Na

Traditional Lahu Na clothing is made of their own homespun indigo-dyed cloth. The woman's ankle-length tunic is trimmed with appliqué patch-work. Generally it opens down the right side; some open down the front. The sides are split to the waist and edged with bands of predominantly red and white appliqué which consists of triangles, squares, and strips with a double row of scallops in red and white. The hemline at the back is embellished with a border of embroidered designs. The sleeves have narrow bands of red and other colours edged with scalloping. A broad band of blue cloth and narrow bands of various colours form the cuffs.

The banded piece which goes diagonally from the throat to just under the right arm and the stand-up collar are encrusted with many rows of silver half-sphere buttons; silver dangles hang from the bottom row. At the back, groups of silver buttons are arranged around the yoke in triangular designs, with more dangles hanging from them. The tunic closes at the throat, shoulder, and under the right arm with round silver buckles.

The black sarong is decorated with strips of brightly-coloured cloth stitched in zigzags and other patterns. A black turban decorated with beads and tassels completes the outfit.

Women wear either wide engraved or narrow molded silver bracelets. Their earrings are similar to those of the Lahu Nyi. For ceremonial occasions the more affluent add heavy silver chains and necklaces with pendants of wheels, fish, butterflies, bells, and tiny grooming tools.

Lahu Na men wear suits of homespun black cloth. The jackets open either in front or down the right side, and the full-cut Chinese pants are ankle-length. Both jackets and pants are decorated with embroidered lines in predominantly red thread. Black turbans are worn for festive occasions.

A black shoulder bag with patch-work appliquéd designs similar to those on the women's tunic is the most distinctive type for this group. Bags of a variety of woven designs are also popular. They like to decorate them lavishly with bright-coloured wool tufting and pompons, those worn by men for the New Year's dancing being especially ornate.

Woman's festive outfit

Back view of woman's tunic

Some women's tunics open down the front

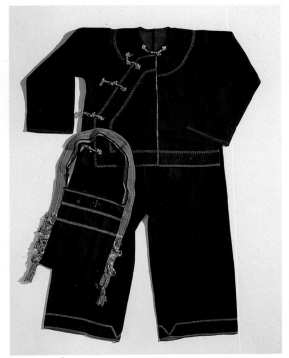

Man's outfit

Woman's tunic

Girl's tunic

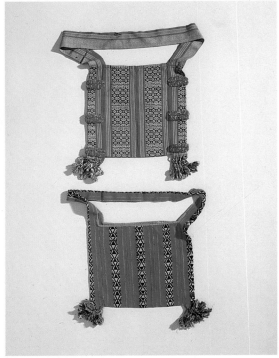

Woven shoulder bags

Lahu Shi

The Christian Lahu Shi women dress like Shan or Northern Thai, while men wear ready-made clothing, usually in Western style. Since 1975 there has been an influx of Lahu Shi refugees from Laos who wear their traditional clothing, made of commercial black cloth. The women's short jackets are flared at the waist. Young unmarried women adorn their jackets with many strips of red cloth set off with white and other colours. Lacy patterns are embroidered between the appliquéd strips, and rows of tiny silver buttons (now aluminium) and cowrie shells are added. Bands of coloured cloth, predominantly red, are sewn to the upper sleeves and cuffs. A row of repousséd silver rectangular buckles closes the jacket in front.

The top section of a young woman's skirt is of Shan or Laotian hand-woven red cloth with vari-coloured stripes. The middle section is of black cloth with strips of appliquéd designs in red and other colours. The lower portion is solid black, with a red hemline border.

The married woman's jacket is similar to that of the single girl, but with fewer red strips and no embroidery. It does not lack for ornateness, however, as there is an abundance of tiny aluminium buttons and dangling silver balls. The skirt has striped red cloth at the top like the young woman's skirt, but bands of coloured cloth or flowered prints are the only decoration on the lower part.

Unmarried women wear black turbans, the ends of which are ornamented with strips of brightly-coloured cloth, buttons, beads and coins. Married women's turbans are less decorative.

Women wear large cylindrical silver earrings and plain silver neck rings. Their throats are wrapped with strands of alternating red and white beads; sometimes waist-length strands of beads are added. Often belts of silver or other metal secure their narrow sarongs.

On festive occasions unmarried Lahu Shi men and boys wear black jackets and pants decorated with strips of red cloth, interspersed with narrow strips of other colours and embroidery. The jacket is ornamented with numerous rows of buttons in front and on the sleeves. The costume is completed with a long-fringed black turban.

Married men wear black with little or no embellishment. A headman, however, often wears a jacket of a shiny material and a pink silk turban.

Lahu Shi weave sturdy shoulder bags on back-strap looms – those from Laos make a simple striped bag; those from Burma weave a wide variety of designs.

All Lahu make delightful caps for their children. Some are made of panels of triangular-shaped cloth which join at the top, and are crowned with a pompon. Caps for little girls are more elaborate than those for boys.

Lahu Shi Ba Lan boy's outfit

Children's caps (Lahu Shi)

Lahu Shi Ba Lan girl's outfit

Lahu Shi Ba Lan young woman's outfit

Lahu Shi Ba Lan young man's outfit

Lahu Ba Keo woman's outfit

Lahu Shi Ba Lan married woman's outfit

Lahu women's turbans and Lahu La Ba woman's jacket

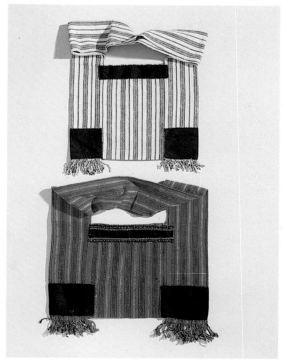

Lahu Shi Ba Lan shoulder bags

Basketry

The Lahu Shi have a good reputation as basket makers. They weave sturdy storage baskets with rattan outer walls and bamboo linings. These covered baskets are either hamper-style or trunk-shaped. They have long been sought after by other tribal people, and are now popular in the crafts market. Some Lahu Shi villages with a source of rattan nearby receive considerable income from the sale of baskets.

All Lahu make back-carrying baskets of open or close weave. Those of the Sheh Leh are of outstanding quality. Some men in each group make superior bamboo containers in round or oval shapes which are used for carrying cooked rice or by the women for keeping sewing supplies.

Musical Instruments

The Lahu musical gourd pipe (*naw*) is made of a gourd inserted with five bamboo tubes of different lengths tuned to the pentatonic scale. At the base of each tube is a finely crafted reed. These instruments are made in various sizes – small ones being in the upper register, large ones descending to low bass.

Bamboo Jew's harps (*a hta*) are used in tuned pairs or threes. Young men and women use both gourd pipes and Jew's harps to 'talk to each other' during courting.

Lahu Na woman making a basket

Lahu Nyi playing instruments in temple

Lahu Na New Year dancing

Lahu men playing musical gourd pipes

Lahu Sheh Leh bridge ceremony

Villages

Traditionally Lahu have preferred living at elevations of 1,200 metres or higher. With the exception of the Sheh Leh most have now moved to lower elevations.

The average number of households per village and people per household differs from group to group. A survey we made in 1981 of all Lahu villages in Thailand showed:

Sub-division	Average houses per village	Average people per house
Lahu Nyi	16.9	6.2
Lahu Na	30.8	5.9
Lahu Sheh Leh	28.9	6.0
Lahu Shi	24.5	5.2

The Sheh Leh have village clusters in areas where there are not many other tribal groups – including other Lahu. There are five major clusters, one each in: Fang and Om Koi districts (Chiang Mai Province); Wiang Pa Pao District (Chiang Rai Province); and the provinces of Mae Hong Son and Tak.

Most Lahu Nyi villages have a temple (*haw yeh*), where semi-monthly rites to worship the supreme deity, G'ui sha, are held. Christian Lahu have a church (*bon yeh*) where they meet for services. These buildings are generally constructed of bamboo and thatch grass similar to their houses, and usually have a prominent location in the village. The Sheh Leh do not build temples, but have a fenced ritual dance circle in the upper part of the village.

Each household must conform to the consensus of the elders' decisions. Those who will not conform must leave. The virtue of unity and 'staying together' is stressed especially at New Year's time, as this is the season when some households are seriously considering whether or not to move to a new village.

In spite of their professed desire for unity, many Lahu villages are not very united. Several households may leave each year on account of economic or social problems. New households may move in, especially if the headman is strong and there is land available for irrigated rice fields. A large village may segment, with one or two groups moving to different areas, leaving the village depleted.

In one Lahu Nyi village three occurrences in quick succession led the elders to move the village: (1) the headman was killed, (2) a child was fatally mauled by a dog, and (3) a young man accidentally shot himself in the foot while hunting. They moved the village four kilometres from the old site and chose a new name, hoping to change their luck.

Lahu Nyi village

Lahu Sheh Leh village

Houses

Lahu build their houses on stilts except for some Lahu Na from China whose houses have dirt floors. The floor plan of the house depends upon the sub-division to which the family belongs, and how many people are in the household.

A plank or notched log leads to an open porch at the front of the house. The only outside door opens from the porch into the main room. The fireplace in the middle of that room forms the social centre of the house. A bedroom is partitioned off for the use of the nuclear family members.

The Lahu Nyi maintain a household spirit altar in a corner of the most protected area of the house, farthest from the door, while the Sheh Leh have a small sacred closet in the same area.

When a Lahu Nyi or Sheh Leh house is finished, ceremonies are performed at which time beeswax candles are burned to drive out the spirits possibly lurking in the building materials. They feast their fellow villagers on rice and pork into the night, believing that the more fun and noise there is, the more prosperous the household will be.

Porch of Lahu house

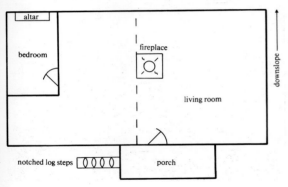

Lahu Nyi house plan

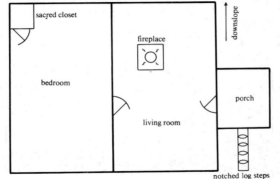

Lahu Sheh Leh house plan

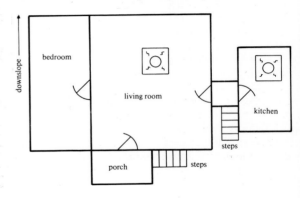

Christian Lahu house plan (one style)

Family and Kin Groups

There are no clans among Lahu, thus no surnames. This creates difficulties in official dealings, so many families, especially the educated ones, are adopting Thai surnames.

Kinship terms are not so complicated or used as much as by other groups. Part of the reason may be that Lahu relationships are counted with equal importance on both the paternal and maternal side of each parent. The general term *aw vi aw nyi* (older/younger kinsmen) is commonly used for all relatives. There are specific kinship terms which are used when pertinent. One context in which it is important to know the exact relationship is when a couple is contemplating marriage. It should not be possible for them to trace a common ancestry within three generations.

Lahu *aw vi aw nyi* are expected to support one another in all circumstances. They can be a formidable force when the political leadership of the village is being challenged – particularly among the Lahu Shi Ba Lan. They try to maneuver their relatives into a position of power, thus enhancing their own chance of 'good fortune' (*bon da ja* – literally 'very good blessing'). Before the selection of a new headman, nightly discussions around fireplaces throughout the village find men trying to persuade others to back their own kinsman.

It is often impossible for the village to remain united, as many strong statements and perhaps even threats will have been made before the selection of the new headman. The relatives of the losing contender may urge him to set up his own village. If someone takes a stand that differs from the majority of his relatives, strong animosity develops, and he is viewed as a traitor.

The Lahu tell a story about the first time *aw vi aw nyi* had a dispute. One day a Lahu man went hunting and killed a sambur deer. As is the custom, he brought the meat back to the village and shared it with his relatives, who enjoyed the meal. Shortly afterwards a relative of his went hunting and brought back a porcupine. He also distributed the meat to these relatives telling them, 'This animal is so small there is only a little meat, but I gladly share it with you'. Later a young female relative of the hunter visited his house and saw the porcupine quills. 'What are these?' she asked. 'Oh, that's the fur of the animal I shot', he replied. She was furious. 'Why, the sambur deer had fur much shorter than this, but we had a lot of meat to eat. Then you killed an animal with fur this big, and yet you gave us only a little. You lie!' she screamed, and straight away went to tell her relatives. 'That was the first time Lahu *aw vi aw nyi* argued and went their separate ways', the story concludes.

There is a unique relationship between husband and wife among the Lahu. Husbands tend to be more considerate to their wives and help around the house more than is true of men of other tribal groups. Once more the Lahu have a delightful story giving the 'reason' for this. Long ago, they say, the Lahu lived in a fortified city in central China, where they were the rulers. The Chinese who lived under them did not like this arrangement, but each time they fought the Lahu they were defeated. One day when the Lahu men were away working in their fields some Chinese men, posing as traders, came to their city. They had lovely Jew's harps which the Lahu women wanted from the moment they heard the beautiful sound. When they brought money to purchase the Jew's harps, the Chinese would not accept it. They would only trade them for the triggers from their husband's crossbows.

The Lahu women wanted the Jew's harps so much they pried out the triggers and traded them. Shortly thereafter the Chinese set out to attack the city. The Lahu men rushed back to defend their homes, only to find that their crossbows were useless. Leaving their wives and children to the Chinese, they fled to a safe area, and began plotting how to win back their families.

Eventually they returned at night, and from outside the city walls communicated with their wives using their musical gourd pipes. At first the wives were not sure they wanted to leave the Chinese and return to their Lahu husbands, for they were being well looked after. So the Lahu men, in order to win their wives back, made elaborate promises to care for them and to provide for their every need. The women, having been won over, got the Chinese men into a drunken stupor, gathered up their children, and ran out to their Lahu husbands. Together they fled to a new country. 'And that is why to this day we men must take good care of our wives', Lahu men will say with a smile. And they do! They share, for example, in the care of children and livestock, as well as in the gathering of firewood and the carrying of water. It is impressive to observe the devotion with which Lahu husbands and wives care for one another in times of sickness and need.

The typical Lahu household consists of a man, his wife, their unmarried children, and perhaps a married daughter with her husband and children. The oldest daughter and her husband are expected to live with the parents until the second daughter is married. Then the first daughter and family move out and build a house nearby.

Lahu Sheh Leh chewing betel

Lahu Sheh Leh village scenes

Marriage

Choice

In all Lahu groups the young people choose their own spouse. The New Year festival is the favourite courting period. It is the time for groups of young men interested in finding brides to visit other Lahu villages. As they approach they call children they find playing, asking them to inform the young women of their arrival. The children race off to tell the girls how many boys are waiting at the edge of the village. The girls come out, usually bringing a chicken and some rice to cook for the boys. After the meal they may pair off and sleep together.

Whenever young men visit in a Lahu Nyi village they are asked, 'Are you married?' If they are not, during the night girls often poke them with sticks through the slats of the bamboo floor, trying to entice them to come out and 'play' with them. If a boy falls in love with a girl from his own village, he may go to her house at night and call her out with his musical gourd pipe or Jew's harp.

We once helped some young Lahu men send a message to their girl friends by recording their gourd pipe music to be played over the tribal radio station. At the time the young men were attending a training programme just north of Chiang Mai town. By means of the gourd pipes they begged their girl friends not to marry anyone else, but to wait for their return. Later we found that the message was received and the request granted – all by means of those melodious pipes.

Arrangements

When a young man has the consent of a girl to marry him, he sends a go-between to ask permission of her father. If the father seems reluctant to permit the marriage, the go-between may point out how much better it would be to give his blessing than to have the couple elope.

Once the father's permission has been granted, they discuss where the couple should live. Traditionally Lahu have observed a custom they call *ma mui* (literally, 'to serve as a son-in-law'), which calls for the couple to live with the girl's parents and the young man to perform bride service for a period varying from three to seven years. Following that the couple may live with the young man's parents for a period of time. Under certain circumstances this practice may be altered. For instance, if the girl's parents already have a son-in-law working for them but the groom has no sister to bring a son-in-law into his parent's home, the couple may live first with his parents. There is considerable flexibility in this system.

Once agreement has been reached as to where the couple will live, a simple betrothal ceremony is held. Village elders are called to the girl's house, and, along with the go-between, are feasted on rice and chicken. Often the engaged couple is not even present – they are 'embarrassed' (*ya taw*). Blessings are pronounced on the two by elders, and strings are tied around their wrists. If the shy couple does not attend, someone goes to them to tie the strings. As one of his final duties, the go-between takes the boy's blanket to the girl's bed. That night they may sleep there, although sometimes they are too bashful to stay together yet. From then on they are regarded as husband and wife, but the marriage is not official until the wedding feast is held.

The next morning the groom must fetch water and firewood for the bride's house. Then if his parents live in the same village the couple goes to their house, where the bride carries water for the groom's family. They return and pound rice for her parents, who then invite the groom to join them for the morning meal as he is now a full member of the family. After that the groom accompanies his bride to one of her father's fields, where they work together. In the meantime, the girl's parents partition an area of the house for the young couple.

The wedding feast

The 'wedding feast' (*hkeh ca*) is held after the family has collected enough pigs, rice, and other supplies to feed the whole village as well as those who come from the boy's village. This may be soon after they start living together, or it might take as long as three years. It is not unusual for the couple to have one or two children by then.

After the feast the most respected elder present pronounces a blessing upon a cup of water saying, 'Let this couple enjoy the blessing of good health and long life. May they have an abundant yield with sufficient to eat and drink. Let them have many children, and may the children have good health. . .'. The cup is then given to each in turn and they drink from it, transferring the blessings into their lives. Lahu used to say that if water spilled while they were drinking it, one child would die for each drop.

In a Christian village the marriage ceremony is much like a Western wedding – with music, exchange of vows, and a Scriptural injunction to the couple. A feast is held following the ceremony, with the groom furnishing the pork and the bride's family the rice and other food.

Divorce

Divorce is fairly common among Lahu during the early years of the marriage. If the girl's parents feel their son-in-law is lazy or disobedient, they may put pressure on their daughter to divorce him. On the other hand, the boy may become homesick for his family or tired of having to work for his in-laws. If he wants a divorce he may simply tell the elders, 'I divorce (literally 'throw away') this woman', and return home. According to custom he is fined 20 silver rupees, and the children remain with the mother.

Polygyny is rare among Lahu, but sometimes a man takes a minor wife after establishing his household. Some Lahu traders who travel extensively take a second wife elsewhere.

Birth

There are no special dietary restrictions during pregnancy. Many women eat a type of fine clay during that time, which may provide some of the minerals missing in the regular diet. However, after the birth they refrain from eating clay as they believe one might become dependent on it.

When a Lahu woman is about to deliver she kneels on a mat, and supports herself by hanging onto ropes or cloths suspended from a rafter of the house. An older woman, or sometimes her husband, supports her from behind, while massaging her abdomen gently so as to aid the birth of the child.

After the baby drops on the mat, the helper ties the umbilical cord and cuts it with a sliver of bamboo. Only white or black thread is used for this, because red thread, which is used in spirit ceremonies, would tempt the spirits to take the baby.

The father buries the placenta beneath the porch steps, and protects it as much as possible to prevent any animal or insect from eating it, which would cause the baby to be unhealthy.

When the cord sloughs off it is carefully disposed of, making sure it will not be burned in the fireplace, for that would cause the baby to die.

The Lahu Nyi often call in a religious specialist (*to bon* or *sala*) if the birth is a difficult one. He first goes to the woman's house, lights beeswax candles, and then offers a prayer, 'Let no tragedy occur here, we beseech you. Let there be neither death nor destruction. Give us the blessing of life. . .'.

For the first cycle of 12 days after the birth a mother must eat only chicken and rice. Chickens with black flesh, which have been raised by Lahu over the centuries for this purpose, are preferred, but have become scarce. In any case the mother would not eat a chicken with white feathers. She wears old clothes, and lies near the fireplace, holding warm stones on her abdomen to keep the blood from coagulating. Lahu women are always quite sensitive to certain odours, but especially following delivery. The new mother is afraid that the smell of soap or some other strong odour might cause her milk to dry up.

Parents in Lahu Nyi villages normally take gifts to the home of the *to bon* shortly after the birth of their child. The *to bon* prays for the child, asking *G'ui sha* to accept the offerings and give protection.

Naming

Lahu Nyi invite elders to name the child on the first lunar holy day after birth. The name given may follow the Lahu, Tai, or Chinese system. In the Lahu system the first syllable of the boy's name is *Ca*, and that of the girls is *Na*. The second syllable may indicate the birth order (*Ui* for the first, *Leh* for the last child, or at least the one they *think* will be last), the time of birth (*Shaw* for morning, *Hpeu* for evening), or the name of the day (*Hpui* for Dog day, *Va* for Pig day, *G'a* for Chicken day).

The Lahu Shi often follow the Tai pattern of naming (*Ai* for boys, *E* for girls). The Chinese system (*Li* or *Law* for boys, *Ci* for girls) is sometimes used by the Lahu Nyi and Na.

It is believed that if a child cries a great deal or is sickly, it is not happy with its name. In such a case the parents call in some elders, serve a meal of rice and chicken, and ask them to choose a new name. Strings are then tied around the baby's wrists and a new blessing is pronounced.

Once a Lahu couple has had a child, they are seldom called by their given names, but are known as the 'father/mother of so-and-so' (the name of their first-born).

Lahu Sheh Leh girl

Lahu Ba Keo boy

Death and Burial

Death

The Lahu say that when a man is near death his dog begins to howl, sensing that his master's soul is about to leave the body. When this happens, the relatives tie strings around the sick man's wrists in the hope of extending his life span, praying for all impurity to be taken away.

When a person dies the soul (aw ha) leaves the body, and goes to the country of the dead. The body is wrapped in a white shroud and placed in the main room of the house. Until the time of burial, cooked rice and chicken meat are kept by the body in a covered basket, a little being added each time the family has a meal. The person placing the food before the corpse says, 'We are feeding you. This is all there is for you to eat. Now eat it, for tomorrow you will be leaving. We eat together now, but you will be leaving, and we will not eat together anymore. You will not be staying with us. You will be leaving, but eat this food for now'. Thus, there is a continual reminder that the deceased is *not* to stay in the home.

Men of the village make a coffin and put the body in it, together with a leg and a wing of a chicken. The deceased is informed that if he becomes thirsty on his journey he can use the chicken leg to dig a well, and if he gets hot he can use the wing as shade.

Burial

The Lahu Nyi, Lahu Na, and Lahu Shi bury their dead. On the other hand, the Sheh Leh cremate, except in the case of a 'bad death'.

Many Lahu select the place for burial by throwing an egg in the air, having asked the corpse to choose the site for its final home. If the egg does not break they throw it in different places until it does. They say the place where the egg breaks will be easy to dig, as the deceased will help. Some Lahu Nyi throw a machete into the air and bury the body where it lands.

After the burial the Lahu Nyi take certain precautions when returning to the village to make sure no spirits follow. Two thorny branches are placed along the path for those in the burial party to brush against, thus leaving behind anything bad which might contaminate the village. When they reach the home of the deceased, branches which

have been brought back from the burial site are dipped in water and everyone is sprinkled so that 'no bad will remain'. Afterwards they all sit on the porch and drink tea, then take a bath and wash their clothes before returning to their own homes.

Post-burial

One cycle (twelve days) after the death of a Lahu Nyi elder, a special ceremony is held. Members of the household and their friends build a little hut for the deceased somewhere between the village and grave, and put in it a new set of clothes along with a chicken which has been sacrificed. The leader says, 'It is twelve days since we buried you. We feed you again, and give you new clothes. This is all we will feed and clothe you. Now go to the other side. We will stay on our side. Don't you seek us, and we won't seek you. Don't yearn for your relatives, and don't call to us. . .'.

We heard of one case where the family did not hold this ceremony. They believed that as a result of this omission the soul returned in the form of birds and rodents and ate up their rice crop.

Lahu are very concerned about weretigers (taw) trying to get to the corpse. If they hear mysterious noises, or see many insects near the grave soon after the burial, they fear that a weretiger may be lurking about. Relatives sometimes wait by the grave with machete in hand ready to attack any weretiger which might try to molest the body.

'Bad death'

A 'bad death', greatly feared by the Lahu, is one resulting from a tragedy, generally involving bloodshed. Death caused by stabbing, shooting, wild animals, childbirth, drowning and lightning are all considered bad death.

They believe that if the victim was calling out at the time of dying the 'bad death' spirit will repeatedly call out in the same manner at that site. Consequently before the body can be buried a religious specialist must be called to drive away the evil spirits.

Religion

Religious beliefs

Basic to the religion of the Lahu is a belief in spirits and souls, as well as in a supreme deity. Along with this is their concept of boon ('blessing/merit'), derived from their Buddhist neighbours.

Many Lahu Nyi have been strongly influenced by a messianic movement which has altered and shaped the form of their religion. Most Lahu Na and Lahu Shi in Thailand have embraced some form of Christianity, while retaining certain animistic beliefs. The Sheh Leh maintain the most traditional form of Lahu religion found in Thailand today.

Some of the basic beliefs are:

1. *Spirits (ne).* There are numerous spirits, with the potential of doing good or evil. The 'house spirit' (yeh ne) protects the members of the household, provided proper offerings and prayers are made. Protection can be withheld if anyone angers the house spirit, or if the proper rituals are not performed. Nature spirits, who live outside the village, are either neutral or vicious. If they are offended they might attack the offender, making him ill. Spirits capable of invading people are greatly feared. When possession takes place they must be exorcised.

2. *God (G'ui sha).* All Lahu believe in a supreme being who is prayed to for blessings of health and good crops. The Lahu Nyi believe that G'ui sha created the heavens, and his wife, Ai Ma (the great Mother), created the earth. Most prayers are ultimately directed to one, or both of them, as givers of all blessings.

3. *Soul (aw ha).* The soul is the spiritual counterpart of the body. If it leaves the body, or is attacked by a vicious spirit, the person becomes ill. Sometimes the soul wanders away in sleep, and has experiences in the form of dreams.

Religious practitioners

The traditional name for the village priest is *paw hku*. The Lahu Nyi usually call him *to bon*, while the Sheh Leh refer to him as *keh lu pa*. The village priest is the main teacher of their religion, and the chief mediator between the villagers and G'ui sha. He is chosen by the people and may serve one or more villages.

The Lahu Nyi who follow the messianic movement have three practitioners ranking below the *to bon:* the *sala* who helps in healing ceremonies; the *la shaw* who drives evil and sickness from the village; and the *a can* who helps villagers receive blessings by the presentation of offerings. The wives of these leaders also play very prominent roles in the religious life of the village.

Among the Sheh Leh, as well as many Lahu Nyi, two specialists deal with matters related to spirits. The first is a *maw pa* (shaman) who has the ability to go into a trance in order to find out which spirit is causing a specific sickness, and then to conduct a ceremony which will 'send the spirit back', often using a pronged metal 'spirit fork' (*meh taw le*). He can also call back wandering souls and perform the necessary rituals to effect cures for the sick.

Lahu believe that some people have the ability to send pieces of animal hide or paper into the body of a person they wish to harm. A victim of this 'black magic' calls a *she pa* to come and suck the object out of him, either through a short bamboo tube, or by applying his mouth directly to the affected place and 'biting' out the offending item. In some cases the *she pa* may spit on the painful area, and then after repeating certain incantations take the saliva between his thumb and forefinger and hold it over the flame of a beeswax candle. As the saliva sputters and hisses the evil is burned away.

Lahu village priests are expected to maintain high standards of conduct; not to smoke opium or drink liquor, and to maintain marital fidelity. If they do not meet these standards the Lahu say that the group would not lose 'blessing', but the erring priest would. On the other hand those specialists who deal primarily with the spirits (*maw pa* and *she pa*) are often opium addicts.

Lahu Nyi priest in temple

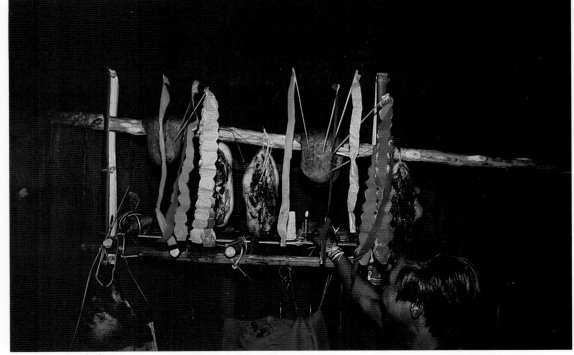

Rice cake altar in home

Religious practices

Prayers, which are important to all Lahu, are addressed to G'ui sha, or to such spirits as *yeh ne* (house spirit), *hk'aw ne law ne* (mountain and valley spirit), or *g'ui ne ha ne* (water and cave spirit). Prayer may be in the form of stylized repetition of formulae passed down from the ancestors, or it may be extemporaneous. The theme is physical and spiritual well-being for one's self, family, livestock, and crops. They also pray that all in the village, big and small, from 'all four corners', be maintained in unity, health and wealth.

Around each Lahu Nyi temple are a number of tall bamboo poles to which white and yellow cloth streamers are attached. They believe that G'ui sha lives in a temple in heaven, and has such streamers flying there as well. Sacred posts, copied from the Tai, are planted in the ground near the temple as a means of enabling the villagers to receive blessings, and be protected from bad luck. Inside the temple is the main altar to G'ui sha where the villagers make their offerings to ensure good health and to avoid tragedy.

Lahu Nyi observe 'holy days' (*shin nyi*) at full moon and new moon each month. The observation starts the evening before, when a member from each household brings water, and pours it into a common vessel in the temple to demonstrate the unity of the village. Then under the direction of the wife of the *sala* the women wash the hands of the villagers to cleanse them from the sins they have committed since the last holy day.

That same evening, someone from each household brings a cup of uncooked rice and pours it into a basket in the home of the village priest. On the morning of the holy day the priest's wife adds her share and cooks it. The priest takes some of that rice to the temple, and after lighting beeswax candles, offers it together with a cup of water to G'ui sha. Throughout the ceremony an assistant is beating the temple gong. A similar offering is made in the evening after which there is dancing in the temple.

The Lahu Nyi have three main holy days during the year when they refrain from work in their fields for two days instead of just one. The first, *sheh k'aw*, occurs after they have burned their fields and before they plant their rice; the second, *hkao,* is held at the time of maize harvest; and the third, *aw*, is held before rice harvest. All

three are borrowed from the Tai, and are observed primarily by those most influenced by Tai Buddhism.

The Sheh Leh observe the same holy days as the Lahu Nyi, at which times they make offerings to the 'Lord of the Land', followed by dancing in the sacred dance circle. Every merit-making ceremony is also followed by dancing. We were present in a Sheh Leh village when 15 such ceremonies were held in one day – mostly for sick people. That evening about 80 villagers gathered to dance. The head of each household which had a merit-making ceremony brought a basket of offerings and put it on the mound of earth in the centre of the dance circle. He then pressed a candle onto its rim and lit it, knelt before the basket and prayed. The dancing stopped each time a basket was presented, and was resumed when the prayer was finished.

The Sheh Leh are enthusiastic dancers. The girls and young women hold hands in groups of four or five radiating out from the central mound and dance around it in a counter-clockwise direction, while the men dance on the outside with exaggerated steps.

Scenes in a Lahu Nyi temple

View of Lahu Nyi village showing temple with streamers flying overhead

Outside a Lahu Nyi temple

Wood carving offered inside temple by individuals

Carved post outside temple to ensure health and stability

Scenes of a Lahu Nyi ceremony in temple

Scenes of Lahu Sheh Leh ritual dancing

Scenes of Lahu Nyi ritual dancing in their temple

Messianic movements

Throughout Lahu history there have been several messianic movements, first in China, and later on in Burma. When Lahu experience economic and political problems of exceptional gravity – such as those caused by Chinese Nationalist troops (KMT), Shan rebels, Burmese political movements, bands of armed robbers, ruthless opium traffickers or loss of land – a messiah-like person claiming to be G'ui sha or his representative is likely to emerge to rally them around a new movement. It may at first be a call to return to 'the true Lahu religion', but as time goes on it often grows into a movement of active political revolt. This in turn might lead to conflict with those in authority and the ultimate defeat of the movement, resulting in even more frustration, paving the way for yet another messiah figure to arise in the future.

After World War II such a messiah, called 'Gibbon God' (*Maw Na G'ui sha*), emerged in the southwestern section of Kengtung State. He gathered a large following, especially among the Lahu Nyi in that section of Burma as well as in northern Thailand. In 1958 he sent word to Thailand that no Lahu was to live any farther south than Fang, and those who could should move back to Burma where he would ensure they had the blessings of 'everlasting food and drink, everlasting clothes and raiment, everlasting youth with no grey hair and no teeth falling out'. When the promises failed to materialize and the Lahu who had moved into Burma did not have enough food, many became disillusioned and returned to Thailand.

As so often happens, the movement on the Burma side turned to armed revolt. By that time, however, *Maw Na* was old and blind, so most of the day-to-day operations were handled by his son and other leaders. *Maw Na* died in 1980, but his movement has survived him – including the concept of the *to bon* and his function in the Lahu Nyi religion.

Christians

One-third of the total Lahu population in Thailand lives within Christian communities. Only a few Lahu Nyi and Sheh Leh have been converted, while nearly all Lahu Na and Lahu Shi are Christians.

Sickness and Treatment

Concept of sickness

An important theme in Lahu culture is health (*cheh sha caw sha* – literally 'live easy be easy'). When Lahu Nyi women bring water to the temple and pour it into the receptacle reserved for that purpose they say, 'Let there be health'. They want the blessing of health to flow like everlasting water. The Lahu Nyi make small mounds of clay, insert bamboo sticks tipped with tufts of cotton, and offer them in the temple with the prayer, 'As this clay is eternal, let me be well forever'. The cotton represents purity which is essential for good health.

Not all sickness, however, is thought to be caused by lack of purity. If a child eats too much green fruit his stomach-ache is not attributed to ceremonial impurity or spirits. An older person's weakness is seen to be due simply to his age. However, if a person who is normally well falls ill and there is no obvious cause, the family may fear that it is due to soul loss or 'spirit biting' (*ne che*).

Treatment

In the event of illness, a Lahu family generally seeks a cure by means of medicines – either traditional or modern. One of the favourite subjects of conversation around evening fires is which treatments are the most effective. Much medical treatment is by trial and error.

Injections have an almost magical quality to the Lahu. They frequently use the services of Chinese and Thai 'injection doctors', but are increasingly purchasing and injecting drugs themselves. They are willing to spend a great deal of time and money on healing.

Together with medical treatment the Lahu Nyi and Sheh Leh frequently resort to one or more types of ritual, especially if there is no evidence of a cure in a reasonable time. One of the most common is the 'soul-calling' ceremony. If this fails the family often holds a 'blessing/merit' ceremony (*bon te*). By serving pork and rice to fellow villagers, the family hopes to gain enough merit to offset the sickness. We met a boy in a Sheh Leh village who had a paralyzed arm. His father had held *bon te* ceremonies for him 18 times, killing a pig on each occasion. The father was dumbfounded because the boy's arm

had not recovered after sharing all this *bon* with the villagers.

Some ceremonies for the sick are held in the temple. An offering is presented to the village priest who then goes to the temple with the sick person. Lighting a beeswax candle and passing it around his lips and inside his mouth, he 'cleanses' his mouth from lies or words spoken in anger before he calls down *bon*. He may burn more candles on the metal 'spirit fork' and pray, 'May all that is impure and unclean be purified and cleansed. May the illness turn into health and strength. . .'.

Sheh Leh blow the musical gourd pipe in healing ceremonies. During the bridge ritual, which is part of the soul-calling ceremony, one man blows the pipe almost constantly. A low drone tone, which always issues from the pipe no matter what tune is played, 'goes all the way to God'. Believing that God brought the first man and woman out of a gourd, they feel it gives him special pleasure to hear men making music for him with a gourd pipe.

Scenes of Lahu Sheh Leh bridge ceremony

New Year

Ceremonial life revolves around the annual New Year festival. The activities and symbolism practiced during those very special days comprise a microcosm of what it means to be Lahu.

The time set for the New Year festival varies from year to year and from village to village. Although some Lahu follow the dates of Chinese New Year, most set it according to other criteria. Timing must be such that the spirits of the ancestors who come to witness the festival leave the village on an auspicious day. Furthermore, the festival must not conflict with a busy agricultural period, as no one is allowed to work in the fields then. If there is a cluster of Lahu villages they all celebrate New Year at the same time, because of the interaction between them during the celebration.

Preparations begin months in advance, as the women must make new clothing for each member of the family. Children and young people in particular wear fine new clothing, with those of marriageable age vying with one another to be the most elaborately dressed. Silver ornaments which may have been buried throughout the year for safe-keeping are brought out for the occasion and are worn mostly by the young. Being the most important time of the year for courtship, each family wants to impress its neighbours with the extent of its wealth.

The New Year festival consists of two main parts: the Women's Year and the Men's Year (also referred to as the 'big year' and 'little year' respectively). Throughout the festivities the male and female theme recurs, pointing up the importance of this relationship in Lahu culture. Walker states, '. . . the harmony between male and female elements is a recurrent theme in Lahu Nyi religious ideology' (1970). We would extend that to apply to all Lahu.

The first activity of the New Year is *Hk'aw tan nyi*, or the 'year beginning day'. In the morning all households exchange portions of uncooked glutinous rice. Then each household combines the rice it has received from its neighbours with some of its own, and prepares it for making 'rice cakes' (*aw hpfuh*). After steaming the rice they pound it until it becomes a glutinous mass, throwing in hands-full of crushed sesame seed. Then they turn it out on a bamboo tray covered with pounded sesame seeds and shape the dough into discs two to three cm thick and 12 to 25 cm in diameter.

Each cake, containing grains of rice from every family in the village, symbolizes the unity and interdependence of the people.

Meanwhile a rice cake altar is constructed inside each house, and decorated with white streamers and paper cut-outs in the shape of a man and a woman. The altar is covered with pine needles (if available), and the rice cakes are placed on them. They are reminders of the time God gave the Lahu his word written on a rice cake. The pine tree is a symbol of new life, or new beginnings, because it puts out new growth at that time of the year.

Later in the day every household presents two beeswax candles twisted together and two rice cakes to each of the other households. These are given in pairs to represent the husband and wife who are the donors. Once more we see the husband/wife theme – the intertwined candles symbolizing the strong marriage bond which is expected of Lahu couples.

Events of the festival follow a prescribed schedule. There is a great deal of dancing, the leader calling the steps by the tune he plays on his musical gourd pipe. Drums, gongs, and cymbals are used by some. Men and women, boys and girls participate in the dancing, but the style varies widely according to the sub-tribe.

Boys and men have great fun spinning hard-wood tops, playing spirited games in which each one tries to knock other tops away while his own continues to spin. Women and girls play a game with large brown seeds from a jungle vine, which involves a routine of throwing the seeds with their feet or shooting them with their fingers to knock down a row of seeds set on edge some distance away. Lahu Nyi women play this game with flat wooden blocks. Young unmarried men and women play catch with black cloth balls made by the girls. They choose partners of the opposite sex and play catch with them for many hours, often leading to the exchange of bracelets. If they continue the relationship, they keep each other's bracelets – otherwise return them.

The drawing of 'new water' is an important part of the festivities. Young people make a game of seeing who can reach the water source first when the new year arrives. They believe old water ceases to flow and the new water begins with the coming of New Year. They maintain that the 'new water' is heavier than the 'old'.

Using 'new water' a female representative from every family goes from house to house washing the hands of the household head and his wife. The recipient in turn pronounces a blessing on the donor's household. Later in the day parents are bathed by their adult children, and elders held in high esteem are bathed by other members of the village. This 'bathing' consists of pouring water, mercifully warmed, over the head and body.

Dancing at New Year's time always takes place around the *Hk'aw ceh* ('Year tree'). For the Lahu Na and some other sub-groups, this will ideally be a pine tree. The Lahu Nyi make their 'Year tree' of four long bamboo stalks complete with foliage which they erect in the form of a square. A shelf attached to these four posts forms an altar. A pig is sacrificed and its head is suspended under the altar. The 'Year tree', whatever its form, represents the 'Tree of Life' which the Lahu see in the shadows of the lunar landscape. They believe that if they possessed even a tiny part of that tree they would be immortal.

The Lahu Na form a line at the lower part of the village, and dance up to the 'Year tree', with a person carrying a small table of offerings following the leader. The table is placed under the tree, and dancing goes on around it for hours. The Lahu Nyi place their offerings on the altar inside the square formed by the four bamboos. As households present their offerings they also pour water into a bamboo section sunk into the ground under the 'tree'.

Just as there is ritual enactment of the interdependence of the people within the village, so the villages within a cluster manifest their mutual support in an exchange of visits during the New Year festivities. Each village forms its group to dance into the other villages, carrying offerings of rice cakes, candles, and pork to the headman.

Offerings are made to G'ui sha and Ai Ma (the male and female deities), and prayers are made asking for good crops, health, plenty of livestock, and the birth of many children in the year to come. Christian Lahu have a worship service in the church to thank God (G'ui sha) for the blessings of the past year, and to pray for new blessings in the year to come.

After four or five days of feasting, dancing, shooting guns, launching fireworks, spinning tops, throwing balls and visiting friends, the Lahu are happily exhausted. Another year has been ushered in. The hardships of the past have been put behind them, and new hope – like the new growth of the pine tree – has been born in their hearts.

Scenes of Lahu Na New Year dancing

Conclusion

The blessings which the Lahu so avidly seek are expressed in couplets, called *taw pa taw ma* (male word, female word), and may be stated either positively or negatively.

Positive

Give us easy minds and hearts.
Give us sufficient food and drink.
Give us health and strength.
Fulfill in us the hopes and longings of our hearts.
Purify and cleanse us so we will have good health.
Unite us in the same purpose and thoughts.
Separate us from evil and deliver us from misfortune.
Protect and care for us.

Give us enough from our toil and labour to live on.

Negative

Don't make us worried or sad.
Don't make us suffer hunger and starvation.
Don't let us fall sick and die.
Don't let evil spirits and people deter us.
Don't let us get the 33 kinds of sickness.
Don't let there be fighting and quarreling.
Don't cause us suffering or tragedy.

Don't let farming tools, wood, and bamboo wound us.
Don't cause us to have to stretch out our hands as beggars and supplicants.

Scenes from Lahu Nyi New Year

Loimi-Akha village

Chapter 7

AKHA (Kaw)

Desire for Continuity

Lah Po has been the village priest of Ho Leh Akha village for over 20 years. There has been much change during that time. Some people have moved on; new households have moved in. The village has changed its location four times, and now they are back almost to the same area where Lah Po was born 60 years ago.

This is the day for building the new village swing for the annual 'swing ceremony'. While the young men go to cut poles for the new one, the elders dismantle the old swing which had been used for last year's ritual. According to Akha custom, Lah Po as the village priest is the first to start digging the hole for the main pole. The new swing is then erected on the site of the old one as the entire village looks on.

Lah Po sees his son making his way through the crowd. He has prepared three bunches of grass and three stones which are to be given the first turn on the swing. These are offerings of thanksgiving to the ancestors. Lah Po is pleased to see his son taking an active part in the ceremony; not all young men are interested in the true Akha customs.

Having given the stones and grass their ceremonial swings, it is now Lah Po's turn. Only after he has had his swing can the villagers have theirs. Somehow the loop at the end of the vine seems higher this year – or is it that he is just getting older? The son helps his father by pulling the vine out straight so he can step into the loop.

Holding tightly to the long vine with both hands, Lah Po launches out – the very first person to use this new ceremonial village swing. As he goes high into the air, the priest looks out over the village, his village. How beautiful the girls and women are in their festive outfits, and rightfully so, since this is the Women's New Year. And isn't that his granddaughter over there? He had not realized that she has been gradually changing into an adult woman's outfit. Why, she will be getting married before he knows it!

He sees the fields on the mountain sides. The rice looks a little scraggly! In two months the whole village will be out harvesting it. Then will come the marriage season, which will bring more babies! 'Ah, the ancestors are good to us', thinks Lah Po in gratitude. 'One day I will leave this life and join them, while my children and grandchildren will continue to carry on the great tradition – the *Akha Way*'.

U Lo, Loimi, and Phami women

Name and language

This group calls itself 'Akha' (with both syllables spoken on a low tone). The Tai groups in Southeast Asia call them 'Kaw' or 'Ekaw' ('Igor'), a name the Akha do not like. In Laos they are often called 'Kha Kaw'. In China and Vietnam they are included in the group referred to as 'Hani' (a name which may derive from the term 'Za Nyi' which they call themselves in their poetic and ceremonial language), although this designation may include other Yi (Lolo) groups.

The Akha language falls within the Yi (Lolo) branch of the Tibeto-Burman family. 'Jeu G'oe' is the dialect spoken by almost all Akha in Thailand, and is the major dialect spoken by Akha who live in Kengtung State, Burma, the southwestern section of Yunnan, China, and in northeastern Laos.

Migration

The Akha originated in Yunnan, where the great majority still live.* One region named in Akha legend is south of the present city of Kunming. Over several centuries many Akha have been migrating southward from their original home. In the middle of the 19th century significant numbers were moving into Kengtung State, the easternmost of the Shan States of Burma, where about 180,000 live today. Others made their way into Laos and Vietnam; the Akha in Thailand came from Burma.

The first Akha village in Thailand was probably established in 1903 in the Phayaphai region of the Hin Taek area near the Burmese border. Other villages followed, but there were probably not more than 2,500 Akha living in Thailand by the end of World War II. In 1964 there were approximately 7,000, and by mid-1983 they numbered 24,000, which means their population has more than doubled three times in 38 years. Some of this is from immigration, but 3% or so a year is from natural increase.

At first the Akha in Thailand lived only north of the Mae Kok River in Chiang Rai Province. In mid-1983 about 7% of them lived in three other provinces; and of the 93% still living in Chiang Rai Province, 15% were located south of the Mae Kok River.

* Reportedly there are about one million Hani in China – how many of these are Akha is not known.

History

Although the Akha have no written history, a rich heritage of legends, proverbs, and rituals gives them a sense of who they are and what being an Akha means. Like some other Tibeto-Burman groups, Akha are able to recite the names of all their ancestors in the male line back to the 'beginning'. They feel these ancestors are the source of life and have provided them with the knowledge of how to cope with daily situations. Seeing himself as a link in this chain of life, an Akha is sustained in the hour of need, and challenged to play his part now so that later others will take care of him as their ancestor.

According to one Akha legend, the earth and sky (*M Ma, M G'ah*) were brought into being by the all powerful 'force', *Apoe Miyeh* (sometimes translated as 'God'). From *M G'ah* came a succession of nine powerful 'spirits' named *G'ah Ne, Ne Zaw, Zaw Zeu, Zeu To, To Ma, Ma Yaw, Yaw Neh, Neh Beh,* and *Beh Sm.* The second part of the parental name becomes the first part of the child's name, which is the way Akha name their children to this day.

Akha legend states that the first human being was the offspring of *Beh Sm,* and was named *Sm Mi O,* from whom all people in the world have descended. The Akha recite the names of *Sm Mi O*'s descendents, who are their direct ancestors, through 13 generations to *Dzoe Tah Pah.* This man is considered the great father of all Akha. As an Akha repeats his genealogy, the name of his clan head is usually among the names he recites.

Repeating one's full genealogy, which includes over 60 names, is usually reserved for special ceremonies, such as the one which takes place after a person has died. At times of crisis, also, the genealogy is repeated and the ancestors urged to 'look down and help'. Normally Akha do not repeat the full list, but when two people of the same clan meet and wish to know just how they are related, they repeat the names of their male ancestors from their grandfather up their lineage to a common ancestor. This is very important when it comes to considering whether a young couple can marry, as they should be able to repeat at least seven patrilineal generations before reaching a common ancestor.

In the same way many Akha remember the names of their male ancestors, they also remember the migration route their ancestors followed in China, Burma, and Thailand. The farther back they go with their recitation of the names of forefathers and former dwelling places, the fuzzier the picture becomes. Even so, Akha from China, Burma, Thailand, and Laos, basically agree in their repetition of genealogy and migration routes. This is amazing for people who have no written language, and are spread over so vast an area.

Phami-Akha girls

Loimi-Akha women and girls

Clothing and Ornamentation

The well-dressed Akha woman looks stunning from the tip of her elaborate headdress to her ornate leggings. The Akha man's clothing is not so elaborate, but there is a certain smartness in the cut of his jacket and the tilt of his turban.

The basic material used in Akha clothing is a firmly woven homespun cotton cloth, dyed with indigo to a blue-black hue. Formerly Akha grew all of the cotton used for their clothing, but now some purchase raw cotton from the Thai. They make it into tufts about 20 cm long, which they carry in a decorated bamboo section or a basket which is tied to the woman's waist. She attaches a tuft to the hook of her wooden spindle which she rolls at high speed on her thigh. When the spindle is released the cotton spins into strong thread. Girls are taught to spin when they are six or seven years old, for the mother alone cannot make sufficient thread to clothe the entire family. Women and girls spin thread constantly – while walking to the field, carrying wood and water, sitting by the fireside in the evening, and during every other available moment. Akha girls like to have contests to see who can produce the most spindles of thread in a day.

The thread is woven into firm cloth 17 to 20 cm wide, using a foot-treadle loom. The cloth is then dyed with indigo which is grown in Akha gardens. It takes about a month of dipping and drying the cloth daily to produce the deep colour typical of their clothing. (See Campbell et al 1978:140 for the process of preparing indigo dye.)

Akha in Thailand have three basic styles of dress. The first, 'U Lo-Akha' (Pointed-headdress) is worn by most of the Akha who have been domiciled in Thailand for many years. Their attire resembles that of the A Jaw Akha in Burma. The second style, 'Loimi-Akha', is named after a large mountain in Burma from which many of them have come, and includes most of those who have migrated recently from Burma. The Akha often call them 'U Bya' (Flat-headdress). The third style is commonly called 'Phami-Akha', named after a village near the border town of Mae Sai. This type is worn primarily by the Mawn Po clan in Thailand, Burma, and China.

The basic costume of an Akha woman consists of: a headdress, a jacket worn over a halter-like garment, a short skirt, a sash with decorated ends, and leggings.

The hip-length jacket is made of two strips of cloth about 20 cm wide, with seams down the back and sides. The wrist-length sleeves are straight, with no tapering or rounding where they are set into the body of the jacket. The front is plain, except for a strip of coloured binding around the back of the neck and down to mid-chest. The back of the jacket and the sleeves are embellished according to the three basic styles. Sometimes a plain white under-jacket is worn for insulation and to keep the wearer's skin from getting blue from the indigo dye.

The knee-length skirt hangs very low on the woman's hips. It is straight across the front and heavily pleated in the back. The halter is a piece of cloth wrapped around the breasts and tied or buttoned at the side. A single string or strap attached to the back on one side goes over the opposite shoulder and loops over a button in front. The width and the embellishment of the halter vary with the style. The U Lo and Loimi styles have a bare midriff between halter and skirt.

The sash is tied around the waist under the jacket, with the ends hanging in front. Being heavily weighted with buttons, coins, and beads, it falls between the woman's legs when she squats or sits, protecting her modesty. Leggings are made by sewing indigo cloth into tubes and decorating them in the appropriate style.

Girls dress similarly to women, except they wear snug-fitting caps, which become more elaborately ornamented as the girls grow older. Pre-adolescent girls do not wear halters or sashes.

Adolescent girls gradually change from the type of clothing worn by a child to that of a woman. This is done during times of ceremonies in four stages: (1) wearing a halter; (2) adding Job's-tear seeds, red and white beads, and silver to her cap; (3) wearing a sash, and (4) changing to an adult-style headdress. Tiny gourds at the waist and on the headdress indicate the young woman is not yet married.

The Akha man's jacket varies in style and ornamentation, using the same needlework techniques as the woman's. The Chinese-style pants are free of embellishment. On occasion some men wear black turbans, which are wound neatly and firmly so that they can be put on like a hat. Some older men wear red or pink silk turbans for special occasions. Boys wear similar clothing, except for a close-fitting cap.

All Akha carry shoulder bags, decorated according to their particular style.

U Lo-Akha woman spins thread

and winds it on frame

Dyeing chicken feathers

Stitching appliqué designs

Making shoulder bag

Weaving

Drying indigo-dyed cloth

U Lo-Akha style

The woman's headdress has two main parts. The base is a wide head band decorated with silver coins, silver buttons, and beads. Above it perches a high conical-shaped framework of bamboo covered with indigo cloth. This is embellished with silver ornaments and chains, coins, beads, red-dyed feather tassels, gibbon fur, seeds, pompons, and unique items that might catch a woman's fancy, such as small, round mirrors. The amounts and types of ornamentation vary according to marital and economic status, age, and how recently the woman has had a baby.

Embroidery consists mostly of a simple running stitch and satin stitch in bright colours. Strips of coloured cloth, seeds, silver buttons and coins are also used.

Men's jackets reach to just below the waist, and have embroidery on the back, and a few lines along the base in front.

Woman's headdress

Woman's outfit

Woman's outfit (back view of jacket)

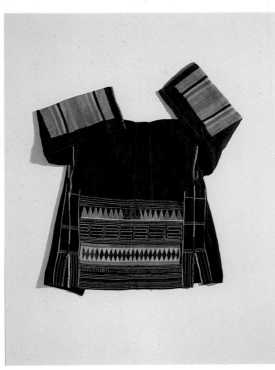

Back view of women's jackets

Woman's headdress

Man's turban

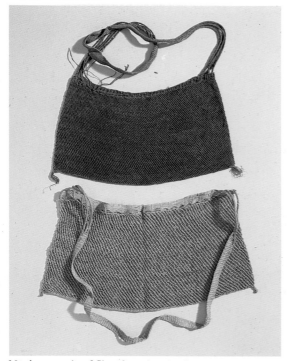

Net bags made of fiber from jungle vine

Shoulder bags

Back view of men's jackets

Loimi-Akha style

The woman's headdress is characterized by a flat, trapezoid-shaped silver piece at the back, and alternate rows of beads and silver buttons over the crown. Strings of hollow silver balls, coins, and beads hang down to the shoulders.

The back of the woman's jacket is decorated with superb appliqué patterns in red and other colours, outlined with couched thread of a contrasting colour. Diamond, triangular, and other shapes of appliqué alternate with bright-coloured embroidery. White shirt buttons, silver buttons, seeds, beads, shells, and tassels are added. Other articles of her clothing are similarly decorated. For full-dress occasions a belt encrusted with cowrie shells and Job's-tear seeds is worn over the jacket, those of unmarried young women being wide with many shells.

Girl's caps are ornamented with silver, feathers, tassels, Job's-tear seeds, gibbon fur, and beads.

The waist-length jackets worn by men and boys have vents at the lower edge on both sides and in the back, and are similarly embellished. Some have a rectangular chest piece bordered with strips of red cloth and closed with a silver buckle.

Woman's headdress

Woman's outfit

Woman's headdress (rear view)

Older girl's cap

Older boy's cap

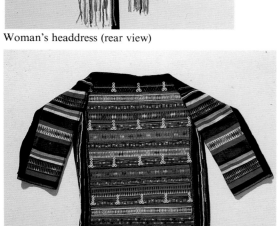

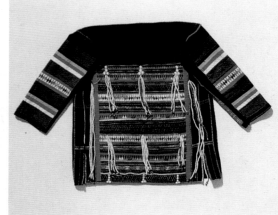

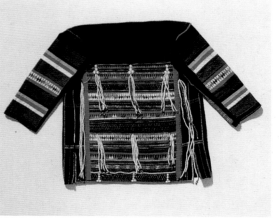

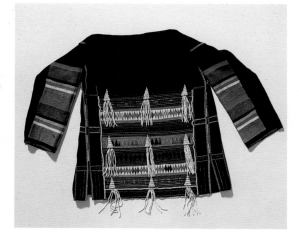

Back view of women's jackets

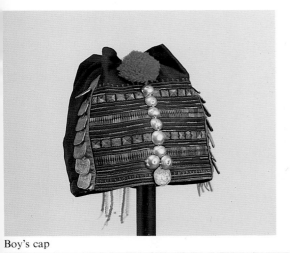

Boy's cap

Boy's cap

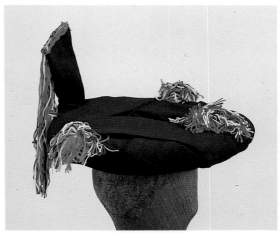

Young man's courting turban

Men's jackets (front)

Men's jackets (back)

Phami-Akha style

The woman's headdress is shaped somewhat like a helmet, and is totally encrusted with silver buttons, coins, and beads. Numerous strings of mostly red beads are attached to the sides of the headdress falling nearly to the waist.

The jacket has numerous overlapping strips of indigo-blue cloth edged with white, stitched in tiers down the back. Each strip is embroidered with delicate patterns. The sleeves are also embroidered, as are the sash, leggings and shoulder bag.

The waist-length halters are covered with round and diamond-shaped silver ornaments and buttons. Girls' caps are covered with similar ornaments, and have strings of beads hanging from the crown to the shoulders in the back.

The man's jacket is long, and is covered with plain overlapping strips of indigo-dyed cloth edged with white. It may fasten either in the front or down the left side. Often a row of silver coins or a silver chain with bells is stitched down the opening of the jacket.

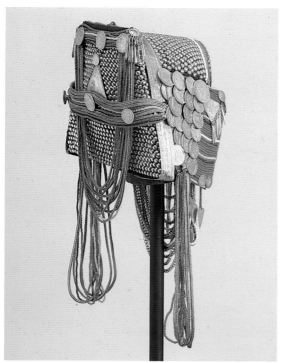

Woman's headdress

Woman's outfit

Girl's cap

Man's jacket (front)

Back view of women's jackets

Man's jacket (back)

**Various styles of Akha women's headdresses
(mainly from Burma)**

Jewellery

Most Akha ornamentation is attached to their clothing. In addition women wear broad flat silver neck rings and wide, plain or engraved silver bracelets. Men wear smooth, round neck rings and bracelets, and sometimes crown-shaped silver rings in their turbans or on their fingers. These days aluminium is often substituted for silver, which has been sold to buy food or opium. In some cases, fear of robbery has caused them to bury their silver, and use aluminium for everyday wear.

Akha elders highly value items of silver which are prestige symbols, such as large hollow silver bracelets, tobacco and betel-nut boxes, and long silver pipes.

Many Akha women wear antique glass beads of Chinese origin, which have been handed down from mother to daughter for many generations. Most of the smaller beads are of European origin, the oldest probably having been traded in China by European traders over several centuries. Some Akha women are selling off their valuable antique beads and replacing them with cheap plastic ones.

The coins used on headdresses and other garments are of several types. Those who can afford them use silver coins, such as silver Indian rupees, Chinese dollars, or French Indochinese piasters. Burmese, Indochinese, and Thai coins of small value are also used.

Villages

An Akha village can be identified at a glance by its gates, the towering village swing, and the distinctive style of the houses with their massive roofs. Ideally, a village is built on the saddleback of a mountain where there is a good breeze, a dependable source of drinking water, and adequate arable land in the surrounding area.

In addition to using the 'three grains of rice' method to test a potential village site (see the first chapter), Akha elders also use the 'egg drop' method of divining the ideal spot where the spirits, ancestors, and the local 'Lord of Land and Water' are willing to let them settle. An area about one metre square is cleared and a shallow hole made in the centre with the dirt being tamped down firmly. The 'village priest' (*dzoe ma*) drops a raw egg from the height of his ear into this hole. If the egg breaks, the unseen forces are granting permission for the village to settle there. If it does not break – and Akha insist that they have seen such instances – they try other places until the egg breaks.

The first house to be built must be that of the village priest. Once his house has been completed the village has been established. The rest of the houses will be grouped around his house in an egalitarian fashion. There is one exception, however. Any family which has ever had 'human rejects' (*tsaw caw*) must build their house on a lower slope below all other houses. 'Human rejects' are twins or any baby the Akha consider to be abnormal. Such families must be at the lowest elevation to ensure that debris from their house will not wash down and contaminate the other houses.

A village will often have more than one name. In Thai it may be named after some physical feature, such as 'Broken Rock Village', and 'Cogon Grass Village'. They prefer Akha names, often the name of the current or former village priest or political headman. When the name or description of the location is used, the word 'Akha' follows, such as 'Law Lo Akha'; whereas when the name of a person is used, the word 'village' (*pu*) is added, as in 'Abaw Tu Seh Pu'.

Everyone in an Akha village should be under the protection of an 'ancestral altar' (*apoe pawlaw*), and participate in the periodic 'ancestral offerings' (*apoe law-eu*). If a non-Akha man marries an Akha woman and moves into her village, he must first become a member of the clan of his wife, or of someone living there. He has to take part in all the ceremonies along with everyone else, and must accept the village priest as having the final word in following the Akha Way.

Choosing site for new village

Leaving old village on way to establish new village

Villages

Houses

There is an aura of sacredness about an Akha house, for in it is kept the ancestral altar, which is the focus for all ceremonies relating to the ancestors. Consequently there is a prescribed way in which household items must be brought into a new home. First all the paraphernalia to do with the ancestral altar must be taken in, along with the three-legged iron cooking stand on which their rice is cooked. After that other household furnishings can be moved in.

Houses are usually built up on posts, although sometimes the side on the upper slope of the mountain is built directly on the ground, while the down-hill side is elevated. The space under the house affords a convenient shelter for the animals, as well as storage space for firewood and equipment. In case of two-level houses, the cooking and eating area is on the ground, and the family sleeps on the elevated portion.

Akha houses have no windows, and the roof is constructed in such a way that the eaves come down very low on both sides. This results in a dark interior, but keeps out the wind and rain, and provides a work space outside under the eaves.

There are two main sections, the men's and the women's, with a shoulder-high partition between the sections extending as far as the central house beam. One area is for sleeping, the other for work and various activites. The ancestral altar is hung on the woman's side of the partition.

Each house has two open fireplaces for cooking. The one in the men's side is used primarily for cooking meat and brewing tea, while rice and vegetables are cooked on the woman's hearth. Usually there is a third fireplace on the woman's side where pig food is cooked.

It is improper for an outsider to walk through an Akha house, entering one door and leaving by the other, just as it is not acceptable for a person to go directly through an Akha village without entering some home and having at least a drink of water. Food or drink will always be offered in an Akha home, and it is important for the guest to partake, even if only a token amount. Otherwise it appears that the visitor is an intruder – perhaps even a thief. Male guests should not enter the women's section of the house unless invited to do so by the head of the household. Women visitors, on the other hand, can enter the men's section along with other visitors.

House construction

Akha house plan

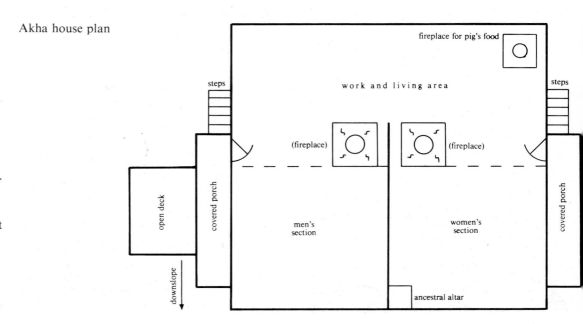

Preparing beam for house construction

Making a basket

Splitting bamboo for wall construction

Ancestral altar above, with basket holding offering paraphernalia

Making the seat of a stool

Drying vegetables

'The Akha Way'

Akha often refer to themselves as those who 'carry the Akha Way' (*Aka zah taw-eu*). They have no word for 'religion', but the term 'Akha Way' covers it – and much more. It includes all their traditions and ceremonies. The Akha Way determines how they cultivate their fields and hunt animals, how they view and treat sickness, and the manner in which they relate to one another and to outsiders. It is all embracing. Any who become Christians, or for any reason discontinue the observance of the Akha Way, are expected to leave the village.

The Akha Way is delineated in their mythology, proverbs, and traditions. The manner in which they carry out the Way may vary from clan to clan and village to village, but the main theme is the same: each is a link in a great chain, a part of the Akha continuum, which must be maintained at all cost.

Myths

Akha myths speak of a great all-powerful being whom they call 'Apoe Miyeh'. The first part of the name means 'male ancestor', which may help non-Akha to understand their concept of this being. At times it is difficult to distinguish whether they are attributing a given quality or activity to Apoe Miyeh or to the ancestors.

Akha believe Apoe Miyeh created the first beings from whom all people descended. According to one myth he called representatives of the various tribal groups to his abode, and gave out 'books' instructing them in his way. The book he gave the Akha was written on the skin of a water buffalo. On the way back to their village the Akha saw several mysterious signs which they attributed to the fact that they were carrying Apoe Miyeh's book. Therefore, they roasted the buffalo skin and ate it. On that day, say the Akha, they lost their book, but they continue to have Apoe Miyeh's wisdom in their stomachs.

Other myths tell of Apoe Miyeh's dealings with the Akha cultural heroes, including instructions he gave them on how to make the ancestral altar and how to perform offerings to the ancestors.

Akha believe that Apoe Miyeh continues to be involved with them to this day. It is by means of his power, for example, that their rice is 'cleansed', thus insuring a good crop. They are

careful not to offend Apoe Miyeh. If a person were to say that a new-born baby is ugly, then Apoe Miyeh would feel they do not appreciate his gift and 'take the baby back'.

Rice steamer

Pounding glutinous rice for rice cakes

Ancestors

An Akha perceives himself as being the link between his ancestors and his progeny. He hopes that after his death his descendants will care for him with offerings as he has done for his ancestors. The place for the ancestral offerings is the ancestral altar (*apoe pawlaw*). It consists either of a section of bamboo tied to a roof support close to the main housepost on the womans' section of the house, or else a small shelf built in the same place. The altar contains the first three heads of rice cut in the previous harvest. A basket containing paraphernalia used for the ancestral offerings is kept beneath the altar.

The offerings 'feed' the ancestors so they in turn will 'feed' or care for the family by providing abundant rice, wealth, good health, and everything else necessary for the continuation of the line. A small chicken and four other items of food and drink are included in each offering. Five small bowls containing these elements are set on an offering table and placed before the ancestral altar. The ancestors are then invited to come and partake.

The man making the offering politely turns his back so the ancestors can 'come down and eat'. Then he calls the family members to come and participate. The one officiating, usually the household head, takes a morsel of each item offered and eats it. Other members of the family are then given a morsel of each offering, which they receive with both hands held together and bring to their mouths to eat. Anyone who has ever killed another person is barred from taking part in the ceremony – indeed is not even supposed to be in the village at the time.

At the completion of the ceremony the one who has made the offering strikes a gong several times. Extra rice cakes might be placed on the mat over the fireplace and later fed to relatives and friends who come to visit during that offering period. Having eaten, they in turn pronounce a blessing on the household.

Each ancestral offering ceremony must begin on a day auspicious for the village priest. A day of the Akha twelve-day week on which any member of the priest's family was born or died is not auspicious.

The most important time for ancestral offerings are New Year, rice planting, the village swing ceremony and rice harvest.

Tying the posts together

Man swinging (U Lo)

Girl swinging (U Lo)

Preparing to swing (U Lo)

Girls swinging (Phami)

Spirits, and the village gate

Although formal aspects of the Akha Way are based primarily on the Akha relationship with the ancestors, in everyday life they are continually concerned about unseen spirit forces (*neh*). According to Akha myth, human beings and these 'spirits' originally lived together in an idyllic relationship. All animals, wild and domesticated, also lived together in perfect harmony. Human beings tilled their fields in the daytime, and spirits tilled theirs at night. Trouble broke out, however, when spirits began to steal chicken eggs from people, and people began stealing cucumbers from spirits. As the conflict grew it was finally decided they should separate – people living in villages and spirits in the jungle. In order to provide a clear demarcation between the human and spirit realms, it was decided that 'village gates' (*law kah*) should be erected at the upper and lower ends of an Akha village.

In compliance with this myth Akha still maintain such village gates. If they follow the ritual requirements fully, they pass through one of the gates each time they enter the village, in order to decontaminate themselves from the spirit powers in the jungle. The gates are sacred, and must not be defiled by anyone, whether villager or outsider. Should someone do so the elders will fine him, since such contamination necessitates a special offering to purify the gates.

The main gate is usually located on the path at the upper part of the village. The primary function of the gate and the wooden figures associated with it is to 'protect the village from hawks and wildcats, leopards and tigers, illness and plague, leprosy and epilepsy, vampires and weretigers, and all other bad and wicked things'.

The village gates are renewed each year under the direction of the village priest. Young men go out, cut timbers, and erect two new posts and a crossbar just beyond the posts erected the previous year. Through time a tunnel of progressively rotting timbers accumulates from the earlier gates leading into the village. Wooden replicas of guns, crossbows, and birds, along with several bamboo taboo signs (*da leh*) are placed on the crossbar of the new gate to prevent spirits from entering. Some Akha have modernized their gates with the addition of miniature airplanes and helicopters. Visitors should not touch these gates or anything related to them. If not planning to enter at least one house, one should not go through the gate or walk through the village, but travel, if possible, on a path which leads around it.

At least one male and one female figure are carved of wood and placed by the main gate each year – the male figure on the upper side of the path, since 'men should not live under women'. Although these figures may have some association with human reproduction, their primary purpose is to indicate that beyond the gate lies the realm of human beings.

U Lo-Akha girls in front of a village gate

U Lo-Akha woman returning from a field ceremony through the village gate

Wooden figures placed by Akha gates

Inside and outside spirits

Akha divide spirits into two main categories: 'inside spirits' (*k'oe neh*), and 'outside spirits' (*nyi neh*). If an Akha is experiencing the effects of 'spirit affliction' (*neh gu la-eu*) he will consult either a 'spirit priest' (*pi ma*) or a shaman (*nyi pa*) who will ascertain which spirit is causing the trouble. If it is an inside spirit, the curing ceremony is held inside the house; if an outside spirit, the ceremony is held outside the house or sometimes beyond the main village gate.

At times both the inside and outside spirits have to be appeased. For example, if a couple has committed adultery the man is fined, and a purification ceremony is held in the woman's house. She has defiled the line, which is a serious matter in a culture stressing the continuity of an unblemished lineage. There must also be ceremonies performed to the outside spirits. Incantations request that '...the channels in Apoe Miyeh's place be repaired'. This is a polite way of asking that she should not be made sterile as the result of her adultery.

There are many types of spirits manifesting themselves in several ways. For example, a powerful spirit lives in swamps and can cause malaria. Each termite hill is believed to have its own spirit. Spirits are present in trees, rocks, and streams. To the Akha these are all animate objects which, when left alone, will cause no harm, but when wronged can bring affliction to the wrongdoer. Akha are especially afraid of two types of spirits: that of a child who died before being named, and that of a woman who died in childbirth. The latter is often thought to appear in the form of a tiger which kills livestock and even people.

Akha feel vulnerable when going into the jungle, because it is the domain of the spirits, but they have developed certain magical means to deal with the spirits on these occasions, such as loudly clearing the throat three times or reciting protective magical formulae. There is one type of spirit which can possess a person. To expel it an elder gently punches the body of the victim with the fang of a wild animal or with a 'lightning bolt' (*tso*), which is actually a Stone Age axe head. Akha believe these 'lightning bolts' have been cast down from the sky, thus have magical powers.

Great powers

The sun and moon, who according to Akha legend are husband and wife, are two great powers. At harvest time Akha 'show' some of the rice to them, and at New Year's, their family wealth. In some of the healing ceremonies they appeal to the sun and moon to 'look down and cure this sick person'.

The *yaw sah* is another power which looms large in the Akha Way. One meaning of this term is 'owner', such as the owner of a pony. Some of this carries over when they speak of *Misah Cusah* ('Lord of Land and Water'). Once a year there is a ceremony to this 'owner/lord'. There are three other great unseen powers in this category. One is in charge of people (*Biyeh*), one of livestock (*Jeyeh*), and the third of rice (*Kayeh*). The *-yeh* in each case is probably related to the final syllable in the name of Apoe Miyeh. These powers are appealed to in various ceremonies.

Wooden 'weapons' used in ceremony to drive spirits out of village, with a 'taboo sign' to prevent their re-entry

Leaders of the Akha Way

Village priest

Each village has a 'village priest' (*dzoe ma*) whose main function is to ensure that the Akha Way is properly followed. 'You cannot have an Akha village without a village priest', is a common saying. Some believe he is next to Apoe Miyeh in importance, and often call him the 'father of the village'.

For their village priest the elders choose a man who is 'ritually pure' (*yaw shaw*). This means he must not have fathered 'human rejects', and has not engaged in conduct contrary to the Akha Way. As he is responsible for the health, welfare, and ceremonial life of the whole village, he must be well versed in the Akha Way. For this reason they prefer a man whose father and grandfather have been village priests before him.

The village priest is not paid for his services, but is granted certain emoluments. He is given a foreleg of every large animal killed in the hunt, for example. Out of respect for his office he is granted precedence on many important occasions.

He is responsible for the sacred sites in his village: the village gate, the swing, the water source, the burial ground, and the altar to the 'Lord of Land and Water'. If there is a crisis affecting a family or the entire village, he is the first to be notified and will take the required action.

The evening before a village ceremony begins, the priest stands on his open porch and calls out to the villagers that they must observe 'ceremonial abstinence' (*lah-eu*), and gives them instructions as to what they must do the next day. He makes an announcement in a similar way when there is a death in the village. In the event of a 'bad death' (*sha shi*), which results from violence away from the village, the priest follows the announcement with instructions for those who will go out to bury the body, for in this case the body will not be brought back.

The priest relates primarily to the great power, Apoe Miyeh, and it is from Apoe Miyeh that he receives his authority. He serves only one village, and everyone must conform to what he, in consultation with the elders, decides is in harmony with the Akha Way.

Blacksmith

The village blacksmith (*ba ji*) ranks second in importance to the village priest. He is the one who forges the sacred knife used by the spirit priest, thus ranks above him. Formerly Akha felt that they could not have a village without at least one blacksmith, because they were dependent on him for tools and sometimes weapons. Each year he makes an offering to the 'Lord' (*yaw sah*) of the bellows to ensure his skill. The villagers give him certain cuts from the spoils of the hunt, and each household donates one day's work a year in his fields. These days many purchase their tools and weapons, so in some villages the position of the blacksmith is largely ceremonial.

Spirit specialists

There are two types of specialists who have learned how to consult with the spirits and to manipulate them to some extent. The first, called *pi ma*, is always male. There is no satisfactory English translation for this term, but because he chants incantations and makes offerings to the spirits, he might be referred to as a 'spirit priest'. When an illness is caused by 'spirit affliction' or 'soul loss', he is asked to repeat spirit incantations, and to call back the wandering soul. When death occurs, the spirit priest recites oral texts by the hour and gives detailed instructions to the departed.

His services are also requested at other times of crisis or special need. For example, a sterile couple may seek his help in begetting children. The family he serves feeds him during the time he is assisting them, and pays him for his work.

For the funeral of an elder it is essential to have a higher-ranked spirit priest (*pi ma*) preside, for only he is qualified to make a buffalo sacrifice. On other occasions a lower-grade spirit priest (*boe maw*) is often adequate.

The second type of specialist, either male or female, is a shaman (*nyi pa*), who is chosen by the spirits and given special powers to communicate with them. The main function of a shaman is that of healing. When called by the family of a sick person, he or she enters into a trance and rides a 'horse' into the 'underworld' where the spirits and ancestors dwell. There the shaman seeks out the soul of the patient and discovers what is happening to it.

Returning from the trance (which always takes place at night), the shaman reports to the family. It may be that the soul was found to have been attacked by vicious spirits. If so the shaman explains what must be done to bring the soul back into the patient, thus ensuring recovery.

Sometimes the shaman informs the family that in the underworld the 'Tree of Life' of the sick person has been cut down and the time of death is near. In such a case the shaman will simply suggest that they 'rest from their exertions'.

Food and money are given for each service. As with the spirit priest, one shaman may serve families in several villages, or there may be more than one in a single village.

Village headman

Although the Akha look to the village priest as their primary leader, they also have a headman (*bu seh*) to meet the requirements of the Thai government. His main duties are to represent the village to government authorities, and to settle disputes of a political nature. In some instances the village priest serves also as the political headman.

Sometimes the duties of the village priest and the headman complement each other. For example, on New Year's Day the village priest is usually asked to throw the dominoes for the first round of gambling, but he leaves soon afterwards because liquor will flow and violent disputes may arise. If trouble develops later, the political headman must arbitrate, for the village priest must not be present when there is potential violence.

Elders

The head of every household normally serves on the village council of elders, although an old man may have his son take his place. The elders choose the village priest and headman, and consult them on village matters.

An Akha myth demonstrates the importance of the elders. When Apoe Miyeh was deciding which positions the sun and moon should take in the heavens, he consulted the first Akha elders, who decided that the sun should be in the east and the moon in the west. When Apoe Miyeh repeated this to the sun and moon they agreed, '. . . because we must do what the people say'. Thus the Akha believe that, 'Even the sun and moon listened to what the elders said'.

During ceremonies there is frequent consultation between the village priest and the elders, as many of them know the rituals as well as the priest. On one occasion we saw village elders laughingly correct the village priest when he made a mistake during the ceremony to the 'Lord of Land and Water'. He accepted their correction – the proper behaviour for even the 'father of the village'.

Rice

Anything related with rice, including its cultivation, preparation and consumption, is given special attention in the Akha Way. To Akha, rice is much more than merely food: it is Life.

Legend of the rice seed

The legend which concerns the receiving of rice seed shows their regard and care for rice. A poor widow, whose only child was a 13 year-old daughter, had to go daily to dig up wild tubers and yams near a large river in order to survive. One day the daughter disappeared and the distraught mother could not find her. Later the mother was digging for food in the same area when she heard her daughter call out from the river, inviting the mother to come and visit her in the water. The daughter had married the Lord Dragon who lived in the river. Having stayed with them for awhile, the mother longed to return home. The Lord Dragon gave her some magical rice seed, specially packaged in a leaf and a hollow reed, promising that if she planted it she would have more than enough to eat and drink.

After she planted the seeds there was such a huge harvest of rice that she was unable to carry all of it home. She returned to ask the Lord Dragon what to do, and he said, 'If there is too much rice, then stand in your field and whistle three times, then clap your hands three times'. When the mother returned to her field and did as her son-in-law directed, the amount of rice diminished and she could carry home in one day all that was left. Akha continue to use the same types of containers for their ceremonial rice seed as the Lord Dragon used, and never clap their hands or whistle while in a rice field!

In common with certain other Southeast Asian groups, Akha believe the rice crop has a soul. While the rice is growing they are careful not to do anything which might cause its soul to leave, for if that should happen it would be necessary to have a ceremony to call it back. While fanning the newly harvested rice they call out, 'Jeu, jeu', which means, 'Increase, increase!' When they carry it home they are extremely careful not to let any of it fall into a river or stream. For they say, 'If the Lord Dragon sees some of our rice drop into the water, he will think we have more rice than we need, and will make it decrease'.

Choosing a rice field

Akha choose a site for a rice field in an area which does not 'see' (or face) a burial place, as that would frighten the soul of the rice causing it to flee. When a potential site has been chosen and marked off, the farmer waits for a sign to indicate whether or not it is auspicious. If during that time he should dream of a Lahu or a Tai, or if he were to see a barking deer or wild pig jump up and run away from the chosen site, he would abandon it and look for another.

Clearing and burning the field

If there are no bad omens, the farmer proceeds to clear the field. The first tree must be felled on an auspicious day. If it somersaults or if any of its branches stick into mud, the farmer would believe the spirits were telling him that the tract is inauspicious, and he must search for an acceptable spot.

After the fields have been cleared, the village elders must choose the day on which to burn them, for adjacent fields must be burned on the same day. They will not set the fire on 'Tiger Day', for then the field would burn in strips like a tiger's stripes. 'Monkey Day' and 'Pig Day' are good, however, because on 'Monkey Day' the fire would jump around, burning everywhere, and on 'Pig Day' the fire would root around like a pig.

Purifying and planting the seed

The day before Akha start planting their rice they make an ancestral offering. As preparation for it, the village priest leads the men in tidying up the village water source, and in putting in a new bamboo spout. After meat and drink offerings have been made to the water source, a container with the first rice seeds to be planted that day is placed under the spout so the water will run over it. Apoe Miyeh is then asked to 'let the waters carry away the bad, and let the good return. Receive this offering of a rooster and a hen, and make the water spout pure (*yaw shaw*), we beseech you!'

Later that day the village priest (or one whom he designates) takes the purified seed to his field. Before planting, a simple little structure of sticks and thatch grass (*k'm pi*) is set up in the centre of the field to serve as a shrine for the soul of the rice while it is growing. Then the first seeds are planted in nine holes made above the rice shrine. (Three is special to the Akha, and nine is three times three.) Other villagers are then free to plant their fields on their own auspicious days.

Care for rice

Three cycles of days (36) after planting, a representative from each household digs up a white grub from his rice field. They then meet at the edge of one field, wrap the grubs tightly in leaves and force them into slits made at the top of bamboo stakes driven into the ground. They call out, 'You who ate the roots before, now try eating the leaves!' After the annual swing ceremony, grasshoppers are caught and a similar ritual is performed, with the admonition, 'You who ate the leaves before, now try eating the roots!' By means of this symbolic procedure they hope to rid their fields of these pests.

If anything offends the soul of the rice while growing, there must be a ceremony to ensure that it will remain and the crop will be good. For example, if a landslide carries away part of the field and leaves a scar of fresh earth, a pig must be killed and incantations made to the spirits.

Harvest

The village priest is the first to begin harvesting. He plucks three heads of rice from that which was first planted above the field shrine to put in his ancestral altar. Three heads are then cut and offered to the field shrine as thanks for protecting the crop. More is then gathered and taken home to be eaten in a 'new rice offering ceremony'. Each family is then free to harvest its rice.

Planting rice in mountain field

Ritual singing calls for God's blessing on the crop

First ritual planting of rice in nine holes near 'shrine'.in
the family field

Courtship and Marriage

Choice

Young people are free to choose their own partners, although the parents must give their permission before the marriage ceremony can take place. The traditional pattern is for a young man to marry a girl from a village other than his own, so during the season between the Akha New Year and rice planting, young men travel around in groups of two or more from village to village looking for wives. Their mothers will have made beautiful jackets and shoulder bags for them, and they will wear silver ornaments in their carefully-wrapped turbans. Silver neck rings, bracelets and chains are added to properly impress the girls, who more than match the boys with their own elaborate attire. The young men stay with friends or relatives in those villages, often working with their hosts in the daytime, which enables them to see the girls in their normal routine.

Courting

After the evening meal the young people often gather at the 'village courting ground' (*deh k'ah*). By the light of a fire, the girls sing and dance as the boys look on. The boys in turn dance to the tune of their gourd pipes and sing courting songs. Benches are conveniently located on two or three sides of the dancing area, and a boy may sit with a girl he fancies and talk to her. Some couples later slip out into the jungle where they spend the night.

Arrangement

Once a young man has chosen the girl he wishes to marry and she has consented, he speaks to his father or an older brother about his intentions. The latter visits the girl's father to arrange the marriage, and he in turn ascertains through some female intermediary how his daughter feels about the matter. As it is expected of a girl to be coy, she generally sends word to her father that she does not want to marry the boy, despite the fact that she has already told the boy she will marry him. When she ultimately consents, the two fathers drink liquor together to seal the agreement. Each of them puts up an agreed amount of money, preferably in silver rupees, which is held by a neutral party to ensure that each side will honour the agreement. If one side backs out, that father loses his bond. If the young people marry as arranged, or if both parties agree to cancel the engagement, each side takes back its money.

A girl must be at least in her 13th year (that is, one full cycle) before she can marry. But Akha proverbs assert that she should be 17 or more. From data we have gathered, it appears that the average age of Akha girls at marriage is 17 (with a range of 13–24), and the boys one year older.

Wedding

After arrangements have been completed and the groom's family has collected sufficient food and drink needed for the wedding feast, the groom and his friends escort the girl to his village, where she will stay overnight with one of his relatives. The festivities begin the next afternoon when she is taken to the groom's house by one of his older male relatives, together with the ritual director of the wedding – usually an elderly woman. Before entering the house, the bride changes into a white skirt which she wears throughout the ceremony. Her headdress is removed and handed, together with her black skirt, to a younger girl who serves as her helper.

Next a lock of the bride's hair is cut off, and she catches it by holding out the bottom of her jacket.

A rain hat is placed on her head, and she proceeds to the house through the men's entrance. As she ascends the steps, an elder beats three times with a long bamboo pole on the thatched roof above her, calling 'Cho! Cho! Cho!' As the bride reaches the top of the steps, she drops the hair clippings she had caught in her jacket, symbolizing that she is cutting off relationships with her clan and entering the clan of her husband.

The couple take their seats on low stools by the fireplace in the woman's section, and an egg is boiled for them. Under the guidance of the ritual director they pass the egg back and forth three times, after which the director feeds it to them. A small chicken is then cooked. After they have eaten it they are considered to be 'joined' as man and wife.

Feast and blessings

The wedding feast, an integral part of the ceremony, lasts for two days, for which at least one pig is butchered. Male guests eat in the men's section and female guests in the women's section of the house. During the feasting young people take soot from the bottom of the cooking pots and wipe it on the faces of the bride, the groom, and some of the guests. This is thought to bring 'good luck' (*gui lah*) to those receiving it.

After the feast the couple sits in the women's section of the house, directly under the ancestral altar. One or more elders, standing on the men's side of the partition, call down blessings on the couple and chant long, detailed instructions regarding marriage and the Akha Way. While chanting, they throw cooked rice over the partition onto the couple, symbolizing the blessings of good health, long life, bountiful rice harvests, plenty of livestock, and many children (phrased as 'five boys and five girls'). Meanwhile the ritual director occasionally throws rice over the partition into the men's section.

The village elders are honoured in special ways. For instance, the groom takes a cup of liquor and lifts it to the lips of each elder in turn as a gesture of respect and gratitude. Each elder then pronounces a blessing on the couple. After the celebrations some pork is ceremonially carried to the home of the ritual director as a thank-you.

Little house

Following the marriage a small house is built for the couple near the house of the groom's parents. They sleep there, but eat with the rest of the family. The bride has now joined her husband's household, and participates in their ancestral offerings. She retains close emotional ties with her own family and is permitted to visit her parents' home, but in the eyes of the Akha, she now belongs to her husband and his clan. As a married woman her main function is to produce children, especially one or more sons, to continue her husband's lineage.

Divorce

Among young couples divorce is rather common, but rare later in life. If the woman commits adultery, it is felt that her husband's line has been defiled. For this reason, such conduct almost automatically results in the dissolution of the marriage, with nothing going to the woman except for the clothes she is wearing. The children remain with the father. The man who wronged her is fined, and may be forced to marry her.

If the wife appears to be sterile, the husband may 'send her away' (divorce her). The desire for continuity of the line is so strong that he will soon remarry. If a wife gives birth to only girls, or if all of her children die in infancy, it may be felt that the marriage is not 'correct', and a divorce often ensues. However, a man may take a minor wife instead of resorting to divorce.

The wife may initiate a divorce simply by running away. This often happens in cases where the husband beats her excessively or is an opium addict. According to the Akha Way she must not leave him when she is pregnant (one Akha word for pregnancy is to be 'under her husband'), but must wait until after the child is born. If she leaves, the children belong to the husband. There are certain exceptional cases where she may be allowed to keep a daughter or two, but only with her husband's permission.

If a husband divorces his wife for reasons other than adultery, and there are children, he must pay certain fines, which are worked out by the elders, often with a great deal of acrimony. Divorced people are in a 'taboo relationship'. They must never speak to each other again. In the event of remarriage the estranged husband or wife should have nothing to do with the new partner of the former spouse.

An egg is boiled for the couple

The future of their marriage is read in the pig's liver

Throwing of rice accompanies the elder's blessing on the couple

Young people gleefully throw mud and dung on couple to initiate them into married life

Birth

It is considered 'good luck' when an Akha wife becomes pregnant. During her pregnancy the couple observes certain taboos to ensure a good birth. Nothing must be done which might focus on her the type of power inherent in such leaders as the village priest, blacksmith, and spirit priest, because that might cause her to miscarry or have an abnormal child.

Delivery

A woman prefers to deliver her child in her own home where her mother-in-law or some other older woman who has had children and understands the birth practices will assist her. However, pregnant women are encouraged to work right up to the time of delivery, so babies are sometimes born in the fields.

The new-born must not be picked up until it has cried three times. These cries are to Apoe Miyeh, begging him for a blessing, a soul, and a long life. Then the midwife picks up the baby and gives it a temporary name, so the spirits will not be tempted to assume the child is unwanted and they can lay claim to it. The naming ceremony takes place later when it is evident that the baby is healthy and will survive.

Naming

A ceremony is held when the child's formal name, which is linked to its father's, is given by an elder. If the father is named *Byeu Seh*, the first syllable of the child's name is *Seh*, and then a new second syllable is given. Thus, *Byeu Seh*'s children might be named *Seh Tah, Seh Peu,* and *Seh Shaw.* Then when they become parents, their children are given names according to the same pattern. This method of naming helps the Akha remember their genealogy. The formal name is not used in daily life, because it has almost a magical significance. It may be changed later if another name is thought to promote better health or good fortune.

Difficult and unusual births

If a birth is difficult, ritual means may be used to facilitate delivery. Akha are particularly worried about the danger that a woman may die in childbirth, as it is considered a type of 'bad death', which necessitates laborious, expensive ceremonies to prevent the deceased woman from causing trouble to the living.

Certain infants are viewed as 'human rejects' (*tsaw caw*). These include twins, or children with an extra thumb or finger, or a child with some body part missing or deformed. Such a birth disrupts the proper order of the cosmos, and is a tragedy for the Akha village as a whole, especially for the household in which it occurs. It is considered to be a judgement of the 'great powers' on the couple for some infringement of the Akha Way. The 'human rejects' must be quickly suffocated, and then buried in a remote spot in the forest. Elaborate purification ceremonies for the couple and the whole village must be held, because such a birth is a threat to the Akha lineage.

Death

Akha see death as a transition from the land of the living to the land of the ancestors. If handled according to the Akha Way, its threat to the living can be overcome, and the continuity of the lineage assured.

Immediately after death the body is washed by the family, and special clothes prepared in advance are put on. Slivers of silver are placed in the mouth, and the deceased is instructed to use it to buy whatever is needed. The body is wrapped in a black shroud and covered with a red cloth. The genealogy of the one who died is recited, preferably by a son, but if he does not know it, by the village priest. This is the first time the dead person's name is included in the recitation of the genealogy. A wake is held each night until the burial, with friends and neighbours coming in for the vigil. At the wake there is gambling, wailing, singing, and the performance of ceremonies having to do with the dead.

Coffin

A large healthy tree is selected from which to make the coffin. It is hewn out of the log in two sections. The bottom is rounded and resembles the hull of a boat. 'Wings' and 'noses' are fashioned into the lid by meticulously hacking the log with sharp axes. Care is taken to make sure the lid fits properly and the coffin sits securely on a specially fitted stand. On completion of the coffin, while it is still outside the house, a member of each household 'washes' the coffin with liquor, then pounds tufts of cotton into both the main section and the lid, to 'keep the person warm'.

After the coffin has been brought into the house and the body placed in it, family members 'wipe the tears away' by brushing the eyes of the deceased with tufts of cotton. Several sets of clothing are laid on the body, the shroud and red cloth replaced, and the lid is put on. The coffin is then bound together tightly and carefully sealed. It is kept in the house while relatives and friends of the deceased are notified, and the family acquires the sacrifices and food needed for the funeral. In most instances the burial takes place within a few days; however, sometimes it may be delayed for months.

Shrouded body in house (men's side)

Making the coffin

Ceremonial feeding of the dead person

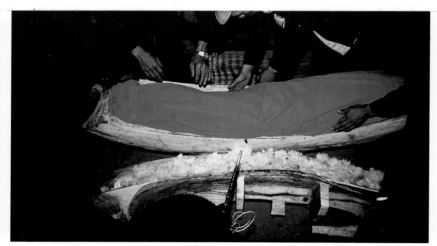

Placing body in coffin

Funeral

A spirit priest is called to take charge of the death ceremonies, which are performed in and near the house before the burial. He chants the Akha death rites for three nights and two days. There must be no mistakes. Careful instructions are given to the deceased regarding which path to take. 'Don't take the upper path, and don't take the lower path – they lead to bad death. Take the middle path, it leads to the land of the ancestors'.

When an important elder dies, one or more water buffaloes are sacrificed. The spirit priest (only a *pi ma* in this case) calls on the spirit helpers and the deceased to aid him in stabbing the buffalo in the proper way. Young men pour water down the buffalo's throat the moment it is stabbed, so it will not moan in death. Its head is then covered with paddy.

Burial

Young men carry the coffin out of the house slung from two long poles (one pole for a child) and take it to the village burial grounds. A grave will have been dug in an east-west orientation the day before. As the body is carried out of the house, some thatch grass is pulled out of the roof and stuck under the cords which bind the two sections of the coffin together. This act symbolically divides the house with the deceased, giving him his share. Later a small section of the rice field is set aside so that the deceased can continue to grow rice.

Certain rites are performed in the graveyard to ensure that the deceased will be able to hear in the world of the ancestors, and weretigers will not be able to dig up the body. A few of the deceased's personal items are left on the grave, such as a tobacco pipe, a tea cup, a water gourd, and appropriate tools, according to whether it was a man or woman. A new shoulder bag containing specially prepared parcels of food is hung on a forked stick at the head of the grave.

There is a 'meal of separation' in the home of the deceased after the burial. This shows the one who died that there is now an unbreachable barrier between the dead and living, and that he or she must not come back to bother the family. A year later however, there is another ceremony at which the family invites this same ancestor back to watch over the household.

Spirit priest commits the sacrificial buffalo to the deceased   Spirit priest repeats incantations before stabbing buffalo

Spirit priest directs soul of the deceased to the land of the ancestors

Spirit priest stabs buffalo

Woman pours paddy over buffalo's head

Coffin is carried out of village

Belongings of the deceased are left on the grave

Girls massage spirit priest and helper

Representative of the mother's brother's side

A death song is sung while following lines on a board

Gambling helps to pass the time during the wake

Bad death

Certain types of death are considered to be 'bad deaths' (*sha shi*). In some cases a special purification ceremony for the body must be held before it can be buried in the village graveyard. But there are three types of 'bad death' which are so serious that the corpse must be buried at the site of death: being killed by a leopard or tiger, death by drowning, or death from smallpox. A dog must be buried over the body to prevent the deceased from calling out later.

When a man dies leaving no male heir (*shm byeh*) certain alterations are made in the funeral ceremony, such as taking the body out of the house through a hole in the wall. As there is now no one to take over the ancestral altar, it must be taken out and thrown into a jungle thicket at the time of burial. The one who throws it away tells the man's ancestors, 'Since you did not take care of this descendent of yours, there will be no one to feed you now!' This illustrates how deeply the concept of continuity permeates Akha thought.

It is generally taboo to talk about death in polite conversation at times other than when there is a death. Certain things are done at the time of death which must not be done at any other time. Akha believe when a person is about to die, he can sometimes be brought back to life by someone beating on a piece of metal near him, whistling in the room, or having his spouse call his formal name. Because these acts are all associated with death, they are not permissable at any other time.

Sickness and Treatment

Akha believe that by diligently following the Akha Way they will maintain good health and have good luck in life. The fact that virtually none of them suffer from leprosy is attributed to this.

Some sicknesses are due to the breaking of taboos having to do with the ancestors. For example, in an Akha village in 1979 ten people died in a short space of time. The villagers concluded that when the first one was buried, his body was placed in the wrong direction, resulting in the death of the other nine.

Illness may be caused by 'spirit affliction' (*neh gu la-eu*). A friend of ours had a severe pain in his shoulder. He was told by a shaman that he had wronged the spirit of a tree by piling his firewood against it. After he pulled down the firewood, he gradually lost his pain.

It may be 'soul loss' (*la ba ba-eu*) that makes a person feel run down and ill. To treat this illness the soul must be called back. An elder leads this ritual, performing ceremonies both inside the house of the patient and outside the village gate. He entices the soul of the sick person in poetic language, begging it to leave the land of darkness and gloom and return to the light and joy of his home. The elder then returns to the home of the patient. Before going up the steps he asks, 'Has the soul returned yet?' Those inside invariably call back, 'Yes, it came running back just a moment ago'. Cotton strings are then tied around the wrists of the sick person to ensure that his soul will not leave his body again.

Akha realise that certain diseases run in families, and conclude that they are inherited. These include tuberculosis, epilepsy, and mental illness. Young men and women belonging to such families often have difficulty finding a partner.

Akha recognize certain symptoms as a sign that the spirits are calling a person to become a shaman. He or she feels ill and is unable to sleep at night, being driven instead to repeat the chants ordinarily used by shamans in a trance. This person cannot eat the same food as others, and has many symptoms which might be diagnosed in the west as psychosomatic. Akha believe the person will become insane if the call is refused. If on the other hand the summons is obeyed, the symptoms gradually disappear.

Not all illnesses are attributed to supernatural forces. Injuries from accidents, such as being struck by an axe, are generally considered to have purely a physical cause and will be treated by herbalists or Western medicine. On the other hand, being struck by a falling branch during a storm may be thought to have been caused by an offended spirit. In such a case, a combination of medicinal and ritual treatment is often used. For ritual cures they may employ bones from animals killed by lightning, or Stone Age axe heads, believed to be 'lightning bolts'.

Ceremonies are sometimes held to protect a whole village from sickness. In one instance, a person who had been jailed for some time returned to his village. Before he was allowed to enter, he had to undergo a ceremony to ensure that he would not bring sickness and bad luck with him. A fire was built on the path just outside the village gate. He was required to step over this fire, and then without looking back, to scrape three lines on the path behind him with a machete, cutting off the potential danger of bringing ill fortune into the village.

Conclusion

When one considers how the unity and integrity of Akha culture has survived, in spite of the hardships and obstacles encountered in their sojourn in five different countries, one can only marvel at their resilience.

As the 20th Century draws to a close, however, the Akha in Thailand are a people in distress. Throughout their history they have found ways to meet every threat to their Akha Way, but the depth and complexity of problems now facing them seem overwhelming.

When we enter Akha homes and see the jaws of animals killed in the hunt hanging in the men's section of the house, we notice there are no fresh ones – the game is no longer there. As we look out at their fields, we observe they are farther and farther from the village. As we witness their daily struggle with economic and political impoverishment, we see more and more of them turning to the comfort of the opium pipe.

Akha often admonish their children to 'Listen to the customs with both ears and obey. Look at the embroidery pattern with both eyes and imitate'. This proverb instructs the young people to follow faithfully the Akha Way. The youth, however, seem to reply, 'The customs were fine for your generation, and the embroidery patterns possible for you to imitate, but how can we follow the ancient Akha Way in today's world?'

Phami-Akha girls dancing and singing

Loimi-Akha women and child

U Lo-Akha women and girls rythmically pounding bamboo sections on overturned pig trough to honour village leaders during swing ceremony

Akha men (note head coverings)

Lisu girl winnowing rice

Chapter 8

LISU (Lisaw)

Lisu young people in New Year garb

Desire for Primacy

Waw Vu was sitting just outside the door of his large house, partly to get away from the commotion going on inside, but also to be able to look out over the village and see what was happening. Perhaps his friend Alepha would join him and they could sit and smoke their homegrown tobacco in their water pipes.

It was an exciting time for Waw Vu's household. He had a son and a daughter both anxious to get married after the New Year celebration.

His wife came and stood in the doorway. 'We need more money to purchase silver for our daughter's New Year outfit'. Reading her husband's thoughts she quickly continued, 'Oh, I know we bought some last month. It wasn't enough. You have never seen such outfits as other girls in the village are making for New Year!' When it came to keeping ahead of the neighbours Waw Vu (as his wife well knew) was second to none.

'Oh, all right, if it's really necessary, go ahead and buy it', he said. Waw Vu could not forget how embarrassed he had been as a young man by his family's poverty. His father had been injured in a hunting accident when Waw Vu was a small boy. As well as having to pay for numerous ceremonies and medical treatments, his father could not work as he had before his injury, so Waw Vu and his brothers and sisters had little silver on their New Year's outfits. Waw Vu had determined then that when he had his own family he would never let anyone outdo him.

'Father, what do you think?' His son came outside showing off the new 'courting bag' his sister had just finished for him. Waw Vu looked at the fine embroidery, the intricate beadwork, and the jingling silver dangles. He thought with pride, 'That is the most beautiful bag I have ever seen'. To his son he said, 'You should be able to bring us a wonderful daughter-in-law with a bag like that!' 'Only the best', the son replied, and went back into the house.

Two girls approached the house chattering and giggling. Each carried her New Year's tunic, wanting to show it off to Waw Vu's daughter. They found her sewing more tassels for the tail of her sash. 'But yesterday you said you didn't need any more', they said in surprise. 'Yes, but yesterday I didn't know that Aluma had more than I did!' Her friends understood at once; a Lisu always wants to be first.

Name and Language

This tribal group calls itself 'Lisu' (both syllables spoken on a mid tone), but is called 'Lisaw' by the Tai. The name has no known meaning.

The Lisu language is in the Yi (Lolo) branch of the Tibeto-Burman family. Only one dialect of Lisu is spoken in Thailand. Much of the vocabulary, some estimate about 30%, has been borrowed from Yunnanese.

Legend

Together with other Southeast Asian groups, the Lisu have a legend about a great flood. The only two survivors were a boy and his younger sister who were saved by riding out the flood in a large gourd. On finding they were the last human beings left in the world, they knew that they were the only hope for the future of mankind. However, they believed an incestuous relationship would be wrong, so they looked for signs indicating whether they should marry or not. First they separated the two stones of a grain mill and rolled them down opposite sides of a mountain. When the stones reached the bottom they kept on rolling around the mountain until they came together. Other tests were made with similar results, convincing the brother and sister that it was proper for them to marry. Their union produced many children who paired up and became the progenitors of all the different tribes. As they were one girl short the Akha man had no wife, so he went into the jungle and married a monkey, according to the legend.

Migration

Lisu believe they originated near the headwaters of the Salween River. Their migrational patterns over the centuries strengthen this hypothesis, as they have tended to follow south along the Salween's general course.

It is difficult to determine when Lisu first migrated into Thailand. We have met elderly Lisu who say they lived in the Fang area by 1905. Hope (from whom much of the Lisu data are taken) has established the date for the arrival of the first four Lisu families in the Doi Chang area as 1921, and 15 more families joined them the following year (Hope 1970:1). All Lisu migrations into Thailand have been from Burma.

Population

In mid-1983 there were approximately 18,000 Lisu living in some 110 villages in Thailand. The 1958 population was about 7,500, an annual increase of almost 3.6% over that 25-year period. Most of this was by natural growth, as immigration of Lisu during that time was minimal.

In mid-1983 the Lisu population in Burma was around 250,000, and in China about 500,000. There are several hundred Lisu households in Northeast India, but none in Laos or Vietnam.

Almost half the Lisu in Thailand (47%) live in Chiang Mai Province; 23% in Chiang Rai; 19% in Mae Hong Son; and 11% scattered in Phayao, Tak, Kamphaeng Phet, Phetchabun, and Sukhothai provinces.

Lisu in Thailand tend to be quite different from those in northern Burma. This is partly due to their isolation from the main population further north for several generations. Moreover, the Thai Lisu have inter-married with Yunnanese over a considerable period, and often refer to themselves as 'Chinese-Lisu'.

Lisu woman's outfit from Burma

Clothing and Ornamentation

Nowhere is the determination to be 'number one' more evident than in Lisu clothing. The coloured strips on the yokes and sleeves of the young women's tunics; the multiplication of strands in the long tassels that hang from their sashes; and the massive amounts of silver with which they adorn themselves are vivid symbols of their consuming desire to outdo one another.

Lisu style of dress, particularly for women, has changed dramatically through the generations. Originally they made their clothing of hand-woven hemp cloth, and indeed Lisu women in the northern tip of Burma and probably many in China still wear heavily-pleated skirts of that material. Various styles of Lisu clothing are to be found in Burma, all differing from that worn in Thailand.

The Thai Lisu woman's outfit is from machine-made cotton or synthetic material. A blue or green tunic, split up the sides to the waist, is knee-length in front, and hangs to mid-calf in back. It crosses over the chest, and fastens under the right arm. The piece across the chest is often made of a different colour from the rest. For instance, if the tunic is basically royal blue, that part might be done in green or light blue.

The yoke of the tunic is made of black cloth cut in a circle. To this bands of cloth in many bright colours are stitched, a pattern repeated in the upper sleeves. The lower sleeves are always red. Older women use wider bands and not so many of them, but the young women vie with each other to see which one can sew the most narrow strips onto her yoke and sleeves.

Women wear knee-length black Chinese-style pants and red leggings trimmed with blue cloth, embroidered with other colours. A wide black sash about six metres long is wound tightly around the waist over the tunic. Looped over the sash in the back is a spectacular pair of tassels, made of tightly rolled multi-coloured strips of cloth about 50 cm in length, sewn with hundreds of delicate stitches in a constrasting colour. At the ends of these rolls of cloth are small pompons of multi-coloured wool yarn. Formerly there were only 25 to 30 strands per side, but the competitive young women have added more and more; today it is common to find clusters of 100 or even as many as 250 per side, totalling 500 strands in a pair of tassels.

A black turban is worn by young girls and women, mainly for festive occasions. A young woman takes black cloth folded to a width of three to four cm, and after measuring the exact size of her head, tightly wraps the strips around her bent knee, layer upon layer, into a neat reel of cloth. After tying it firmly together in four places, she wraps a wider strip of good-quality black cloth (sometimes velvet) which crosses over and under the reel, and is stitched carefully in place. To this turban she attaches long strands of multi-coloured yarn which she wraps over one side, under the front of the turban, and back over the other side. The portion passing across the front of the turban is strung with glass beads, and embellished with pompons. An embroidered red triangle to which masses of yarn are attached hangs from the back of the turban. The yarn is spread out over the back of the head and hangs to the shoulders. Older women wear unembellished black turbans, loosely wrapped.

Lisu woman plying thread for weaving

Girls dressing up for New Year dancing

Binding a turban and dressing up for New Year

Young woman's outfit

Older woman's outfit

Old style women's outfits and turban (note aprons)

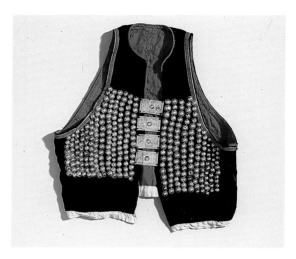

Young woman's velvet vest adorned with silver

Young Lisu woman's turban for festive occasions
(Front and back view and two details)

At New Year the young women bedeck themselves with massive amounts of silver jewellery. They wear waist-long black velvet vests over their tunics with many silver buttons sewn on, closed in front with a row of rectangular or round silver buckles. A cloth collar with silver buttons and dangles attached is worn around the neck. Silver neck rings and necklaces are also worn, falling in tiers down the woman's chest. She wears silver hook-shaped or dangle earrings through her pierced ears, to which wool tassels are attached. A silver chain of several strands hangs from one earring to the other passing under her chin. Wide bracelets with beveled edges are worn on both wrists, and silver rings on her fingers.

Lisu girls in their New Year finery

The man's outfit consists of a black jacket, blue or green pants, and black leggings. Elderly men usually wear black pants. White-lined black velvet jackets, worn for dress occasions, have many silver buttons stitched to them, the ideal being 1,000. A red sash is tied around the waist, and on festive occasions tassels similar to those of the young women are looped over the sash in front.

At New Year men have traditionally worn turbans made of red, blue, yellow, and black silk cloth. These are now seldom seen, instead a white turkish towel folded around a piece of cardboard standing about 20 cm high serves this purpose.

Men wear a single silver earring in their pierced left ear and a plain round silver bracelet on each wrist.

Man's outfit

Lisu man's traditional New Year's silk turban

Young Lisu man's outfit for festive occasions

Lisu young man's jacket adorned with silver
(back and front views)

Shoulder bags are woven of white or unbleached cotton thread on back-strap looms, and have vertical stripes of red and other colours. Work bags, of a coarse weave and unembellished, are frequently attached to a woven rattan strap which is worn across the forehead. Bags of fine cotton thread are used for dress, with red 'ears' attached to the bottom corners. These 'ears' are squares of cloth delicately embroidered, the patterns differing widely as they represent the 'signature' of the maker. Often a small silver button is attached to each corner of the 'ear'. Narrow banding of coloured cloth is added to the top of the bag to a width of three to four cm. Strips of torn red and blue cloth hang from the lower corners, while strands of coloured yarn may dangle from the seams.

The most elaborate shoulder bag used by the Lisu – or any other tribe, for that matter – is the young man's 'courting bag'. It is made like the bags described above, but the face of it is covered with a network of tiny multi-coloured beads. Hanging from the 'ears' are wide richly-embroidered strips of cloth about 20 cm long. Yarn of many colours hangs from the bottom and an array of silver buttons and dangles are attached across the top.

Children's clothing is similar to that of the adults, except that boys to the age of three or four wear triangular-shaped rompers which tie around the neck. Snug-fitting caps adorned with exquisite bands of patch-work are made for babies and small children by their mothers.

Work bag with rattan strap

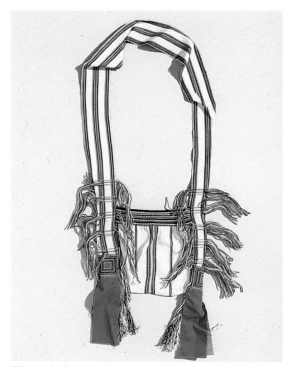

Woman's shoulder bag

Burmese Lisu style shoulder bag

Man's shoulder bag

Young man's courting bag

Girl's outfit

Rompers for small boy

Villages

Lisu like to plant rice at an elevation of about 1,000 metres, and opium at about 1,600 metres. Thus, those who are still opium cultivators like to live about halfway between these elevations.

One of the big considerations in locating a village site is an adequate water supply for daily needs, but Lisu are concerned about the mystical power residing in water. The setting they like most is one where they can live on one side of a ridge, with a stream on the other. This makes it possible to bring water around the ridge into the village by means of bamboo aqueducts, without exposing themselves unduly to this mystical power. They are also anxious to live in an area with plenty of *lu khwa*, a type of ragweed, for this is used in many of their ceremonies.

Lisu try to locate their villages where they can have political independence and freedom from harassment. At the same time they want to be near Northern Thai villages where they can purchase rice when their crop is not adequate, and to Karen and Lahu villages, where cheap labour is available. They like to have other Lisu villages in the area for security and companionship, and they do not want to be too far away from the Yunnanese who will buy their opium.

Having considered the political, social, and physical aspects of a site for a new village, an advance party performs a divining ceremony to make sure it is 'clean from disease and evil influence'. They use a star-shaped arrangement of rice grains, as is done by other tribes, and in the centre insert a blade of grass to represent a tree, an important theme in their culture.

Lisu tend to move their villages often due to social, economic, political and religious factors; pressure to find adequate land for opium cultivation; emergence of competing factions in a village which has grown quite large; and dissatisfaction with the political headman.

Lisu village scenes

Lisu men set gun trap

Going hunting

Making rice cakes for the New Year festival

Lisu woman collecting herbs

Guardian spirit shrine

Every Lisu village must have a 'village guardian spirit shrine' (*Apa mu hi*) above the village. The guardian spirit (*Apa mu* – literally 'Old Grandfather') inhabiting this shrine protects the village by keeping out bad influences, robbers, evil spirits, drought, and disease. If villagers violate Lisu customs, such as disobeying the village priest or committing sexual sins, they believe the guardian spirit will take some kind of revenge. This roofed shrine is located in a fenced area above the village, and is built underneath a leafy tree. On a shelf in the shrine are kept four small rice bowls containing water, one for each point of the compass. In addition there is a bowl of water for each clan represented in the village.

In this sacred compound, which females cannot enter, are two other less elaborate altars – to the 'Lord of the Land' (*Mi suh da ma*) and the ruler of the area (*Ida ma*). In some cases there is another altar below the shrine to *Xwa suh*, who is the brother of the guardian spirit.

Communal worship of the guardian spirit helps to bind the village together. There are many annual offerings at this shrine, as well as special offerings for the purification of the village whenever the priest decides they are needed. Individual families also feel a responsibility to the guardian spirit, and derive some protection from him. A new family moving into a village makes an offering to *Apa mu* to announce their arrival, and to ask for his protection. A family moving away also makes an offering to the guardian spirit, explaining their departure, and requesting his blessing. A special ceremony is conducted to obtain his blessing when a child is born – also for a colt or a litter of pigs. Meat is offered to him from the first pig in a litter to be butchered.

Village guardian spirit shrine

Lisu house plan

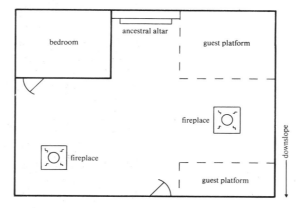

House construction

The ridge-pole of a house follows the contour of the hillside. The only door is always made in the middle of the lower side, opposite the 'ancestral altar' (*ta bya*). This places the altar on the uphill side of the house, so it is 'above the people'. At ceremonial feasts the most respected elders sit nearest the altar, while the younger men sit nearer the door. No house in the village may be built directly in front of another, as that would obstruct the unseen 'spirit path' that goes through the door to the altar. Lisu tend to build their houses far enough apart so that if one should burn, the fire would not spread to other houses.

There are two types of houses: 'ground houses' (*micha hi*), with packed earth for the floor; and 'elevated houses' (*kacha hi*) built on posts. Houses built on the ground are more popular at higher elevations, as they are warmer. In both types the main bedroom is on the uphill side, next to the ancestral altar. The other bedrooms (if any) and guest areas are constructed according to need and available space. In some clans the fireplace must not come between the door and the ancestral altar.

The size of the house depends on the number of people living in it. Small children sleep with their parents in the main bedroom. Children from the age of about 10 to puberty sleep on the guest platforms, girls on one and boys on the other. When there are guests the girls go to the house of a relative to sleep. Girls who have reached puberty are given a bedroom of their own. A married son living with his parents has a separate bedroom for his family.

Lisu welcome guests into the main room of the house, and look after their needs. They expect the guests to stay out of the bedrooms, not to interfere with the ancestral altar, and not to sleep with their heads toward the fire, which is sacred.

The first fire in a new house must be started by an older person (the older the better). It should be someone who has parented at least one child.

When the altar is installed, the ancestral spirits are asked to take up residence. Two cocks and a hen are sacrificed, and meat from them, some cooked and some raw, is placed on the altar. During special ceremonies the ancestral spirits residing in the altar are addressed by the terms, 'You who rule the gold, you who rule the silver', for it is through their blessing that the household can gain wealth.

Headman

The Lisu political headman (*xwa thu pha*) should be a person who has a 'good heart and good mind'. When the elders choose him, they kill a pig or chicken and have a feast. They pray that he will have a long life and be taken care of 'seven times a day by the sun, and nine times a night by the moon', their poetic couplet signifying 'forever'. They also pray that the people not separate, and that more people will move into their village. At the end of the ceremony they tie a string around his neck to ensure good health, and to keep his soul from leaving him, being overwhelmed by all this attention.

Lisu want their headman to be more of an arbiter and judge than a ruler. For example, if one person's pigs get into another person's field and eat some rice, the aggrieved man complains to the headman, who then sets a time when both sides, with their friends and any witnesses, should meet at his house. Each faction tells its version of the incident, and the headman decides what should be done. The spirit of competition is so volatile in Lisu society that serious arguments are likely to ensue. The headman may appeal to the elders, who almost automatically align themselves according to clan and family, thus the side with the most clansmen nearly always 'wins' the case.

At the conclusion of the discussion, the headman exacts a fine, which may simply be to donate a bottle of liquor to be enjoyed by participants. In the case of a monetary fine the headman takes a share, and the balance goes to the wronged party. Often the defendant refuses to pay the fine, and the case continues unresolved. The headman must attempt to gain the cooperation of all concerned, because failing to do so might result in disgruntled villagers moving out. It has been reported that headmen have been killed by parties losing a case, for Lisu are determined to be winners.

Making liquor

Maize being prepared for liquor making

Cooking a meal

Clan and Family

Kinship is based on a system of patrilineal clans. Six of them are traditionally Lisu, and have Lisu names: 'Honey' (*Bya*), 'Wood' (*Suh*), 'Fish' (*Ngwa*), 'Bear' (*Wu*), 'Buckwheat' (*Gwa*), and 'Hemp' (*Dzuh*). The Honey clan is the largest, and has three segments. There are a further nine principal clans which have evolved from inter-marriage with Yunnanese: Li, Yang, Wang, Tao, Wu, Ts'ao, Ho, Cu, and Cang. Of these the Yang and Li are the largest.

There are no formal heads or chiefs, but the oldest male member of a clan is accorded a place of special respect by the clan members of that village. He may be called upon to arbitrate disputes within the clan to keep the matter out of the headman's jurisdiction. At festivals, such as the New Year, this respected elder is accorded special honour by those in his clan.

On the last night of the old year a Lisu family often gathers around the fire, and the oldest member of the household tells the history of the family and clan, relating names and incidents which go back many generations.

There tends to be rivalry and conflict among clans. Members of the Honey clan, for example, believe that they are far superior to the Fish clan members, and vice versa. If there is a lawsuit, clan members of both parties side with their kin and try to make sure he wins – guilty or not. If tensions become too severe, one or more families may move out of the village, bringing about a measure of stability.

Certain clans in Thailand tend to be ostracized by the others. Rumours are spread, for example, that many of the women in the Hemp and Buckwheat clans are possessed by weretigers. There are cases where a village (usually small) is made up entirely of members of one of these ostracized clans. It has even reached the point where it is difficult for their girls to find Lisu husbands – often they end up marrying Yunnanese men.

On some occasions there have been feuds between clans. In one year six people were killed in such a feud in the Doi Chang and Tak areas. If such feuding goes on undeterred, villages may disintegrate; but as long as they respect the priest and continue to unite in their worship of the village guardian spirit, they can usually function as a community.

Serious animosity sometimes develops in a family, the most serious being between a son and his father. The Lisu ideal is for the son to show his father utmost respect and obedience at all times; he is dependent on him for most physical, social and religious needs. When the son wants to marry, the father pays the bride price. If a son and his family are still living in the father's house, and one of them falls ill, the father decides whether or not to call a shaman.

If the father is a domineering type, serious tensions build up, sometimes to the point where the son kills him. Between 1958 and 1966 there were at least six such incidents. The main factor which deters such behaviour is the knowledge that when the father dies he will become one of the son's ancestral spirits, and will be able to take revenge.

Sometimes younger/older brother conflicts develop. A younger brother should accept inferior status. The older brother takes charge of the household in the absence of the father, assigns work to his younger siblings, and even makes commitments they are expected to honour. This often arouses resentment in the younger siblings, and the theme of 'primacy' rears its head.

Lisu children

Religious Beliefs

Lisu religion embraces beliefs and practices related to various categories of spirits, the village guardian, and an all-powerful being called Wu sa.

Wu sa and Ida ma

Wu sa, the Creator (comparable to the Lahu G'ui sha), is the 'High god'. He looks after the living, and never brings trouble to them. He determines each person's lifespan, and sends a letter when his time has come. This is expressed in a song they sing to a person when he dies:

'Today you die... Wu sa made this be your time to die. He makes the sky take your strength, and he makes the earth take your bones. Wu sa wrote the date for you to die. Now your letter has arrived. Today Wu sa's letter reached you. Always stay with Wu sa and do whatever he asks you to. He needs food, so you must find it for him. May you get water and food for Wu sa... Wu sa wrote this letter for you to die. His letter has come, and you must go up there...'

There is also a being called the 'Great One' (Ida ma), who is especially concerned with sickness and curing. In various ceremonies he is asked to take care of the villagers, and to drive away sickness in the area.

Village guardian

The 'village guardian', whose domain is the village as a whole, is both powerful and potentially fierce. He sees all, and is greatly feared. Lisu are expected to observe the polite 'avoidance' behaviour toward him and his shrine.

Spirits

There are four categories of 'spirits' (*ne*): ancestral spirits, forest spirits, owner spirits, and bad death spirits. Spirits are believed to lead a life which mirrors the Lisu culture. If wronged, they expect the one responsible to apologize and make restitution. Lisu sometimes make contracts promising that if the spirits help in a given situation, they will make a sacrifice to them.

The ancestors are powerful spirits who play an important role in the daily life of the family. They are represented on the ancestral altar by small bowls which had been placed on their graves at the time of their burial. The ancestors must be fed regularly with offerings of meat, rice, and water. If neglected, they may cause trouble to the household; when cared for properly, however, they help in many ways, ensuring good health and bountiful crops. Joss sticks are burned and *lu khwa* leaves are placed on the altar when communicating with the ancestors.

Other spirits which concern the Lisu are: tree spirit, sun spirit, moon spirit, gun spirit, crossbow spirit, and bellows spirit, all of which may attack people with or without provocation. Lisu are especially afraid of the 'bad death' spirits (*cha*), because they are souls of dead people who have not yet gone to the land of the dead, but continue to roam the earth. When hungry they attack people in order to obtain meat offerings.

Each hill has its own spirit, so before cutting down a large tree a Lisu farmer first makes an offering to the spirit of the hill. Each field also has a spirit. If a dispute arises over who is going to plant a certain field, Lisu tend simply to divide the land to prevent an argument. They fear that if the spirit of the field heard them arguing, a poor crop would result.

Weretigers and vampires

Lisu believe two types of beings may take possession of a person: weretigers (*phi pheu*) and vampires (*phu seu*). Family members of a person possessed with a weretiger might also become possessed. For this reason, when Lisu boys go to a village to court the girls, they first ask if there is anyone in the village possessed by a weretiger, because they want to avoid courting a girl related to such a person. If a boy should marry a girl considered to be possessed by a weretiger, he would be disowned by his parents and forced to leave the village. Sometimes a possessed person causes the essence of the weretiger to go into some valuable object, such as a silver ornament or a piece of fine fabric, and leaves it lying on a path. Anyone who picks up that object will in turn be possessed by the weretiger.

From time to time the weretiger leaves the person in whom it dwells and attacks someone else. If a person becomes very ill and it is believed that the illness is caused by a weretiger, a relative may cut or burn off a lock of the patient's hair. If indeed it was a weretiger, the hair will have grown back by the next morning, but a corresponding lock of hair will be missing from the one in whom it dwells. The person being harassed, upon being asked who the 'owner' is, may speak out the name. If the owner is from another tribe, a Karen for example, the possessed person, though having never learned a word of Karen, will speak in the Karen language, as it is really the weretiger who is speaking.

To accuse someone of being possessed by a weretiger is an extremely serious matter, as it can result in no one being willing to marry a member of the possessed person's family, and ultimately the family may be driven from the village.

A person possessed by a vampire (*phu seu*) takes the shape of a cat, a dog, or some other animal, and goes around biting and sucking the blood of people and animals, both the living and the newly dead. On the morning after a Lisu corpse has been buried someone goes to the grave and shoots a gun over it, and then tells the deceased, 'The vampire is dead'. Lisu believe that if there is a vampire in a village many children will die.

Lisu ceremonies

Religious Practitioners

As the Lisu religion combines ancestor worship and spirit propitiation, two types of practitioners are necessary in carrying out religious functions: the 'village priest' (*mu meu pha*), and the shaman (*ne pha*).

Village priest

The village priest is chosen by the elders to direct ceremonies and to be the go-between in all dealings with the village guardian spirit. One of his most important duties is to announce the special days in the Lisu calendar, such as the semi-monthly holy days, various ceremonies, and most important of all, the New Year festival. He directs the men in caring for the altar of the village guardian spirit, as well as all other religious affairs of the village, and is given the highest status (very much like the Akha *dzoe ma*). Any improper behaviour towards him on the part of the villagers endangers everyone, for he is virtually the incarnation of the guardian spirit.

Durrenberger tells of one priest who did not change the water at the village shrine and neglected other duties. One day while he was fishing with explosives an accident destroyed one of his eyes. This was taken as a sign that the guardian spirit was angry and wanted to kill him, so the elders chose a new priest to take his place.

Shaman

Whereas the priest serves as the representative between the villagers and the guardian, a shaman serves as the link between the human and spirit world. The shaman belongs to his spirits, just as the priest belongs to the village guardian, but only the shaman becomes possessed.

Any male may become a shaman who shows an aptitude for contacting ancestors and spirits and passes an initiation test given by other shamans in the area. A shaman is chosen by the spirits of his clan. The first manifestations are that he is physically weak, wants to play in the fire, and prefers staying at home rather than going to the fields. If he eats food denied to a shaman, such as onions, garlic, or fried foods, he will become insane for a short time, and a sacrifice must be made to the household spirits to bring

him back to his senses. This is proof that he has been 'called' to be a shaman.

The main function of a shaman is to divine the cause of illness or misfortune, then sing away the spirit who is responsible. When called to someone's house to go into a trance and be 'ridden by the spirits', he first changes the water in the bowls on the ancestral altar, and then lights joss sticks. Bending over with his hands on his knees, he whistles for his spirits to come, and sings himself into a trance. The spirits ride him as if he were a horse, and they speak to the people assembled in the house through him. He finally falls unconscious to the floor, which is a sign that he has sung the spirit out of the patient into himself. As the shaman sleeps in a coma the spirit returns to its abode.

In the event of a serious illness, the shaman may be asked to perform the 'spraying' of the sickness. A pan of lard is placed on the fire, and while it is heating he sings himself into a trance. He then scoops hot fat into his mouth, and sprays the fat over a torch he carries, making big fireballs – a most spectacular sight in a dark house. Then he moves to the door and blows fireballs out of the house.

While the shaman is in a trance the spirits speak through him telling those assembled what offering is required to bring healing – usually a pig or chicken. The following day the sacrifice is made to the ancestor or other spirit causing the sickness. The ancestors most commonly associated with sickness are those who have recently died, especially fathers and mothers.

When there are clear signs that a man is called to be a shaman, other shamans in the area gather with him in the jungle outside his village to hold an initiation ceremony. One of the older shamans calls down some of the powerful yet potentially benevolent spirits, such as the village guardian spirit, to ride the new shaman. Lisu say they do this so the wild, fierce spirits will not come to ride him first, as it is 'just like when someone gets a new horse, everyone wants to ride it'. The good spirits keep away the evil spirits, until the shaman is strong enough to deal with them.

Ceremonies

New Year

The most important festival is that of the New Year, when they celebrate the turning from the old to the new. Many hours and considerable sums of money are devoted to the making of new outfits for the young people. Silver ornaments are cleaned, and silver buttons are sewn onto the clothing. Quantities of liquor are distilled, each step in the process being punctuated by shooting a gun.

The New Year festival begins with the announcement by the village priest that on the following day they must make 'rice cakes' (*pa pa*). The household of the village priest is the first to make the cakes then a gun is shot as a signal that the other villagers can start making theirs. Each family gathers around its pounder and together makes the cakes to be used in New Year offerings, and to be eaten by the family.

During the day the young people make excursions to the fields to collect large quantities of vegetables, and men from each family go to the jungle and cut a New Year tree (*leh dzuh*). After sunset the priest calls out from the guardian spirit shrine that the sun has set, then each family ceremonially plants its tree in front of the house. The 'Old Year' celebration is observed, in preparation for which each house is 'purified' by being swept thoroughly and having all leftover food discarded.

That evening hard-boiled eggs and strings, one of each for every person in the household, are placed in a basin of uncooked glutinous rice. The oldest man in the household takes the basin outside and calls the souls of the household members to come into it, then takes it back inside, gives an egg to each person to eat, and ties the strings around the necks of adult family members and the wrists or elbows of children and guests.

Later in the evening the senior shaman goes into a trance for his household and the village as a whole. While in the trance he blows fireballs of lard, and sprays water from his mouth in order to drive the 'bad' of the Old Year away, so that everything will be clean and good for the New Year. The spirits speak through him, emphasizing that everyone must make a break with the old, so as to enter into the New Year free from sickness and evil. He says such things as, 'People, don't separate. Wherever you go, whatever happens, stay together and be united'. This theme is expressed in other ways as well, because there may be families who plan to leave the village soon after the New Year.

Later that night people congregate at the village priest's house. While elders drink and sing, young people first dance around his New Year tree then go in procession from house to house throughout the night, dancing around each tree, thus 'sweeping out' the bad and impure elements from the entire village.

At cockcrow the next morning, women from the village priest's house go to the water source and make offerings of joss sticks, rice cakes, and pork, then bring 'New Year water' back to the house. This 'new water', considered to be special, is used to fill the cups on the ancestral altar, and to cook offerings for the ancestors. The priest and his wife wash their faces with some of this water by their New Year tree to 'wash away the evil of the old year'.

Later that morning men from each household go to the village shrine with the priest to present offerings of rice cakes, liquor, and pork to the guardian spirit. During the offering the priest prays, '. . . like a stream, like clear water, let us have no trouble or sickness. . . . Let us not separate. Come receive this offering. Sha-a-a'.

Later similar offerings are sent to the priest by each household. He arranges these on the platform under his altar, and then prays again in the same fashion. Strings are tied to the necks of those present, then dancing resumes. Some of the elders inside the priest's house sing songs asking for unity, good health, and other blessings for the New Year.

On New Year's day there is almost constant dancing around the village priest's tree. The music is provided by men playing either musical gourd pipes or lutes, the type of dancing varying according to the instrument used and the tune played. At one celebration we observed the headman and other adults started the dancing in the morning; later small children joined in. It was not until early afternoon that young women, who had spent the morning hours dressing in all their finery, came to the dance area. Towards evening the young men, also in their finest attire, joined in. The next day the site of the dancing shifted to the headman's house and continued all day.

Two or three men in the village are appointed to be 'idiots' (paka) who tease those who are not dancing to get them back into the group whenever the number drops too low. They throw dirt on people, grab their drinks, and generally carry on to make it a happy, festive occasion.

During the celebration it is important for the villagers to maintain friendly relations. Quarrelling and bickering are taboo. There is much visiting with clan members and friends. Lisu used to put up a 'taboo sign' (ta leo) at the entrance of the village during the New Year celebration so no outsiders would enter. Since the 1960s the Lisu have gradually dropped this, and now visitors are no longer prohibited.

At the next dawn the village priest announces that the 'sun has risen', and the New Year celebration is over. Each family ties a piece of pork and two rice cakes to its New Year tree and casts it out into the jungle, ending the festival.

Lisu girls all dressed up for New Year celebrations

New Year dancing (note courting bags)

Tree renovation ceremony

Another important ritual in each Lisu village is the annual 'tree renovation ceremony', similar to those held for the 'Lord of Land and Water' by Karen and Akha groups. The priest leads the elders to the compound of the guardian spirit shrine above the village; they clean up the area and build a new fence. They carve miniature wooden weapons, such as guns, crossbows, swords, knives, spears, and clubs, for the guardian spirit to use in defence of the village against evil.

In the evening the elders bring trays of eggs and other food to offer at the shrine. While they kowtow with their foreheads to the ground, the priest chants a prayer to the guardian spirit.

After dark these offerings are paraded through the village by the children. Calling to the spirits in high-pitched voices, they go in procession along the trail leading from the village, just beyond the taboo signs which have been erected to keep outsiders away. There the trays are overturned, and the eggs broken. The children then run back to the village as fast as they can, while the evil spirits which have followed the procession feast on the food. As the taboo signs prevent them from returning, the village is purified of these evil spirits.

Sickness and Treatment

Lisu have adopted certain measures to avoid sickness. These include building bridges over streams so they will not be exposed to the power of the water spirit by wading through them; and wearing charms, either home-made or purchased in local markets. When illness occurs, they first determine the cause – whether by spirits, black magic, the breaking of a taboo, the person's soul leaving the body, or some natural reason.

When spirits are suspected of causing an illness, certain older people are called upon to 'read' the lines of a pig's liver or the alignment of holes in the thigh bones of a chicken. They thus determine which spirit has been wronged, and what type of offering must be made to bring healing. Lisu keep many pigs and chickens to have ready when offerings to the spirits are needed. They say, 'If you are lazy, you cannot carry out Lisu customs, for you will not have enough pigs, chickens, and money to perform all the ceremonies'. Durrenberger found that in one medium-sized Lisu village in the Pa Pae area, 100 pigs were sacrificed in one year for curing ceremonies. The meat from those sacrifices was of course eaten by the villagers, thus providing protein in their diet.

In more serious cases a shaman may be called in to communicate with the spirit world to determine the cause of the illness and how it can be cured. He first calls his spirits to ride him. When they have come, the patient tells them the symptoms. They in turn consult with other spirits if need be, and then inform the patient through the shaman what must be done to effect a cure. It is usually found that two or perhaps three different spirits have been offended, so offerings must be made to each. If the patient does not get well, the family simply tries something else until he does. The return of good health indicates that the spirits are now satisfied.

When a person feels weak and off-colour, Lisu believe that his soul has left him, so there must be a ceremony to call it back (tsuh ha khu). As a part of this ceremony the elder in charge builds a 'bridge' along the trail near the village, then calls the soul and entices it to return to the owner by crossing the 'bridge', which is a plank of wood with streamers and cords tied to it. He calls the soul repeatedly while returning to the house of the sick person. The patient sits in the area between the door and the ancestral altar while the elder prays for him and ties strings around his neck.

According to Lisu belief much sickness is caused by a person or spirit sending an object (tai') into a patient by means of black magic. This object causes severe stabbing pains in the area where it is located, and if it is not sucked out quickly by a skilled person, death may result. There are some, usually shamans, who claim to be able to extrude the tai' and send it back to plague the person or spirit who sent it. Lisu become frustrated when Western-trained doctors give no credence to the theory of tai'.

Each clan has its own curing ceremonies. Lisu prefer to live in a village where there are many other members of their own clan so they will have friends who know those ceremonies. For example, only Fish clan members lay a thread on the sick person which must not be removed for seven days and nights.

Lisu realize that some illnesses are the result of natural causes. In such cases they may seek the services of a medical practitioner, such as someone trained in Western medicines, an 'injection doctor', or a local herbalist. We know a Lisu man who as a boy was saved by the ministrations of a Lahu herbalist, and as a result his name was changed by his father to that of the Lahu practitioner.

In the past Lisu were not willing to take their sick to hospitals, fearing that they might be bitten by 'vampires', for they believe wherever many people are sick and dying, vampires must be present. Another fear was that if they went to a hospital they might be fed to a huge ogre (phi ya). These beliefs have been changing gradually so that today many Lisu avail themselves of hospital and clinic services.

Making an offering at ancestral altar

Reading the lines of a pig's liver

Bridge ceremony

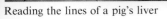

Above: After calling the soul back, strings are tied around the patient's neck

Courtship and Marriage

A Lisu man cannot marry any girl he would call *ci ci* or *nyi ma*, – an older or younger girl of his own clan, or a daughter of his mother's sister. This latter type of marriage does sometimes occur, however, but the groom is required to pay a 'fine' in addition to the bride price.

Courtship

Courtship centres around the rice pounders in the evenings. As the girls gather to pound rice for the next day's meals, young men join them and a lot of teasing and flirting ensues. As the girls take turns resting, a boy may sit with one he likes. They may eventually exchange bracelets or some other token of their love, which they keep hidden in a pocket of their jacket or tunic.

Courting also takes place during working parties in the fields. The girls pass word to the boys where they will be. All go to the fields in their finery and the 'singing of songs' begins. The leader of the group sings the first line of the song, and his or her friends join in for the rest of the verse. The lyrics, all sung to the same tune, are traditional poems with highly figurative meanings. The boys might begin:

'In the sixth month it drizzles,
In the ninth month it pours, yes it does.
In the sixth month I'm nostalgic,
In the ninth month I'm sad, completely'.

The first two lines refer to two important months: the sixth is auspicious, and the ninth is dangerous, when epidemics occur. The latter lines refer to the fact that when lovers have been apart for only a short while they feel nostalgic and long for their sweethearts, but after a long time this turns to sadness, and the longing changes to bitterness. There is an implied warning, 'Don't let me dangle on a string too long, or my love for you could turn to hatred'.

After a few such verses the girls take their turn, then it goes back to the boys. As the singing progresses it becomes harder and harder to remember the appropriate verses without repeating. If one side sings a verse to which the other cannot reply or repeats itself, the singing ends, and the news of who won the contest soon spreads through the village.

When a couple becomes interested in marriage, their families usually sense what is taking place and serious tension may develop. The Lisu view the men of the clan as being the 'tree', and the women the 'leaves'. When the men see the threat of a leaf being 'stolen' from their tree, they feel compelled to try to prevent it.

Marriage

Lisu marriage has evolved into a fascinating drama. Each person is expected to play his or her role in accordance with the master script, although minor variations are acceptable if they fit into the pattern of Lisu custom.

The first act is for the boy to present 30 silver rupees to the girl, which she keeps personally. This is known as 'putting a flower in her hair'. Then they agree on a date when he will 'steal' her. On that evening the girl goes out to pound paddy, and disappears with the boy to some field hut. Neither family must know about this. If their plotting is discovered by the girl's family they can add a 'fine' to the bride price.

Early the next morning the young man sends a go-between (often his paternal uncle) to the girl's house. As he approaches he shouts, 'Your daughter is no longer your daughter'. He assures the parents that she has been taken by a man, 'not by a tiger'. The father, playing his part, refuses to believe this. He may reply, 'Boys often lie to girls and say they want to marry them'.

The go-between then takes his leave, in order to give the father time to gather his family and clansmen. Later in the day he returns, bringing a tray with two bottles of liquor and a parcel of tea leaves.

Having offered the tray to the father and his kin, he tells them what clan he belongs to, and explains that he is looking for a 'gold word and a silver word', because his clan has carried off a daughter of the household. The girl's father continues to deny that any such thing has happened, even though he knows it has. Meanwhile he praises his own clan, declaring how numerous and powerful it is. Both sides are making clear from the start that if litigation takes place later as a result of this union, there are plenty of clan and family members who will rally round to ensure victory.

In accordance with the proper progression of the drama, the go-between continues to say that the girl has been 'stolen', but the girl's father insists that it is not so, and does not accept the liquor and tea. Finally, after many refusals, the father accepts the gifts, indicating that he is ready to enter into the next phase of the drama: The discussion of bride price and bride service.

They first discuss the amount of black cloth which is to be given the girl's family. It is the type used for men's jackets and the yoke of women's tunics. The girl's father demands two pieces, one for the 'tiger's bite', and one for the 'thunder's rumble'. The 'tiger's bite' refers to the anxiety which has been caused by his daughter being 'stolen', and the 'thunder's rumble' to the scolding which the girl's father has refrained from delivering. After this discussion the go-between leaves, having shown extreme courtesy throughout.

When he returns a little later, he brings the tray with another bottle of liquor and a small packet of salt. He claims to have difficulty in raising the money. The girl's father refuses to believe this, but finally announces the amount he requires as a 'down payment' on the bride price, upon which the go-between leaves – again in a flurry of politeness.

The next time he returns, he brings, together with the usual liquor, a portion of the money demanded as a down payment. The father refuses to accept this, and in the course of the bargaining demands an additional seven silver rupees for the 'breast price' – payment to the mother for the period she breast-fed the girl. Possible fines are also discussed. For example, if the young man marries a younger daughter before an older one is wed, a fine of 30 to 40 silver rupees, or its equivalent, will be exacted.

Many such visits ensue during the day, with various fines being demanded, until finally the girl's father states the sum of money he wants for the bride price. In the Doi Chang area, noted for its highly desirable girls, the price may start at around 2,000 silver rupees. In other areas it may be closer to 1,000 silver rupees. The bargaining becomes serious after an actual figure has been stated, and in the end a payment of 700 to 800 rupees for girls in Doi Chang, and 150 to 300 rupees for girls from other areas is agreed to. Because of the scarcity of silver rupees, however, more and more Lisu have been paying the equivalent in Thai baht. The value of a silver rupee currently varies from about $3.50 to $4.50.

Upon payment of the first installment of the bride price, a date is set for the 'kowtow ceremony' (literally 'knocking of the head'), when the balance is paid. Even though the couple may have lived together for some time, they are considered man and wife only after this ceremony. A mat is spread before the ancestral altar in the girl's house. The couple get down on their knees and the boy knocks his head on the floor in front of the girl's father and mother. While their heads are bowed, the father and mother ask an elder to bless them. The couple then share water and rice to complete the ceremony.

This final rite of the marriage drama accomplishes two purposes. First the 'tree' and the 'leaf' factions are reconciled, mending the relationship between the two families and thus their clans. Secondly, the ancestors are informed that the girl is leaving her parent's home and entering the home of another clan.

After the 'kowtow ceremony' a feast is held for family and friends, with the bride and groom helping to serve. A bowl of water is set near the door for guests to drop coins in as they enter. Often someone from the groom's party stands close by watching, and makes comments if someone gives a small amount. Towards the end of the day one of the go-betweens pours the water and coins over the cupped hands of the groom, leaving the coins in his hands. The groom in turn places these coins into the outstretched end of his bride's turban. The Lisu consider this to be 'seed' money to give them a start in married life.

Blessings are called down on the couple in prose and song. One wedding song reveals Lisu respect for their traditions. The lyric states that the girl's father does not ask for money because he is poor, but because 'it is the custom'. A plaintive theme, occurring in many of their legends, is repeated in this song: 'We Lisu have no writing, no irrigated rice fields, and no country of our own'. In contrast to this negative theme, however, is a positive statement declaring that their customs and their ways of doing things are the very best.

Birth

A Lisu mother delivers her baby either in her bedroom or close to the main fireplace. One or more village women help her. If the labour is extended, an offering may be made to one of the 'bad death' spirits to facilitate the birth. The woman must not drink cold water, for fear her blood might become cold, making her unable to deliver.

After delivery she must lie by a 'mother-roasting fire' for a month (Hope 1970:37). For seven days a taboo sign is kept outside the door to prevent visitors from entering. During this period the baby is not considered a human being, but still belongs to the spirit world. The placenta is either placed high in a tall tree in the jungle, or buried under the spot where the 'mother-roasting fire' is built.

The day after the birth the family kills a pig, and the priest makes offerings of pork and other items to the village guardian while praying, 'By your blessing we have a new baby. Look after the village and let nothing happen to it. Give the child your blessing. We ask you for a name for him. Let him become big, like a huge cucumber. May he have no sickness. Give him long life and much power'.

The village priest then returns to the house where the child was born, and while making offerings to the ancestors prays to them in a similar way.

Naming

After the offerings and prayer, a low table is brought in with a bowl of water and two bowls of liquor. The priest drops a silver rupee into the water, then uses two cowrie shells to divine a name. As he calls out names, first using those of the most famous ancestors, he drops the shells into the water. When one of the shells falls with the closed side up and the other with the open side up, the name just called becomes the official name of the child.

For everyday use, however, the child is usually called by a Lisu name indicating its birth order.

	Sons	Daughters
First	Abe pha/Ata pha	Ami ma
Second	Ale pha	Ale ma
Third	Asa pha	Asa ma
Fourth	Asuh pha	Asuh ma
Fifth	Avu pha	Avu ma
Sixth	Alu pha	Alu ma
Seventh	Atsuh pha	Atsuh ma
Eighth	Apa pha	Apa ma
Ninth	Atyoe pha	Atyoe ma
Tenth	Ashui pha	Ashui ma

These birth-order names are used in direct address, but in the person's absence, when there is a need to be more specific, the official name is used.

Seven days after the birth the mother is purified by a 'sizzling the body ceremony' (Hope 1970:38). She sits inside a tent of blankets on an overturned pig trough, thereby imparting fertility to the livestock. Water containing *lu khwa* leaves is then poured on hot rocks, and the woman is engulfed in steam. After this ceremony she may again drink cold water, and cook for herself, although not yet for her husband.

At the end of one month the 'mother-roasting fire' is extinguished, and the ancestors are informed of the new member of the clan. If the baby has been ill or weak, a 'soul-calling' ceremony is performed. The mother now returns to normal life. She can cook for the family, carry water, and use tools which were taboo to her.

An unwed mother often rears the child herself, but most Lisu ostracize such a mother. If the girl's father discovers who has fathered the child he will fine him, enabling his grandchild to belong to its father's clan. If it is not known who the father was, the child will remain clanless until grown up. A boy can then request a bowl from the altar of a household belonging to a clan different from the one in which he was reared, thus becoming accepted in Lisu culture.

A Lisu woman who dies in childbirth is considered to have died a 'bad death' – the same as being killed by lightning, a leopard, or smallpox. Her body will not be buried, but cremated.

Death and Burial

Lisu believe that when a person is born Wu sa writes in his book how long he or she will live. When the time is up, the person dies – unless a shaman, under the guidance of the benevolent household spirits, can 'write a letter' to extend that person's life span.

When an old man is in a death coma one of his children puts nine grains of rice and nine small pieces of silver in his mouth. For an old woman seven grains of rice and seven pieces of silver are used. As they put them in they say, 'If you don't want to stay here, go on. Don't be lonely. We allow you to go'. In cases when a baby is very sick and unconscious, the parents may put some cooked rice into its mouth saying, 'If you want to stay here, come back. If you want to go away, then go now'. They believe that shortly after this the baby will either die, or begin to recover.

A gun is fired to announce death; the corpse is washed and a coffin made. The first night after a Lisu adult dies, the 'death song' is sung, instructing him, 'Go away, and don't come back!'

Burial

From the time of death until the morning after the burial a wake is held each night in the dead person's home. There is drinking, feasting, gambling, and sometimes dancing. The purpose of the wake is to keep the relatives of the dead person from feeling sad. The corpse is kept in the house for a shorter time for one who has never been married. Burial may even be on the day of death in the case of a child.

Young men are appointed to carry the coffin to the burial site. An older man accompanies them carrying a basket which belonged to the deceased, in which some rice, strips of cloth, gourds filled with water, and an old knife are placed. The departure is marked by the firing of a gun.

On arrival at the burial site, which is often on the middle of three parallel ridges, someone drops an egg to divine the exact location where the body wishes to be buried. If the egg does not break they will try other sites until it finally does. This type of divining for a burial site is common among the Yi (Lolo) tribes. If the deceased was a young person, he or she will be buried far from any path, as it is felt the spirit might pester people walking along the trail.

The coffin is lowered into a shallow grave, covered with earth, and a cairn of rocks built on top. A small bowl of water is placed in a protected niche in the cairn. The water is changed daily for ten days.

The basket (mentioned above) is left hanging on a pole at the head of the grave. The man who carried it for the family is customarily given one silver rupee. The poles used to carry the coffin are chopped up and left on top of the grave. This 'sends' the soul of the deceased to the land of the dead. The burial party pours water over it all and returns to the village.

On the way back members of the burial party repeatedly splash water on the trail, and the young men and women splash it over one another as well. This helps to keep the soul of the deceased from bothering them. When the burial party reaches the village, another shot is fired, this time in the direction of the burial ground; everyone then goes indoors.

Later a shaman leads a special ceremony to separate the living from the dead. He encircles the family with a long string, and prays that the one who is dead will not come back to haunt the living. Then he goes into a trance and sprays the family with water from his mouth. He emphasizes to the soul that he or she is indeed dead, and is not to come back to bother the living.

A month later the bowl of water which had been kept on top of the cairn is returned to the house and placed on the ancestral altar while joss sticks and beeswax candles are burned. The spirit of the dead person is then recognized as a family ancestor and reunited with his clan.

Once a year for three years following the death of an adult, a special ceremony is performed. The family members and friends gather at the grave, and an elder sings the 'orphan's song', which states:

'This soul has gone to the sky, these bones have gone to the ground. Why did you take this person's soul? Now this person has become a big spirit. You, dead person, you do not see your children, because you live in the jungle. Now your children are like worms, they know nothing. Other children can see their parents when they call them. Your children call, but they cannot see you . . . .'

Then an elder prays to the 'Lord of the Grave' (*Xeu thu seu pha*):

'Come and sit down here. We offer you water and tea. Come receive flags and joss sticks. Come receive a three-year old cock. Take care of us. Let us be able to work well, let us be able to keep pigs. Let us not have trouble in the future. Let us be rich, and not have misfortune or be sick. Let others have to borrow money from us. Here are the offerings . . . .'

An offering of a pig and two chickens is made, and those present have a feast at the site. Boys and girls in the party chase each other, throwing dirt and mud all the way back to the village.

Homicide

The rate of homicide is probably higher among the Lisu than any other tribal group. Not only do killings occur within their own tribe, but also between Lisu and lowlanders, Yunnanese, and other tribal groups. This is often a result of their determination to get their 'just rights'. On occasion Lisu families or groups of families (in one case a whole village) have moved from a situation where murder would surely have taken place had they remained.

Suicide

The suicide rate among Lisu also seems to be higher than among other tribes. A young woman whose husband is addicted to opium, for example, might commit suicide because she feels her situation is hopeless. One who believes he has been denied justice might commit suicide if he feels he has no redress. One Lisu man became very angry at a group of fellow villagers whose horses got into his rice field and ate a large amount of grain. He tried to persuade the village leaders to force the owners of the horses to reimburse him. When that failed he took the case to local Thai officials, but again with no result. In total frustration he put a gun into his mouth and pulled the trigger.

Conclusion

Lisu are not shy and withdrawn, like some of the tribal groups. When they are around everyone knows it. They travel in large boisterous groups. When selling they employ the hard-sell technique. When buying they are vociferous bargainers.

Being hard workers they disdain those whom they consider to be lazy. They enter into every aspect of their lives with enthusiasm, whether it be farming, making of crafts, seeking a husband or wife, celebrating the New Year, or fighting a court case.

If a family member is in a hospital, often the entire extended family goes to visit. When women have needlework to sell, men, women and children troop to town, and all raise their voices if the price offered is not deemed sufficient. A craftsman will extol his or her work as being highly superior to that of others.

For every Lisu wants to excel.

Relaxing at the end of the day

Two Karen drums, Akha drum, bamboo flutes, Hmong mouth organ *(left),* Lahu Sheh Leh musical gourd pipe *(middle),* and four musical gourd pipes as used by Lahu, Akha, and Lisu

Chapter 9

Musical Instruments, Baskets and Utensils

Never short on resourcefulness, tribal people through many generations have learned to fashion from the products of their environment tools, utensils, containers, weapons, and musical instruments necessary for survival and recreation. Before manufactured products became so easily available to them in market towns, they could manage quite satisfactorily by using woven baskets for rice plates, bamboo sections split longitudinally for curry dishes, bamboo cups for tea and liquor, and bamboo or wooden chopsticks, spoons, and ladles. Tools and instruments for making thread and weaving cloth, for trapping and hunting, and for working in the fields are produced within the household, or obtained by barter from skilled fellow-villagers. While metal for making knives, tools, and guns must be purchased, traditionally they have been hammered out on the anvils of the village blacksmiths.

The Karen bronze ceremonial drum is hundreds of years old. There is much mystery regarding the origin of such drums. Some Karen believe they were made and given to them by the spirits

Stringed instruments made by Karen, and three *(bottom)*
used by Lisu, Lahu and sometimes Akha

Mien bells, oboes, drum and two buffalo horns *(right)*

Buffalo horns *(left)*, gongs, and cymbals are used by all the tribes

Jew's harps, in varying styles, are used by the Sinicized tribes

Lahu baskets: Lahu Shi and Lahu Nyi covered storage baskets; small open baskets used as rice plates or for weaving and sewing supplies; and woven bamboo boxes

Open-weave carrying baskets are used by Lahu, Akha, and Lisu. The closely woven ones pictured are made by Lahu Sheh Leh

Lower left: Lahu Sheh Leh table
Winnowing trays, *(lower middle),* are used by all the tribes

Karen baskets *Upper right:* Basket for collecting wild honey, with wooden shoulder pieces and head-strap for carrying. *Lower right:* Open basket used for holding weaving and embroidery paraphernalia. Other baskets are used for storage. (Notice green beetle wings decorating basket in *upper left*)

Karen baskets and betel-nut boxes. Karen often apply
lac to waterproof their baskets. The two in the *upper left*
are used as back-packs for carrying clothing

Akha bamboo and rattan work: Bamboo sections and baskets *(at left)* used for holding cotton tufts and spindles at woman's waist. Small open baskets hold tea and tobacco. Sun/rain hats and small stool *(at right.)* Bamboo tobacco boxes, and woven rattan needle and thread boxes *(lower centre)*

Hmong back-carrying baskets (two White, one Blue); Hmong carrying-board; bamboo water pipe (used by all Sinicized tribes); utensil holder and bamboo dishes; and Akha wooden yoke (*lower left*)

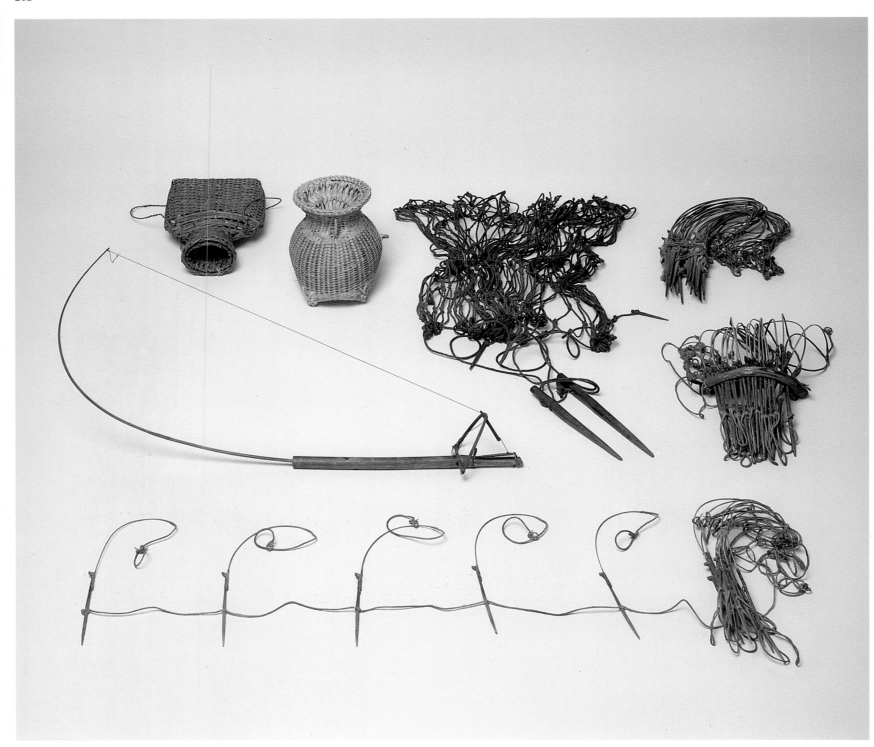

Fishing creels *(upper left)* , snares, and traps, used by all
tribes – with modifications

Knives, machetes, crossbows with arrows, sling-shot and guns. Karen knives *(far left)* have bone handles and aluminium cases. Type of crossbow *(on left)* used by Lahu, Akha, and Lisu – the other by Karen. Other items used by all tribes

Tools for producing textiles   *Upper row:* Karen spinning wheel, Akha loom parts, and Karen cotton gin.

Lower row: Hmong batiking tools, Akha spindles, and boar's bristle brushes for smoothing thread on loom

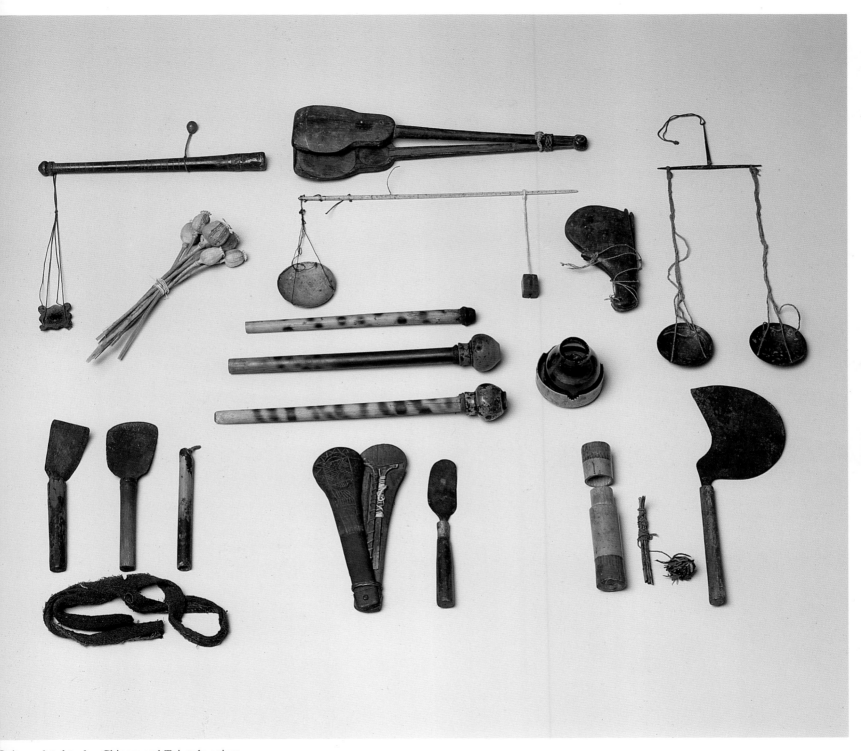

Opium-related tools Chinese and Tai-style opium
scales *(top row)*. Dried opium pods, opium pipes and
lamp *(centre)*. Opium harvesting tools *(bottom)*

Bright-coloured pick-up trucks break into traditional
village scene

Chapter 10

Signs of Change

More and more tribal people are buying pick-up trucks and motorcycles

Hmong girls selling in Chiang Mai night bazaar

Radios and cassette players are common in tribal villages

Rice mills replace foot-treadle paddy pounders in some villages

Graffito T-shirts have become popular among tribal people

Akha girl adds modern pictures to traditional jewellery

Page 289 top: Tourists invade many tribal villages

Middle: An increasing number of tribal children are going to school

Bottom: Strings are cut and tribal religious paraphernalia burned as family converts to Christianity

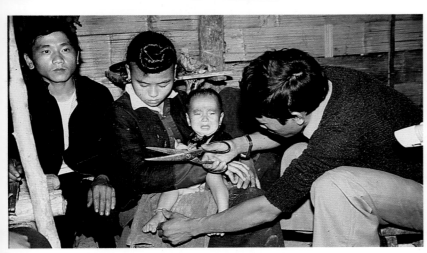

Top left: Sewing machines replace hand-stitching for some tribal women

Top right: Tribal chief adds aspects of Buddhism to his traditional religion

Bottom left: Groom wears modern running shoes with traditional wedding garb

Bottom right: Christian symbol is added to a traditional coffin

The future of the tribal people in Thailand hinges to a large extent on how they respond to the challenging problems confronting them.

1 Population   If the population of tribal people increases by 3% a year (including migration and natural increase), the present 415,000 will swell to 685,000 by the year 2,000 – a 65% increase!

2 Land   Land available to tribal people for agricultural purposes is decreasing at an alarming rate due to: reforestation; exhaustion of the soil; over-population; dam construction; road building; and valley dwellers moving into the hills.

3 Economy   Although they work hard and some receive benefits from development programmes, most tribal people face serious economic problems due to: lack of funds with which to purchase land; lack of capital with which to diversify their agriculture; and constant exposure to economic loss from robbery and exploitation.

4 Education   Under the existing situation, it is impossible for most tribal children to receive an adequate education due to: lack of primary schools in most villages; lack of dedicated teachers in the few schools there are; lack of official documents needed by children to enroll in town schools; and inadequate boarding facilities for tribal students in towns and cities.

5 Political status   While the number of tribal people being granted citizenship is slowly growing, the majority remain stateless people: they are 'fined' at check-points when they cannot produce citizenship papers; they cannot own their fields; they cannot get licenses for the motorcycles and trucks some are buying; and their children cannot qualify to sit for school examinations.

6 Health   In spite of significant Government upgrading of medical care throughout the nation, tribal people have serious health problems due to: decreasing jungle areas where they can collect foods and traditional medicines; less game to add protein to their diet; malnutrition from reduced crop yields and increased consumption of polished rice; and the increasing rate of opium addiction in some groups.

7 Religion   In many cases tribal religious beliefs and practices are beginning to break down, due to: modern medicine increasingly supplanting ritual healing; modern agriculture replacing ceremonies to ensure good crops; scientific education undermining their traditional view of the cosmos; and few young people being willing to become religious practitioners.

The changes currently taking place among these six tribes will no doubt continue at an ever accelerating pace; problems will certainly multiply in the days ahead. Amidst this, however, there are signs of hope: some tribal children are getting an education; some tribal farmers are making irrigated rice fields; some families are accepting family planning help; some opium addicts are detoxifying; and some Government officials are helping the tribal people get needed citizenship papers.

The resilience of these people has served them well in the past; may it be adequate to preserve their integrity in years ahead. Our hope for them can be expressed in this tribal blessing:

Wherever you go, in all you experience;
May your feet not stumble, your arms not falter.
May your words prove true;
Your hopes be fulfilled.
May your labours sustain you;
And all you undertake flourish.

Bibliography

ANDERSEN, KIRSTEN EWERS
1980 *Davong Guu, en karénlandsby i Thailand,* København: Nationalmuseet.
BERNATZIK, HUGO ADOLF
1947 *Akha und Meau,* (2 volumes) Wagner'sche Universitätsbuchdruckerei, Innsbruck.
BINNEY, GEORGE A.
1968 *The Social and Economic Organization of Two White Meo Communities in Northern Thailand,* ARPA Publication ARPA-T10, Washington D. C.
BOON CHUEY SRISAVASDI
1963 *The Hill Tribes of Siam,* Bangkok: Khun Aroon.
BRADLEY, DAVID
1979 *Proto-Loloish,* Scandinavian Institute of Asian Studies, Monograph Series No. 39, London and Malmö: Curzon Press.
1979 *Lahu Dialects,* Oriental Monograph No. 23, Canberra: Australian National University Press.
BRUKSASRI, WANAT, AND JOHN MCKINNON, editors
1983 *The Highlanders of Thailand,* Kuala Lumpur: Oxford University Press.
BUTLER, JACQUELINE
1970 *Yao Design,* Bangkok: The Siam Society.
CAMPBELL, MARGARET, NAKORN PONGNOI, CHUSAK VORAPHITAK
1978 *From the Hands of the Hills,* Hong Kong: Media Transasia.
CHINDARSI, NUSIT
1976 *The Religion of the Hmong Njua,* Bangkok: The Siam Society.
COOPER, R. G.
1976 *Resource Scarcity and the Hmong Response: A Study of the Settlement and Economy in Northern Thailand,* Ph. D. Dissertation, University of Hull.
DEPARTMENT OF THE ARMY
1970 *Minority Groups in Thailand,* Ehtnographic study Series, Department of the Army Pamphlet No. 550-107, Washington: U. S. Government Printing Office.
DESSAINT, ALAIN Y.
1971 *Lisu Migration in the Thai Highland,* *Ethnology* 3: 329–348.

1980 *Minorities of Southwestern China. An Introduction to the Yi (Lolo) and Related Peoples and an Annotated Bibliography,* New Haven: HRAF Press.
DESSAINT, WILLIAM Y. AND ALAIN Y.
1975 *Strategies in Opium Production,* *Ethnos* 1–4: 153–168.
DURRENBURGER, E. P.
1974 *The Regional Context of the Economy of a Lisu Village in Northern Thailand,* *Southeast Asia*
EMBREE, JOHN, F. AND LILIAN OTA DOTSON
1972 *Bibliography of the Peoples and Cultures of Mainland Southeast Asia,* New York: Russel and Russel, 2nd. edition.
GARRET, W. E.
1974 *The Hmong of Laos: No Place to Run,* *National Geographic,* 145 No. 1: 78–111.
GEDDES, WILLIAM ROBERT
1970 *Opium and the Miao: A Study in Ecological Adjustment,* *Oceania,* September 1–12.
1976 *Migrants of the Mountains: The Cultural Ecology of the Blue Miao (Hmong Njua) of Thailand,* Oxford: Clarendon Press.
GRUNFELD, FREDERIC V.
1982 *Wayfarers of the Thai Forest: The Akha,* Amsterdam: Time-Life Books.
HAMILTON, JAMES W.
1976 *Pwo Karen: At the Edge of Mountain and Plain,* St. Paul: West Publishing Co., The American Ethnological Society Monograph (60).
HANKS, JANE RICHARDSON
1968 *Rite and Cosmos: An Akha Diary,* North Bennington, Vermont 05257. (Mimeographed)
1969 *The Akha Patrilineage,* North Bennington, Vermont 05257. (Mimeographed)
HANKS, LUCIEN M.
1975 *Gazeteer for 1964, 1969, 1974: Maps of Ethnic Settlements of Chiengrai Province North of the Mae Kok River, Thailand,* Ithaca, New York: Department of Asian Studies, Cornell University.
HANKS, LUCIEN M., AND JANE R. HANKS
1975 *Reflections on Ban Akha Mae Salong,* *Journal of the Siam Society.* 63(1): 72–85.
HANKS, LUCIEN M., JANE R. HANKS, AND LAURISTON SHARP, editors
1964 *A Report on Tribal Peoples in Chiengrai Province North of the Mae Kok River,* Bennington-Cornell Anthropological Survey of Hill Tribes in Thailand, Bangkok: The Siam Society (Data Paper No. 1)

1965 *Ethnographic Notes on Northern Thailand,* Data Paper Number 58, Southeast Asia Program, Department of Asian Studies, Ithaca, New York: Cornell University.
HINTON, E. M.
1974 *The Dress of the Pwo Karen of North Thailand,* *Journal of Siam Society,* 62: 27–50.
HINTON, PETER, editor
1969 *Tribesmen and Peasants in North Thailand,* Chiang Mai: Tribal Research Centre.
1975 *Karen Subsistence: the Limits of a Swidden Economy in North Thailand,* Ph. D. Thesis, Sydney University. (Unpublished)
HO, R. AND E. C. CHAPMAN, editors
1973 *Studies in Contemporary Thailand,* Canberra: Australian National University, Department of Human Geography, Monograph HG/8.
HOPE, E. R.
1970 *Ethnographical notes on Lisu Culture and Society,* (Unpublished)
JOINT THAI-U. S. MILITARY RESEARCH AND DEVELOPMENT CENTER.
1969 *Meo Handbook,* Bangkok, Thailand.
KACHA-ANANDA, CHOB
1971 *The Akha Swinging Ceremony,* *Journal of the Siam Society.* 59: 119–128.
1976 *Etude Ethnographique du Groupe Ethnique Yao en Thailande du Nord,* Thesis: University of Paris. (Unpublished)
KEEN, F. G. B.
1973 *Upland Tenure and Land Use in North Thailand,* Bangkok: SEATO.
KEYES, CHARLES F.
1977 *The Golden Peninsula: Culture and Adaptation in Mainland Southeast Asia,* New York: Macmillan Publishing Co. Inc.
1979 Editor, *Ethnic Adaptation and Identity: The Karens on the Thai Frontier with Burma,* New York: Institute for the Study of Human Issues (ISHI).
KUNSTADTER, PETER
1967 Editor, *Southeast Asian Tribes, Minorities, and Nations,* Princeton: Princeton University Press. (2 volumes)
1972 *Spirits of Change Capture the Karens,* *National Geographic* 141: 2, 267–285.
KUNSTADTER, PETER, E. C. CHAPMAN, AND SANGA SABHASRI, editors
1978 *Farmers in the Forest,* Honolulu: University Press of Hawaii.

LARSEN, HANS PETER
1975 *Musik og mennesker i Thailands bjerge,* København: Musikhistorisk Museum.
1976 *The Instrumental Music of the Lisu in Northern Thailand,* Lampang Reports 225–268, Copenhagen: The Scandinavian Institute of Asian Studies.

LEBAR, FRANK M., GERALD C. HICKEY, JOHN K. MUSGRAVE, editors
1964 *Ethnic Groups of Mainland Southeast Asia,* New Haven: Human Relations Area Files Press.

LEMOINE, JACQUES
1972 *Un Village Hmong Vert du haut Laos,* Paris: Centre National de la Récherche Scientifique.
1972 *Les Ecritures du Hmong,* Bulletin des Amis du Royaume Lao No. 7–8: 123–165.
1982 *Yao Ceremonial Paintings,* Bangkok: White Lotus Co., Ltd.

LEWIS, PAUL W.
1968a *The Role and Function of the Akha 'Village Priest',* Behavior Science Notes 3(4): 249–262.
1968b *Akha-English Dictionary,* Ithaca, New York: Cornell University Southeast Asia Program, Data paper 70.
1968/70 *Ethnographic Notes on the Akha of Burma,* 4 volumes. New Haven: Human Relations Area Files.

LOMBARD, S. J., AND H. C. PURNELL Jr.
1968 *Yao-English Dictionary.* Ithaca, New York: Cornell University Southeast Asia Program, Data Paper 69.

McCOY, A. W.
1973 *The Politics of Heroin in Southeast Asia,* New York: Harper and Row.

McKINNON, JOHN
1977 *Shifting Cultivation: Who's afraid of the big bad wolf?* Paper prepared for 77th Seminar in Agriculture in North Thailand Series.

MARLOWE, DAVID H.
nd *Notes on a Mountain Flower: Thoughts on the Epidemeology of the Cultivation and Use of Papaver Somniferum in Certain Hill Areas of North Thailand.* (Unpublished)

MORÉCHAND, GUY
1968 *Le Chamanisme des Hmong,* Bulletin de l'Ecole Française d'Extrême-Orient 54: 53 294.

MILES, DOUGLAS
1967 *Report on Fieldwork in the Village of Pulangka,* Chiang Mai, Thailand: Tribal Research Centre. (Mimeographed)
1974 *Marriage, Agriculture and Ancestor Worship Among the Pulangka Yao,* Ph. D. Dissertation, Sydney University. (Unpublished)

MOTTIN, J.
1980 *The History of the Hmong (Meo),* Bangkok: Rung Ruang Ratana Printing.
1980 *Fêtes du Nouvel An chez les Hmong Blanc de Thaïlande,* Bangkok: Don Bosco Press.
1980 *Contes et Légendes Hmong Blanc,* Bangkok: Don Bosco Press.

PUBLIC WELFARE, DEPARTMENT of
1966 *Report on the Socio-Economic Survey of Hill Tribes in Northern Thailand,* Bangkok: Department of Public Welfare, Ministry of Interior, Royal Thai Government.

RENARD, RONALD
1976 *Notes on the Karen.* (Unpublished)
1977 *Changing Patterns of Karen Life.* (Unpublished)

ROUX, HENRI
1924 *Deux Tribus de la Région de Phongsaly,* Bulletin de l'Ecole Française d'Extrême-Orient, 24: 371–501.

SCHOLZ, FRIEDHELM
1969 *Zum Feldbau des Akha-Dorfes Alum, Thailand,* Jahrbuch des Südasien-Instituts der Universität Heidelberg 3: 88–99, Wiesbaden: Otto Harrassowitz.
1974 *Begräbnis eines Knaben – Miao (Thailand, Tak-Provinz).*
1974 *Batiken eines Kindertragtuches – Miao (Thailand, Tak-Provinz).*
1974 *Flechten eines Deckelkorbes – Akha (Thailand, Chieng Rai-Provinz)*
1977 *Tanz am Neujahrsfest – Schwarze Lahu (Thailand, Tak-Provinz).*
1977 *Weben von Tragbändern für Schultertaschen – Schwarze Lahu (Thailand, Tak-Provinz).*
1980 *Tanz am Neujahrsfest – Lisu (Thailand, Tak-Provinz),* Encyclopaedia Cinematographica, Göttingen: Institut für den Wissenschaftlichen Film.

SCHWÖRER, GRETEL
1982 *Die Mundorgel bei den Lahu in Nord-Thailand. Bauweise, Funktion und Musik,* Beiträge zur Ethnomusikologie Band 10, Hamburg: Karl Dieter Wagner.

SHIRATORI, YOSHIRO
1978 *Visual Ethnography: the Hill Tribes of South East Asia,* Kodansha, Japan.

STERN, THEODORE
1965 *Research upon Karen in Village and Town, Upper Khwae Noi, Western Thailand. Selected Findings, Report to the National Research Council of Thailand,* Bangkok. (Mimeographed)
1968a *Aria and the Golden Book: A Millenarian Buddhist Sect among the Karen,* Journal of Asian Studies 27(2): 297–328.
1968b *The Cult of the Local 'Lord' among the Karen,* Paper presented at the 67th Annual Meeting of the American Anthropological Association. (Mimeographed)

SUWANBUBPA, ARAN
1976 *Hill Tribe Development and Welfare Programmes in Northern Thailand,* Singapore: Regional Institute of Higher Education and Development.

TAKEMURA, TAKUJI
1976 *An Ethnological Study of the Yao Religious Systems in Northern Thailand,* National Museum of Ethnology, Osaka, Japan.

TELFORD, J. H.
1937 *Animism in Kengtung State,* Journal of the Burmese Research Society 27(2): 85–238.

UNITED NATIONS
1967 *Report of the United Nations Survey Team on the Economic and Social Needs of the Opium-Producing Areas in Thailand,* Bangkok: Government House Printing Office.

WALKER, ANTHONY R.
1970a *Lahu Nyi (Red Lahu) Village Society and Economy in North Thailand,* (2 volumes), Chiang Mai: Tribal Research Centre. (Mimeographed)
1970b *The Lahu Nyi (Red Lahu) New Year Celebrations,* The Journal of the Siam Society 58/1: 1–44.
1975 Editor, *Farmers in the Hills: Upland Peoples of North Thailand,* Penang, University of Malaysia.
1976 *Lahu Nyi (Red Lahu) New Year Texts – III,* The Journal of the Siam Society 64/1: 1–40.
1982 Editor, *Studies of Ethnic Minority Peoples, in Contributions to Southeast Asian Ethnography,* Double-Six Press Pte Ltd., Singapore.

WONSPRASERT, SANIT
1977 *The Socio-cultural and Ecological Determinants of Lahu Population Structure,* Chiang Mai: Tribal Research Centre. (Mimeographed)

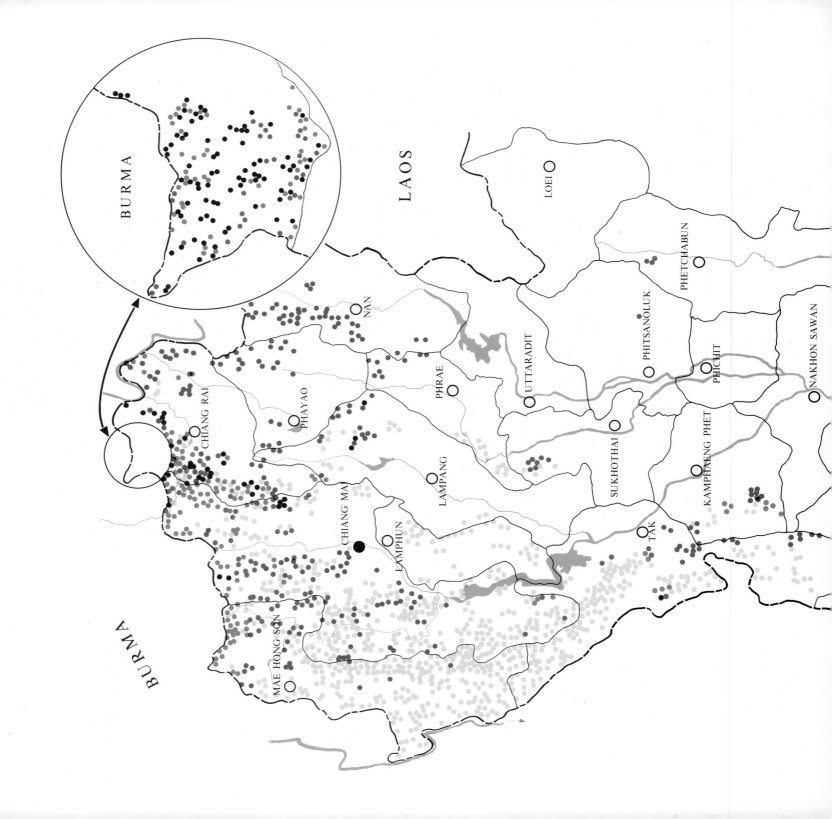

BURMA

LAOS

BURMA

LOEI ○

PHETCHABUN ○

PHITSANOLUK ○

UTTARADIT ○

NAN ○

PHRAE ○

PHICHIT ○

NAKHON SAWAN ○

CHIANG RAI ○

PHAYAO ○

LAMPANG ○

SUKHOTHAI ○

KAMPHAENG PHET ○

CHIANG MAI ●

LAMPHUN ○

TAK ○

MAE HONG SON ○

Distribution of Major Tribal Village Settlements
in Thailand

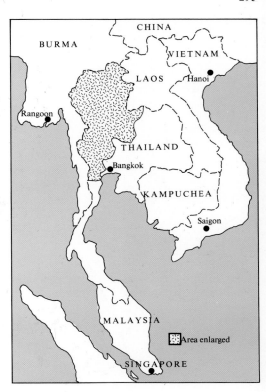

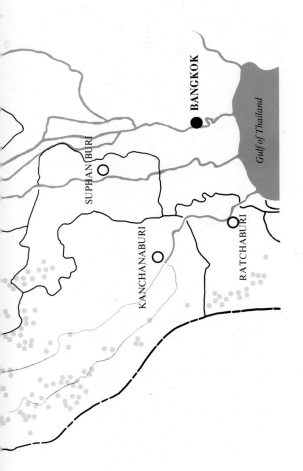

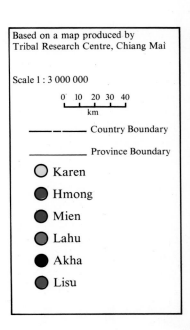

Based on a map produced by
Tribal Research Centre, Chiang Mai

Scale 1 : 3 000 000

0 10 20 30 40
km

— · — · — Country Boundary

———— Province Boundary

○ Karen

● Hmong

● Mien

● Lahu

● Akha

● Lisu

296

Acknowledgements

Photographs appearing in this book were taken by:

We wish to thank the following for the use of their translations of poems and songs:

ED HUDSPITH AND THRA LAY HTOO for the Karen songs on page 88 and 96, from an unpublished manuscript.

PETER KUNSTADTER for the Karen prayer on page 97, from a mimeographed report to the Tribal Research Centre.

ANTHONY WALKER for the Lahu prayer on page 171, found in Walker 1976: 37. (The translation is ours.)

E. P. DURRENBURGER for the Lisu song and prayers on pages 260 and 270, from mimeographed reports to the Tribal Research Centre.

MICHAEL FREEMAN: 17 A, 18 b, 18 c, 19 b, 19 c, 20 a, 21 b, 22, 23 a, 23 d, 26 b, 29 e, 95 d, 170, 171, 173 c, 174 a, 185 a, 185 d, 186 b, 189 a, 189 c, 189 d, 189 e, 189 f, 198, 234, 235, 236 a, 240, 245, 249 b, 249 c, 249 d, 254 c, 255 a, 255 c, 255 d, 257 b, 257 c, 258, 259, 261, 267, 272 b, cover f.

JOHN HOBDAY: 2, 6, 73 b, 82a , 92 f, 103 e, 105 c, 118, 135, 139 a, 202, 205 e, 241, 243, 254a , 256, 257 a, 264 f, 265 b, 265 c, 265 f, 271 a.

JACQUES LEMOINE: 132 a, 160.

PAUL LEWIS: 11 a, 12, 16 a, 16 c, 17 c, 21 a, 23 b, 24, 27 c, 29 a, 29 c, 72 b, 72 c, 73 a, 85 b, 87 a, 87 b, 87 d, 90 b, 90 d, 91 e, 93 d, 93 e, 93 f, 94 a, 94 b, 94 c, 103 a, 103 c, 117 b, 117 e, 119, 120 b, 124, 125 b, 125 d, 148, 149 a, 149 b, 149 c, 151, 154, 155, 172, 173 c, 173 d, 173 e, 175 a, 175 b, 175 c, 184 b, 184 c, 185 b, 185 c, 186 a, 189 b, 191, 193, 194, 195, 197, 200, 201, 204, 205 a, 205 b, 205 c, 207 b, 207 c, 217, 219 a, 219 b, 221 a, 221 c, 221 d, 221 e, 222, 223 a, 223 b, 225 a, 229 a, 229 b, 229 c, 233, 236 c, 238 a, 238 c, 239 b, 239 d, 239 e, 242, 244, 249 a, 254 b, 255 b, 255 e, 264 b, 264 c, 264 d, 264 e, 265 a, 287, 288, 289, 290 a, 290 b, 290 c, cover c, d.

HANSJÖRG MAYER: 15 b, 69, 92 d, 94 d, 100, 117 c, 122, 221 f.

HEINI SCHNEEBELI: 11 b, 11 c, 14 a, 17 a, 17 b, 17 e, 18 a, 20 b, 25 b, 25 c, 26 a, 27 a, 27 b, 29 b, 68, 71 72 a, 73 c, 73 d, 82 b, 83, 84, 85 a, 85 c, 85 d, 85 e, 85 f, 87 c, 90 a, 90 c, 90 e, 91 a, 91 b, 91 c, 91 d, 92 a, 92 b, 92 c, 92 e, 93 a, 93 b, 93 c, 94 e, 95 a, 95 b, 95 c, 95 e, 95 f, 98, 99, 105 b, 116, 117 a, 117 d, 121 a, 123 a, 123 c, 123 d, 125 a, 125 c, 132 b, 134, 138, 139 b, 149 d, 149 e, 162, 163, 164, 165, 166, 167, 168, 173 d, 175 d, 175 e, 175 f, 184 a, 187, 203, 219 c, 219 d, 236 d, 239 a, cover a, b, e.

FRIEDHELM SCHOLZ: 4, 14 b, 15 a, 16 b, 16 d, 17 c, 19 a, 20 c, 23 c, 25 a, 101, 103 b, 103 d, 104, 105 a, 105 d, 105 e, 105 f, 117 f, 120 d, 121 b, 121 c, 121 d, 123 b, 128, 130, 131, 174 b, 174 c, 174 d, 188, 196, 206, 107 a, 207 d, 207 e, 218, 220, 221 b, 223 c, 223 d, 224, 225 b, 225 c, 225 d, 225 e, 226, 229 d, 231, 236 b, 238 b, 239 c, 263, 264 a, 265 d, 265 e, 290 d.

ALI SUMLUT: 217 a, 223 e, 286.

Map on page 294/295 by Nick Downes.
Map on page 8 and house diagrams drawn by Andreas Karaiskos.

Edited and designed by Hansjörg Mayer

Index